GRAPHIC STYLE

FROM VICTORIAN

TO NEW CENTURY

3RD EDITION

SEYMOUR

GRAPHIC STYLE

FROM VICTORIAN TO NEW CENTURY

3RD EDITION

STEVEN HELLER
SEYMOUR CHWAST

ABRAMS
NEW YORK

For Louise and Paula

Pushpin Editions
Producer: Steven Heller
Designer: Seymour Chwast
Associate Designers: Roxanne Slimak/
Jeremiah Boncha
Researchers: Barbara Dominowski/
Diana Litchfield
Design Assistance: Myoah Son/Cindy Goldstein
Cover design by Seymour Chwast © 2011

Abrams
Editor, new edition: Eric Himmel
Editor, original edition: Margaret Donovan
Art Director, original edition: Samuel N. Antupit

Unless otherwise stated, illustrations are from the
authors' collections.

Library of Congress Cataloging-in-Publication Data
for the previous edition

Heller, Steven.
Graphic style: from Victorian to digital / Steven
Heller & Seymour Chwast.
p.   cm.
Includes bibliographical references and index.
ISBN 13: 978-0-8109-2984-5 (pbk.)
ISBN 10: 0-8109-2985-8 (pbk.)
1. Graphic arts—History—19th century. 2. Graphic
arts—History—20th century. 3. Commercial
art—History—19th century. 4. Commercial art—
History—20th century. I. Chwast, Seymour. II.
Title.

NC998.2.H448 2001
741.6'09'034—dc21 00-045125

ISBN, 3rd Edition: 978-0-8109-9791-2

Original edition published in 1988 by Harry N.
Abrams, Inc. Second edition published in 2000 by
Harry N. Abrams, Inc.

Printed and bound in China
10 9 8 7 6 5 4 3 2 1

THE ART OF BOOKS SINCE 1949
115 West 18th Street
New York, NY 10011
www.abramsbooks.com

CONTENTS

GRAPHIC STYLE TIME LINE	6
PREFACE	8
INTRODUCTION	9
VICTORIAN	14
British	16
American	20
French	28
ARTS AND CRAFTS	30
British	32
American	38
ART NOUVEAU	40
French/Belgian	42
Jugendstil	52
Glasgow Style	58
Vienna Secession	60
American	64
Italian	70
EARLY MODERN	72
Plakatstil	74
Wiener Werkstätte	80
EXPRESSIONISM	82
German	84
MODERN	88
Futurism	90
Vorticism	96
Constructivism	98
De Stijl	110
Bauhaus	112
New Typography	118
ART DECO	126
French	128
German	136
Swiss	140
Eastern European	144
Italian	146
English	150
American	154
Streamline	160
Dutch	166

DADA	168
HEROIC REALISM	176
LATE MODERN	182
Swiss	184
English	186
American	190
Swiss International Style	198
Corporate Style	200
Revival	202
Eclectic	204
Polish	206
Psychedelic	210
Japanese	214
POST-MODERN	220
Memphis/Basel/Zurich	222
American New Wave	224
American Punk	228
American Post-Modern	230
European New Wave	232
DIGITAL	234
Deconstruction	236
Emigre	238
Fontism	241
Controlled Chaos	244
Rave	248
Kinetics	250
New Simplicity	255
NEW CENTURY	259
Neo-Modern	260
Ornamental	263
Information	264
Street Art	268
Hand Lettering	271
Political	272
SELECTED BIBLIOGRAPHY	275
INDEX	278

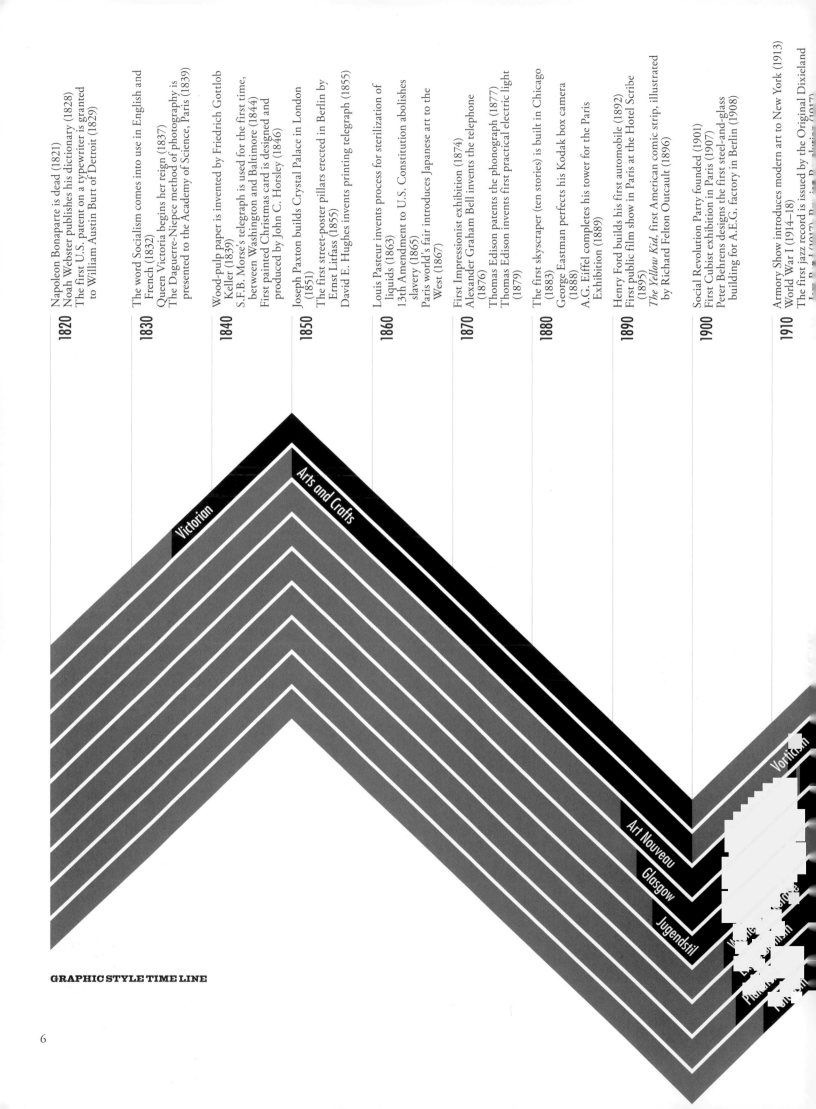

1820
Napoleon Bonaparte is dead (1821)
Noah Webster publishes his dictionary (1828)
The first U.S. patent on a typewriter is granted to William Austin Burt of Detroit (1829)

1830
The word Socialism comes into use in English and French (1832)
Queen Victoria begins her reign (1837)
The Daguerre-Niepce method of photography is presented to the Academy of Science, Paris (1839)

1840
Wood-pulp paper is invented by Friedrich Gottlob Keller (1839)
S.F.B. Morse's telegraph is used for the first time, between Washington and Baltimore (1844)
First painted Christmas card is designed and produced by John C. Horsley (1846)

1850
Joseph Paxton builds Crystal Palace in London (1851)
The first street-poster pillars erected in Berlin by Ernst Litfass (1855)
David E. Hughes invents printing telegraph (1855)

1860
Louis Pasteur invents process for sterilization of liquids (1863)
13th Amendment to U.S. Constitution abolishes slavery (1865)
Paris world's fair introduces Japanese art to the West (1867)

1870
First Impressionist exhibition (1874)
Alexander Graham Bell invents the telephone (1876)
Thomas Edison patents the phonograph (1877)
Thomas Edison invents first practical electric light (1879)

1880
The first skyscraper (ten stories) is built in Chicago (1883)
George Eastman perfects his Kodak box camera (1888)
A.G. Eiffel completes his tower for the Paris Exhibition (1889)

1890
Henry Ford builds his first automobile (1892)
First public film show in Paris at the Hotel Scribe (1895)
The Yellow Kid, first American comic strip, illustrated by Richard Felton Outcault (1896)

1900
Social Revolution Party founded (1901)
First Cubist exhibition in Paris (1907)
Peter Behrens designs the first steel-and-glass building for A.E.G. factory in Berlin (1908)

1910
Armory Show introduces modern art to New York (1913)
World War I (1914–18)
The first jazz record is issued by the Original Dixieland

Victorian

Arts and Crafts

Vorticism

Art Nouveau

Glasgow

Jugendstil

GRAPHIC STYLE TIME LINE

1920

(1922)

Al Jolson appears in *The Jazz Singer*, the first full-length talking film (1927)

Wall Street crash initiates a worldwide economic crisis (1929)

1930

Adolf Hitler is first appointed German chancellor (1933), then Führer (1934)

Spanish Civil War begins (1936)

Henry Luce begins publication of *Life* magazine (1936)

1940

The first automatic computer, or electronic brain, is developed in the U.S. (1944)

Atomic bomb is employed in war; World War II ends (1945)

The transistor is invented at Bell Laboratories (1948)

1950

Korean War begins (1950)

Color television is first introduced in the U.S. (1950)

Elvis Presley has his first rock 'n' roll hit (1956)

Soviets launch Sputnik I, first Earth satellite (1957)

1960

U.S. scientists develop laser (1960)

President Kennedy assassinated (1963)

U.S. bombing of North Vietnam (1965)

Apollo 11, first manned lunar landing (1969)

1970

U.S.-South Vietnam and North Vietnam sign a cease-fire agreement (1973)

First test tube baby born, in England (1978)

Anwar Sadat and Menchem Begin sign Camp David accords (1978)

1980

Space shuttle flights begin with the *Columbia* (1981)

Relativity high temperature superconductors developed (1986)

Glasnost policy is implemented by Russian Communist Party Chairman Gorbachev (1987)

1990

Reunification of East and West Germany (1990)

The first McDonald's opens in Moscow (1990)

South Africa ends apartheid (1991)

Windows 3.0 is introduced by Microsoft (1991)

Member nations in the European Union (EU) officially adopt the euro as its common currency (1999)

2000

New Century is a period of style-less style where universal mannerisms are no longer as consistent as during the twentieth century.

2010

Swiss International Style

Revivalism and Eclecticism

Polish Style

Late Modern

New Typography

Polish Modern

Streamline

Japanese Modern

Basel

Psychedelia

Post-Modern

Punk

Deconstruction

Memphis

Digital

Rave

New Simplicity

New Century

Any book whose scope is historical will become obsolete after one or two decades (or less). This arguably goes double for graphic design, which shifts and morphs in briefer segments owing to the ephemeral nature of the subject. If the authors are lucky enough to be alive when the need for revision occurs, they are called into service. As it happens, we are both alive.

There was always the belief that *Graphic Style* would require more than one edition. In fact, in 2000 after the flurry of design activity that occurred during the computer revolution, we were anxious to develop a section that built on the shifts in digital technology and its impact on design style. We were given a full-color signature to summarize the field and decided to highlight some common stylistic manifestations. Much of what we observed in the design firmament had to do with the chaos in type and image that emerged in print and on the newly fertile Internet. We followed the jumbled path that was set out for us, but we concluded the new section with a counter-intuitive return to simplicity. And why not? After all the pyrotechnics and complexities born of the digital boom were over, simplicity and minimalism seemed the logical result.

In this third edition, we begin with simplicity—or what we call neo-Modern—not as a style so much as an ethos. We continue with ornamental and handwritten mannerisms because we've determined that there is no overarching stylistic manifestation at this current time, only various preferences drawing on a broad range of stylistic options. The preferences we've highlighted are based on common traits we've observed. There is an overriding prevalence in graphic design for alternately the simple and the complex, and it comes out through this past decade's trends in street art, political design, and information architecture.

It may be too early to write an accurate history of the graphic design of the past ten years. There has not been enough time to do a proper analysis. But we are not writing history as much as charting style—or perhaps the death of style.

Graphic design is in more flux in 2010 than ever before. The media have changed and the term graphic may not efficiently encompass what is occurring. Rather than style, we see genres of design. We also see that replacing universal or international styles—like Art Nouveau or Art Deco, which were also commercial styles—we have "narrative." All the artifacts selected to represent the 2000s are visual stories. They are conveyed on posters, through typefaces, in billboards, and on the sides of buildings. They don't say one thing, but many things. They don't have one style but are comprised of numerous manners and conceits. What we call New Century style is a cumulation and culmination of all the styles that came before. Maybe this will be the last *Graphic Style*—then again, where there's life, there's always style.

Steven Heller and Seymour Chwast
June 2010

All art is at once surface and symbol.
Oscar Wilde, *The Picture of Dorian Gray,* 1891

The humblest as well as the most exalted ornaments may one day become elements in that revealing whole, the decorative style of an epoch.
Emile Gallé, Nancy, France, 1900

Style is the signal of a civilization. Historians can date any artifact by its style, be it Egyptian, Grecian, Gothic, Renaissance, Colonial, American or Art Nouveau. It is impossible for man to produce objects without reflecting the society of which he is a part and the moment in history when the product concept developed in his mind.... In this sense everything produced by man has style.
Sir Micha Black,
The Tiffany/Wharton Lectures, 1975

Style, in its most general sense, is a specific or characteristic manner of expression, design, construction, or execution. As it relates to graphic design, style suggests the dominant visual aesthetic of a particular time and place. The word has also been used to refer to a specific graphic designer's signature: his or her preference for a certain typeface or family of faces, for a characteristic color palette, and for either a decorative or a functional approach. Style is further defined by the material being designed and the audience for whom it is being produced: corporate style differs from editorial, news style from advertising, polemical style from commercial, and so on.

The graphic designer is basically organizing and communicating messages—to establish the nature of a product or idea, to set the appropriate stage on which to present its virtues, and to announce and publicize such information in the most effective way. Within this process, style is a transmission code, a means of signaling that a certain message is intended for a specific audience. By manipulating visual forms into an appro-

priate style, the designer can attract the right audience for a product or idea. In 1969 strategists in the reelection campaign of New York Mayor John Lindsay commissioned Peter Max, then guru of the commercial youth style, to design a psychedelic poster to attract the newly enfranchised baby-boomers. Likewise, in 1972, the promoters of George McGovern's presidential campaign used a Larry Rivers poster to lure a similar group; in the opposing camp, Nixon's publicity men came up with their own version of a youthful-looking poster. While the two presidential candidates proffered distinctly different points of view, their posters thus had similar graphic styles.

Simply defined, *graphic style* is the surface manifestation or the "look" of graphic design. This book is concerned with how that look has evolved and been reapplied since commercial art had its beginnings as a result of the revolutions in industry and commerce during the nineteenth century. Yet, even with such a narrow focus, a linear examination of style is still complicated by the fact that artists and designers do not always dutifully follow the arbiters of taste in their respective periods. What we call the Victorian style, for example, covers a period of seventy-five years and has countless nuances and variations; Art Deco, the decorative arts movement dominant between the two world wars, also is an amalgam of distinctly different methodologies. Upon close examination, however, there are enough visual charac-

teristics common to most products of each period to justify the use of the *Victorian* or *Deco* umbrella.

In studying and analyzing style through the ages, historians have developed a system of classification that commonly focuses on painting, sculpture, architecture, furniture, and clothing and pays only scant attention to graphic design. Nevertheless, the advertising, posters, packages, and typefaces of a period, as well as its illustrations and cartoons, are equally, if not more, indicative of the society in which they were produced. As mass communication, commercial art is often a synthesis of other arts and technologies, demystified and made accessible to a broad audience. In fact, a vernacular graphic style usually indicates popular acceptance of visual philosophies that were once inaccessible, avant-garde, or elitist.

The farther one backtracks in history, the more singularly representative of its epoch a style appears to be (partly, of course, because lack of documentation tends to force generalization). Our relatively recent past is notable for a myriad of styles that occupy comparatively brief, concurrent periods and come and go with such speed that a kind of cultural detonation results when one collides with another. The question that now concerns graphic style is whether today's new technologies, like those of the Industrial Revolution, will change the substance, and not merely the surface, of graphic communications. While designers hope for a more

1. Will Bradley. *The Masqueraders.* Poster, c. 1894.
The Metropolitan Museum of Art, New York. Gift of Fern Bradley Dufner

coherent future, the buzzword that best sums up contemporary graphic style is "life-style." Design itself has become a commodity: more than ever before, decorative graphic design is assigned the task of seducing the customer into buying products.

From the Victorian era to the present, graphic design has had to serve various economic and cultural masters, and thus there have been numerous ways in which graphic styles have evolved. Certain styles were developed for aesthetic reasons (Art Nouveau), while others were politically motivated (Dada). There are those based on the need for corporate identity (Swiss International), on commercial requisites (Post-Modern), and on moral and philosophical foundations (the Bauhaus). Some were influenced by the fine arts (Art Deco), others by industry (Plakatstil). Some national styles became international movements (Futurism). A few styles enjoyed long duration—two or three (Constructivism, Expressionism, Surrealism) exert influence even today—though most were comparatively short-lived. And many historical styles have been revived, reinterpreted, and misused by succeeding generations.

Graphic designers today freely rummage through a big closet of historical styles looking for ones that are adaptable for their purposes. Sometimes, as they reprise a vintage graphic style, it will be an appropriate and graceful use—the product image is enhanced by being linked to another place and time. More often, designers without distinctive visual characters of their own attempt to adopt a once viable style without regard for the factors that brought it about in the first place.

As early as 1856, in an essay titled "The True and False in the Decorative Arts," Owen Jones condemned the contemporary practice of trying to make "the art which faithfully represents the wants, the faculties and the feelings of one people represent those of another people under totally different conditions." In the sixties a revival of French Art Deco gave rise to a hybrid decorative manner in American design. While creative practitioners took

2. Vassily Komardenkov. *Storm Cavalry*. Cubo/Futurist design for a book of poems, 1920. Courtesy Ex Libris, New York

the time to understand Deco's formal aspects, to make them unique and even expressive, most designers carelessly mimicked Deco's lightning bolts,raybands, and display typefaces. At best they produced a nostalgic conceit that said little about the time in which it was produced and less about the product or idea being newly presented. More recently, the radical form language of Russian Constructivism endured a similar "reappreciation." Instead of using the style to influence and shape a new vision—in the way Constructivism inspired the Swiss rationalist design of the forties and fifties —contemporary designers employed Constructivism's dynamic asymmetry and primary colors as casual toys, copying the surface qualities without regard for original intent. This tendency, however lamentable, may be regarded in one way as a logical and inevitable response. Although style divorced from its *raison d'être* by time and circumstance is just an empty shell, some designers may see it as a tempting refuge when faced with the necessity for original thinking.

Of course, this kind of appropriation is not unknown in art history, which is marked by periods of innovation and

then—years, decades, even centuries later—of reappreciation or revival. Along with the revivals that are merely shallow borrowings and those that honestly attempt to reestablish forgotten standards, there are still others that prove to be gateways to new discovery. The Pre-Raphaelite Brotherhood of English painters, for example, sought in the nineteenth century to emulate the purity of Italian religious painting during the Early Renaissance. To a period of predominantly realist art, the Brotherhood brought back the important and virtually neglected element of the imagination and thus was able to make a meaningful historical contribution. About the Pre-Raphaelites' direct influence on Surrealism, Marcel Duchamp said that they "lit a small flame which is still burning despite everything." Hermann Broch, on the other hand, argues that a preponderance of neo-this and neo-that in any period of art really signifies that the false or fraudulent is pervasive. Broch applies such a judgment to the Neo-Gothic and Neo-Baroque of the late nineteenth century, despite their impact on architecture, fashion, and applied arts. Such stylistic contrivances, he says, are nonstyles, because they do not truthfully represent their time and place.

Although Art Nouveau was, in fact, the first true modern international style, the term *Modernist* is commonly reserved for the antibourgeois, utopian art movements of the early twentieth century. The design innovations of the Modernist movement were the ones most obviously woven from whole cloth rather than patched together from imitations of the past. The unprecedented Cubist experiments of Picasso and Braque from 1908 to 1913 stimulated painters, fashion designers, and graphic artists for decades to follow. For designers the Cubist letter/image collages, in which word fragments were made by juxtaposing unrelated letter forms, suggested an original and expressive method of typographical communication. Employed for poetry, manifestoes, and exhibition announcements, these types were essentially advertising tools, their ultimate purpose the propagation of a new vision. Their marriage of word and image eventually helped bridge the gap between the fine and applied arts that had grown ever since the early days of printing.

From the Modernist tree grew many branches, each more or less supported by a formal design language and a philosophical underpinning disseminated through an official periodical. Though Theo van Doesburg's unadorned De Stijl typography differs visually from Solomon Telingater's Constructivist lettering, both adhered to the basic tenets of reductionism: ornament was a sin (as Viennese architect Adolf Loos declared); simple linear and geometric forms were virtues; and asymmetry was everywhere dominant. In Germany, Paul Renner's geometric sans-serif type, Futura, offered an exciting alternative to the antiquated and fussy blackletter Fraktur; in Russia, typographers

3. El Lissitzky. *Die Kunstismen.* Book cover, 1924. Courtesy Ex Libris, New York

used dynamic type arrangements to powerfully symbolize the Productivist age.

Such innovations were not without their critics. In speeches before design organizations in the twenties, Thomas Maitland Cleland, a renowned American typographer and advertising designer in the classical tradition, zealously decried the New Typography. Its "alluring shortcuts and seductive philosophies—a disturbing Babel of undigested ideas and indigestible objectives" were, Cleland

stated, the result of "the relentless craving for something new.... Typography is a servant of thought and language to which it gives visible existence. When there are new ways of thinking and a new language, it will be time enough for a new typography." Such critics refused to believe that a new way of designing, free from the shackles of formality, could be effective for conventional advertising purposes or that their classical approach, though beautiful in the right hands, represented past, not present, achievements. The New Typography, like most Modernist innovations, wasn't simply a matter of style for its own sake but rather style resulting from necessity.

Among those answering such charges was the German Jan Tschichold, who codified the Constructivist-influenced, asymmetrical typographic approach into a form language in his "Elementare Typographie" of 1925. Tschichold declared, "The rules of the old typography contradict the principles of fitness for purpose in design. Unsymmetrical arrangements are more flexible and better suited to the practical and aesthetic needs of today." Championing these forces of graphic innovation and criticizing those who copied past styles, Wassily Kandinsky said, "Such imitation resembles the antics of apes."

Of course, the virtues of any style, like those of any typography, are determined by how and to what purpose it is applied. In the wrong hands an otherwise beautiful stylistic mannerism can be made trivial and ugly. For example, the elegant typefaces developed in the eighteenth century by François Ambroise Didot and Giambattista Bodini were bastardized two centuries later by tasteless Victorian commercial job printers. While a few serious typographers tried at the time to maintain standards, they were undercut by the increased need for fast and economical commercial printing and by the proliferation of craftsmen without aesthetic training. Thus, graceful classical forms were made to serve the cluttered visual look of the age.

Even in its own time, the widespread use of a style by untutored practitioners

usually degrades the style, although it may increase its visibility and public acceptance. To fill his famous retail store with expensive inventory, Arthur L. Liberty shamelessly stole and altered original Art Nouveau designs. He did create an unprecedented market for the style but also contributed to its demise through overexposure. A few decades later the Bauhaus encountered a similar problem. Displeased with the irresponsible execution of Bauhaus-like wares by commercial firms, the school's director, Walter Gropius, railed against "imitators who prostituted our fundamental precepts into modish trivialities."

Yet it is inevitable that the moment a unique creation becomes a style, the great leavener called fashion comes into play. Some of the styles discussed here began as honest individual efforts with distinct purposes that ultimately became officially or universally adopted. In some cases, the individuals originally responsible for the styles were willing participants in their popularization; in others, they believed that to be true to their ideals required abandoning the popularized styles for purer forms.

Vanguard art has often been transmuted into commercial style, despite the best intentions of artistic pioneers to keep it out of the mainstream. German Expressionism was avowedly radical—in its aesthetic before World War I and in its pacifist polemic during the war. For years, its artists were criticized and rejected by the art establishment. Eventually, however, Expressionist works came to be perceived and honored as Germany's first contributions to Modernism; after the war Expressionism virtually became Germany's national style. Its emblematic hardedged woodcuts formed the basis for much of the stylization in modern advertising and printing, a fact that quickly led to its obsolescence as an avant-garde form.

Even Dada—which in Germany rejected the artistic pretensions and emotional excesses of Expressionism and asserted an antiart position—could not escape being usurped by stylists. Through its distribution of mass-produced advertisements, periodicals, books, and posters, 11

Dada propagated a distinctive collage, montage, and typographic style that has been borrowed by less politically committed designers, then and now. Today the Dada style, as reflected in Punk and Neo-Expressionist design, is an effective code for conveying the tempests of contemporary youth.

Some of the most significant twentieth-century avant-garde art movements were successful in propagating their ideas through the popular commercial media, only to find their radical visions overexposed and trivialized. Italian Futurism was formulated in 1908 by F. T. Marinetti as a striking contrast to the Neoclassical Novocento Italiano style, but it was also wed to Benito Mussolini's emerging Fascist party. The influence of Futurism's forceful interpretation of the Machine Age grew as did Mussolini; it flourished as both a national and a commercial style after his power was secured. Yet the obvious requisites of an authoritarian regime—especially once Italy entered the war—ultimately caused Futurism's subordination to party needs. What remained of the original graphic style was merely a decorative Futurist veneer.

The past half-century has witnessed a proliferation of design styles, some enduring, others short-lived. The rise of the Nazi party and later the beginning of World War II had a direct impact on many design forms. Though many Modernists were forced to flee Europe or go into hiding, the disbanding of the dominant art and design movements only briefly interrupted the stylistic continuum of graphic design. Indeed, during the war, many significant designers developed individual styles consistent with Modernist thought, among them the Americans Paul Rand and Lester Beall and the European immigrants Herbert Matter, Alexey Brodovitch, and Herbert Bayer. Others, like the Swiss Max Bill, Josef Müller-Brockmann, and Armin Hofmann, built a new form language from the legacy of the Constructivists and the Bauhaus.

Various postwar graphic styles grew up around the efforts of such innovative stylists, many of whom were prolific writers on the theory and process of their vision.

4. Paul Rand. *Modern Art USA*. Book cover, 1956

From the ashes of war sprang new industrial states, with distinct communications needs. No longer simply an offshoot of other disciplines and media, graphic design served a primary role in establishing and maintaining the identity of business. Within the dominantly rationalist ethic exemplified by the Swiss, design in the fifties also saw a flowering of eclecticism and revivalism. No single style dominated: rationalist design found a home within the expanding corporate universe; eclecticism was ideal for certain advertising, publishing, and merchandising needs; and, later, the Psychedelic style, an original synthesis of Secessionist, Symbolist, and East Indian motifs, expressed the vibrant but brief life of the youth culture.

Through Punk, New Wave, Japanese, and the Basel School, we have arrived at Post-Modern, a resurfacing of classical forms clothed in updated traditional ones. At once symbolizing respect for the past, obsession with the present, and perhaps fear of the future, Post-Modern has replaced Art Deco as the latest international style.

Graphic design has come full circle in the eighties. It has evolved from the primordial clutter of Victorian Neo-Gothic, through the austere functionalism of Modernism, and back again into a mélange of Neoclassical layering. Although analysis of art history from this perspective reveals interesting cultural data, *Graphic Style* does not aim to offer new, scholarly methods for the study of popular culture. Rather, it is the first book to present an annotated chronology of the most significant stylistic movements, schools, and trends in printed communications from the nineteenth century to the present. Neither an inclusive nor conclusive history, it is more a map with which to navigate the continually changing topography of graphic design.

As such, *Graphic Style* is primarily concerned with the image, not the image-maker. Rarely is one man's or woman's genius solely responsible for the development or popularity of a significant style. While we discuss some individuals who provided prototypes for a style, we consistently emphasize the formal, emblematic visual characteristics of a design period. Thus, for instance, a designer who worked in several stylistic periods may be represented only in the one in which his or her work first appeared. Some of the work illustrated is attributable to a specific designer, but there is an equal number produced by unknowns. Graphic design is first a service, not an art, and most quotidian printed matter is unsigned and often anonymous. The apprentice and journeyman designers of any period followed the dominant forms and standards set down by established printers or in manuals, and this is the work that has most frequently survived.

Graphic Style therefore addresses how and why elements of Arts and Crafts, Jugendstil, Constructivism, Expressionism, and the other significant methodologies became conventions used by printers, layout artists, and advertising designers for commercial and business purposes. By tracing the roots and development of style, we aim to show how graphic design has interacted with the material culture, how it has served both as an adjunct to and as the vanguard in the development of broader period styles. In effect, we are tracing nothing less than the evolution of the popular tastes of a period.

Steven Heller

GRAPHIC STYLE

5. Designer unknown. *Sutton's Compound Cream of Ammonia.* Advertisement, 1907. Courtesy Chris Mullen

lthough Queen Victoria was crowned in 1837, the style of architecture and decorative arts that bears her name actually began in the 1820s and continued in England, America, and much of Europe until 1900. Victorian style was not the invention of this iron-willed matriarch, but rather the aesthetic response of a society to industrialization.

The Industrial Revolution was a mixed blessing in Britain. Along with technological revelations, it brought crime, urban blight, and the rise of a self-indulgent *nouveau riche* class. Between the end of the eighteenth century and the middle of the nineteenth, the once profound English sense of social, civic, and artistic responsibility diminished. Wealth became in effect the motivating cultural force. As the desire for unlimited comfort spread from the wealthy to the middle class, popular aesthetics were increasingly devoid of any critical standards.

With contemporary aesthetic standards in decline, Victorian artists turned to the past for inspiration. Taking special delight in medieval ruins, they saw parallels in the Gothic art and architecture of previous centuries to their present-day Christian virtue. Yet the borrowed elements in Victorian style were completely detached from their original culture. In *Analysis of Ornament* (1856), Ralph Nicholson assailed the revivalists, stating, "A designer might...produce a perfect arrangement of forms and colours, and yet show the grossest stupidity in its application."

The early Victorians reveled in ostentation. After the Great Exhibition of 1851, the taste for ornamentation based on historical forms was passionately indulged. Victorians believed that the corpulent display of material gain gratified the eye; ornament appeased their need to have visible evidence of their social status. The exaggerated embellishment of virtually every article in the Victorian home created an atmosphere of unshakable comfort and contributed to the decidedly cluttered look of the style. While ornament might seem simply to have offered Victorians status and aesthetic pleasure, one contemporary critic argued that it served to hide the "more aberrant lusts of human nature." And, as if industrialization were the metaphor for these perverted desires, Victorians disguised the advancements of their engineers under decorative excesses that mimicked natural forms.

Victorian taste was confused by the belief that ornamentation and design were identical functions. The art critic and architect Augustus Welby Northmore Pugin criticized this idea: "How many objects of ordinary use are rendered monstrous and ridiculous simply because the artist, instead of seeking the most convenient form and then decorating it, has embodied some extravagance to conceal the real purpose for which the object has been made." Another Victorian commentator proudly replied, "Disguise is the spice of life."

Although England is recognized as having originated the Victorian style, other burgeoning commercial centers in Europe and America felt its influence, which was disseminated to all classes through the printed mass media. The surpluses created by the Industrial Revolution led to increased competition in the marketplace, as sellers sought to educate buyers to the virtues of products and services. To this end, advancements in the simultaneous printing of text and image fostered the new medium called advertising, which soon became the clarion for announcing the rewards of the Victorian life-style.

The standards governing the production of graphic arts, like those guiding the other decorative arts, were few and unequal to the strides made by technology. Victorian commercial printed matter was characterized by the era's pervasive ornamentation, often imitating contemporary architectural eccentricities; images were frequently crudely drawn and engraved; typography was decidedly poor. If a compositor lacked a lower-case *g*, for example, he would not hesitate to use an upside-down *b* in its place.

Sometimes, however, a merchant's demand for distinctive announcements did result in truly original display faces, composed of odd, and even ingenious, woodblock letters. Designers of new display faces savaged the elegant eighteenth-century Bodoni and Didot types, distorting and making them larger and blacker. These bastardizations, called Fat Face types, became emblems of the Victorian look. As wood engravers mastered their medium, outline, whiteline, and shadowed letterforms gained greater exposure. The Egyptian faces—squared serif letters apparently influenced by the revival of interest in that country after Napoleon's excursions—joined the Fat Faces as one of the most original typographic forms of the century. Wood display types were popularized in Britain and abroad through frequent use by commercial printers. And the distinctive Victorian style of layout—extreme variations of type size and weight crammed within a single headline—was an invention of expedience, allowing the printer to utilize every inch of precious space.

By 1845 the high-speed steam press had so increased the volume of printed matter that many townscapes were blighted by bills and posters covering every inch of available wall space. Legislation was enacted and taxes levied to counter these graphic assaults, and advertising was ultimately restricted to special areas. Yet advertisers persisted and their trade became a fact of life, eventually elevating with it the role of commercial art. By the 1860s, an influx of academically trained craftsmen and artisans had entered the commercial arts, with the result that printed matter became more visually appealing and more conceptually sophisticated—some of it even quite beautiful.

The technological advances that ushered in the Victorian style continued to alter its look throughout the century: first, as chromolithography advanced in Germany and America in the 1870s, and then, at the close of the century, as the camera gave birth to photoengraving. Little by little, designers came to rely on standardized motifs and generic ornaments sold through printing catalogues. Victorian woodcuts and engravings, and the slab-serif and Gothic types, ultimately gave way to more sinuous, organic, and curvilinear forms. Indeed, during the seventy-five years that Victorian style was dominant, it evolved from a nostalgic Gothic revival into a precursor of Modernism.

BRITISH

Today the decorative excesses of the Victorian style seem very quaint, for, detached from the art and politics of the epoch, this printed material has a simple, nostalgic beauty. Yet the Victorians suffered from a confused belief that ornament and design were identical. Their century witnessed a decline in the stringent Renaissance standards of typography, a decline typified here by the posters and broadsides featuring Fat Face bastardizations of Bodoni and Didot types as well as Egyptian slab-serif display faces. Had the word *functionalism* been coined, Victorian designers would have rejected everything it stood for. For them, decoration was a virtue that symbolized the comfortable Victorian lifestyle, here exemplified by the cover of *Punch,* England's premier satiric journal, and the excessive Rococo styling on Arthur Dixon's store sign.

6. Designer unknown. Wood-engraved food packaging labels, c. 1870

7. Richard Doyle. *Punch.* Magazine cover, May 26, 1883

8. Designer unknown. Storefront sign for chemist/druggist, c. 1835. Courtesy Chris Mullen

9. Designer unknown. *Phrenology. Physiology.* Lecture poster, 1861

10. Designer unknown. *Russia, Constantinople…* Poster, c. 1852

6

7

8

TWO EXTRA LECTURES

PHRENOLOGY. **PHYSIOLOGY.**

MESSRS.

Fowler and Wells

WILL GIVE

TWO EXTRA LECTURES,

AS FOLLOWS, IN THE

TEMPERANCE HALL, HARTLEPOOL.

On FRIDAY Evening, July 19th, 1861,

HOW TO TRAIN UP A CHILD.

On the Right Government, Training, and Proper Education of Children, with Advice to Young Men and Women on Self Culture and Personal Improvement. Every Parent, Teacher, and Youth should hear it.

On SATURDAY Evening, July 20th, 1861,

THE

Perfection of Character,

Or the Moral Nature of Man, including his relations to Society and to Deity.—A future state—power to control and direct our propensities and passions, and to resist temptations—how to acquire respect, moral prudence and circumspection—the true or scientific interpretation of FAITH, HOPE, and CHARITY.

Tickets—Front Seats, 1s.; Second do., 6d.; Back do., 3d.

Doors open at Half-past Seven, to commence at Eight. Each Lecture to close with Public Examinations.

☞ PRIVATE EXAMINATIONS. ☜

Professional Delineations, with Charts and full written Description of Character, and advice in regard to "WHAT TO DO," or the most appropriate occupations and pursuits in life; Faults, how to correct them; Health, how to secure and retain it; the Management of Children; Self-improvement, Marriage, &c., given during the day in private reception rooms of the Temperance Hall. Persons desiring the services of Messrs. FOWLER & WELLS, should call early, as their stay in Hartlepool terminates soon, and another opportunity may not occur.

9

Will Open on Monday Next August 24th,
IN THE

WESLEYAN REFORM CHAPEL,

REGENT SQUARE, CHARE HEAD FIELD,

HARTLEPOOL,

FOR THREE NIGHTS ONLY!

Monday, Tuesday, and Wednesday, August 24th, 25th and 26th.

Fashionable Day Performance on Wednesday

AT TWO O'CLOCK, DOORS OPEN AT HALF-PAST ONE

M. GOMPERTZ, respectfully announces to the Nobility, Clergy, Gentry, and Inhabitants of Hartlepool and its Vicinity, that he has made arrangements to Exhibit his Colossal Panorama, in the Wesleyan Reform Chapel, as above stated, there being no Room in the Town sufficiently large for the erection of this Stupendous Production, which he has just removed from the Athenæum, West Hartlepool, were it was last Exhibited.

M. GOMPERTZ'S

NEW AND COLOSSAL PANORAMA, ILLUSTRATING

THE WAR WITH

RUSSIA

Painted from Drawings & Military Plans, made on the Spot, by both FRENCH & ENGLISH OFFICERS.

ACCOMPANIED BY A SPLENDID BESSON TUBA BAND.

The Panorama commences with a series of Views, illustrating the routes of the Magnificent City

CONSTANTINOPLE.

DESTRUCTION AT SINOPE

SEBASTOPOL

LANDING of the ALLIED ARMIES in the

CRIMEA

BATTLE OF ALMA

Triumphant Attack of the Guards and Highlanders

UPON THE PRINCIPAL REDOUBT.

FIELD OF THE ALMA THE EVENING AFTER THE BATTLE.

CAVALRY CHARGE AT

BALAKLAVA

RETURN OF THE REMNANT OF LIGHT CAVALRY.

Field of Balaklava the Night after the Battle.

COMMENCEMENT OF THE BATTLE of

INKERMAN

THE COMMANDERS IN CHIEF WATCHING THE PROGRESS OF THE BATTLE.

DESPERATE STRUGGLE in the VALLEY of INKERMAN !

FINAL REPULSE OF THE RUSSIANS

CAPTURE OF THE

Malakhoff

ASSAULT UPON THE REDAN.

Pictorial Chart of the Crimea,

CRYPT of the HOLY SEPULCHRE

10

17

11

12

18

UPPINGHAM

HORTICULTURAL SOCIETY.

THE NINTH ANNUAL

SHOW

OF

FLOWERS, FRUIT, AND VEGETABLES

WILL BE HELD ON THE

LEICESTER ROAD FIELD,

ON

THURSDAY, JULY 16TH, 1885.

FAIRFIELD GARDENS & AVIARY

Will be open to Visitors (by kind permission of the Rev. E. THRING).

A CRICKET MATCH,

UPPINGHAM & DISTRICT C.C. v. the PRESIDENT'S XI.

Will be played on the adjoining Victoria Ground, on THURSDAY and FRIDAY, July 16th & 17th.

THE

BAND OF THE MUTUAL IMPROVEMENT SOCIETY

WILL BE IN ATTENDANCE.

THE SHOW WILL BE OPEN AT HALF-PAST ONE O'CLOCK AND CLOSE AT SEVEN.

ADMISSION : Before Four o'clock, ONE SHILLING ; after Four, SIXPENCE.

Schedules may be obtained of the Secretary, MR. H. DEAKE, Uppingham.

Contributed by A. C. Cooke, Foreman, with John Hawthorn, Uppingham.

13

14

15

16

As consumerism grew during the nineteenth century, the production of advertising announcements was left to commercial printers untutored in aesthetics. Serving their needs were an amazing variety of unique display typefaces. The printing historian Michael Twyman writes, "The jobbing and periodical printers were faced with new problems…new processes and materials…new clients…and new kinds of information to translate into print. What emerged was a new approach to design which distinguishes the 19th century printer from his 18th century counterpart, and leads to the new profession of graphic design." Owen Jones's book *The Grammar of Ornament* (1856) provided Victorian designers with examples of ancient patterns and designs used in architecture and graphics. These motifs were standardized in specimen books and sold as stock designs to the printers who serviced small businesses. The specimens also provided models from which to make customized designs like the one for the Boltonian Under-vest poster.

11. Designer unknown. *Dutch Flower Bulbs.* Type specimen from *The Printers' International Specimen Exchange,* vol. VII, London, 1885. Courtesy Chris Mullen

12. Designer unknown. *W. J. Cummins Calendar.* Type specimen from *The Printers' International Specimen Exchange,* vol. VII, London, 1885. Courtesy Chris Mullen

13. Designer unknown. *Uppingham Horticultural Society.* Type specimen from *The Printers' International Specimen Exchange,* vol. VII, London, 1885. Courtesy Chris Mullen

14. Designer unknown. *Charta Spartica Envelopes.* Type specimen from *The Printers' International Specimen Exchange,* vol. VII, London, 1885. Courtesy Chris Mullen

15. Designer unknown. *Boltonian Under-vest.* Advertisement, 1888. Courtesy Chris Mullen

16. Designer unknown. *S. G. Chalfont, Artistic Printer.* Type specimen from *The Printers' International Specimen Exchange,* vol. VII, London, 1885. Courtesy Chris Mullen

AMERICAN

The dominant American graphic style of the nineteenth century drew inspiration from contemporary English and German lettering and decoration, especially as reflected in the scores of illustrated periodicals initiated around mid-century. The typography of these publications was conservative, while the editorial illustration proved to be a more important stylistic signpost. Wood engraving and lithography were the primary means of reproducing the usually over-rendered visual narratives. When *Harper's Weekly* first began publishing in 1857, its wood-engraved illustrations were limited by their mandate to represent newsworthy events as accurately as possible. Imagination came to the surface when the German-born cartoonist Thomas Nast joined the staff in 1862 and marked the periodical with his distinctive, cross-hatched editorial cartoon style. In 1871 Joseph Keppler, a Vienna-born political cartoonist trained in European lithographic techniques, founded the acerbic satirical weekly *Puck,* which not only raised the quality of American illustration but also introduced chromolithography (color printing) to cartoons. The work of Nast and Keppler also influenced the style of cartoonists working in rival (and often imitative) periodicals, such as *Judge, Jingo,* and *Truth.*

17. Rummler. *Truth.* Magazine cover, January 19, 1895

18. Designer unknown. *Harper's Magazine.* Magazine cover, December 1883

19. Grant Hamilton. *The Judge.* Magazine cover, March 22, 1884

20. Designer unknown. *Harper's Weekly.* Magazine cover, February 12, 1876

21. Designer unknown. *Jingo.* Magazine cover, October 1, 1884

22. Designer unknown. *The New York Fashion Bazar.* Magazine cover, September 1885

23. E. N. Blue. *Puck.* Magazine cover, March 23, 1887

17

18

19

20

21

22

VOL. XXI.—No. 524.

NEW YORK, MARCH 23, 1887.

PRICE, TEN CENTS.

"What fools these Mortals be!"
MIDSUMMER-NIGHTS DREAM.

Puck

TRADE MARK REGISTERED 1878.

KEPPLER & SCHWARZMANN, Publishers.

PUCK BUILDING, Cor. Houston & Mulberry Sts.

ENTERED AT THE POST OFFICE AT NEW YORK, AND ADMITTED FOR TRANSMISSION THROUGH THE MAILS AT SECOND CLASS RATES.

A CONTRAST.

PUCK.   I don't wish to make any invidious comparisons, Auctioneer Hilton; but — Mr. W. W. Corcoran is universally respected and esteemed.

25

26

24

27

28

22

29

30

AMERICAN

With the swing toward consumerism in America after the Civil War, the need to educate the public concerning a variety of new products caused a shift in emphasis from simple announcements to full-blown "advertisements." The same technological advances that had originally created the market surpluses and the need to compete in business also provided new economical printing methods. Chromolithography was first used for trade cards in 1840 and became a truly efficient process by the 1870s; it soon proved a formidable means of seizing viewer attention. Since advertising agents were more brokers of space than creative decision-makers, the owners of small companies themselves determined early Victorian advertising images on the basis of what they instinctively thought would be effective. The most popular themes included nationalism, patriotism, progress, and work as well as comic vignettes of all kinds. Printing firms, like Julius Bien Co., Currier and Ives, and Louis Prang and Company, eventually assumed a creative role in conceiving and producing custom and stock cuts and chromos for trade cards, song sheets, packaging, posters, and greeting cards.

24. Designer unknown. *Heinz Sweet Pickles.* Trade card, c. 1887

25. Designer unknown. *Ring de Banjo.* Sheet music cover, 1851

26. Designer unknown. *Cleveland's Baking Powder.* Trade card, c. 1886

27. Designer unknown. *Soapine.* Trade card, c. 1896

28. Designer unknown. *Arm & Hammer.* Trade card, c. 1880

29. Designer unknown. *Muzzy's Starch.* Trade card, 1882

30. Designer unknown. *Rose Leaf.* Trade card, 1865

31. Designer unknown. *Vinegar Bitters Almanac.* Book cover, 1874

32. Designer unknown. *Best in the World Superior Silk.* Trade card, c. 1880

33. Designer unknown. *Ivory Soap.* Packaging, c. 1895

32

33

31

23

AMERICAN

The makers of early Victorian posters were primarily concerned with conveying verbal messages and gave scant attention to artistic design. Typography was often a conglomeration of different styles, usually with broken fonts. Broadsides would feature various discordant typefaces, often within the same word; occasional small woodcut vignettes added some interest to an otherwise dull typographical arrangement. Some of the more amusing and successful concoctions were those announcing theater and circus performances, lectures, and auctions. Another reason for the poster's lack of artfulness was that the Victorian businessman could not see his high ideal of art, modeled after Italian Renaissance paintings, as having anything to do with the ephemeral needs of practical selling. Before the end of the century, however, type designers working with foundries like the American Type Founders Co. began to teach printers how to make type more readable. And pictorial posters became fashionable when businessmen finally came to realize that pictures attract an audience more easily than words.

34. Designer unknown. *American National Caravan*. Poster, 1831. Courtesy American Antiquarian Society, Worcester, Mass.

35. Designer unknown. *Payn & McNaughton*. Poster, 1847

34

PAYN & McNAUGHTON,

SIGN OF SEVEN HEADS, NEXT E. CORNING & CO.'S. No. 7 BROADWAY,

ALBANY, N. Y.

P. & McN. having received the Highest Premium from the New-York State Agricultural Society, as Manufacturers of the best articles above named, beg leave to assure the public, that their

TOBACCO, SNUFF, CIGARS,

CHOCOLATE & COCOA,

bearing the accompanying Stamps, are in no way inferior to that submitted to the Agricultural Society, but confidently believe it to be

SUPERIOR TO THAT MANUFACTURED ELSEWHERE.

We Use Rogers' Patent Tobacco Cutting Engine.

Sold

Here

36

37

38

26

39

40

In his book *The Democratic Art,* Peter Marzio quotes a social critic of the 1870s who attacked the chromolithograph as "the quintessence of the democratization and, therefore, debasement of high culture. It represented a 'pseudo-culture,' being one of a plethora of evil media—newspapers, magazines, lyceum lectures, small colleges—that diffused through the community a kind of smattering of all sorts of knowledge, a taste for art—that is, a desire to see and own pictures." The chromo did bring cheap reproductions of great paintings into the average home, but it also provided the means for colorful imagery to enhance the most quotidian advertising and publishing. Despite their naive aesthetic prejudices, businessmen realized that color helped increase sales. For the Victorian consumer, color printing—like color television almost a century later—was a metaphor for progress and affluence.

36. Designer unknown. *Uncle Sam's Little Dinner Party.* Poster, 1876. Courtesy New-York Historical Society

37. Designer unknown. *Robert Heller, Prestidigitateur.* Poster, c. 1895

38. Designer unknown. *Merchant's Gargling Oil.* Trade card, 1894

39. Designer unknown. *Cock Robin.* Pages from children's book published by McLaughlin Brothers, 1896

40. Designer unknown. *The Hanlons, "Le Voyage en Swiss."* Poster, c. 1880. Courtesy New York Public Library, Lincoln Center

A

FRENCH

Like England and the United States, France benefited from the Industrial Revolution and the subsequent rise of a middle class. From the 1830s, the country also experienced a betrayal of republicanism and a return to authoritarian rule. Early French Victorian graphic style is best represented by the satirical political and social lithographs of Charles Philipon, Honoré Daumier, Grandville, Henri Meunier, and others, which were published in journals like *La Charivari* and *La Caricature* under the censorship decrees of the "citizen king," Louis Philippe. Later, during the rule of Louis Napoleon, cartoonists such as Alfred Le Petit and André Gill popularized the "big-head, little-body" caricature. In advertising, the emphasis was on the word over the image, except for the occasional comic vignette. Poor standards in typography prevailed until around 1870, when Jules Chéret singlehandedly began a poster revolution that involved the marriage of text and image and supplied the basis for French Art Nouveau.

41. Alfred Le Petit. *Les Contemporains.* Magazine cover, 1889
42. Alfred Le Petit. *Les Contemporains.* Magazine cover, 1889
43. Rouchon. *A l'Oeil.* Poster, c. 1845. Musée de la Publicité, Paris
44. Rouchon. *Punch-Grassot.* Poster, 1845. Musée de la Publicité, Paris
45. Jules Chéret. *Aux Buttes Chaumont.* Poster, 1885. Musée de la Publicité, Paris

41

43

44

45

46. William Morris. *The Canterbury Tales.* Page, published by Kelmscott Press, 1896

housands of visitors from England and the Continent thronged to the colossal Crystal Palace in 1851 to view the remarkable products made by the most advanced manufacturing machinery the world had ever known. Yet they found that the only truly remarkable revelation was the poor aesthetic quality of virtually all the wares on exhibit. Rather than improving industrial goods, modern machinery had virtually stamped out taste by eliminating the role of the artist in the production process.

For the English middle class, born in the wake of the Industrial Revolution, industry symbolized the final break with everything associated with the medieval social system. By the mid-nineteenth century, handicrafts and craftsmen, the last remnants of the medieval artistic tradition, were seen as beneath contempt. The essential unity and interdependence of all artistic activity was utterly rejected. An article in an issue of *The International Studio* deeply lamented this popular view, "In former days there was no demarcation between the artist and the craftsman.... In modern times we make a distinction as arbitrary as it is invidious between 'fine' arts, thereby indicating exclusively painting and sculpture on the one hand and on the other those arts which we call 'minor' or more usually 'handicrafts' or 'industries.' And if we deign to name him 'artist' at all who is neither a painter of pictures nor a modeller of statues, we apply the term to him with little more significance than we should do in the case of a cook or hair-dresser."

While most Victorians remained apathetic to this situation, social reformers—including artists, architects, and writers—did try to reestablish aesthetic standards by developing a coherent national style. The art critic Henry Cole began publishing the *Journal of Design and Manufactures* in 1847, stating in its pages that "ornament must be secondary to the thing being decorated." In *The True Principles of Pointed or Christian Architecture* (1841), Augustus Welby Northmore Pugin championed the idea of honesty in architecture and design and announced that all ornament should constitute an enrichment of the essential form. The influential artist and critic John Ruskin argued that fitness of purpose was a moral obligation, that ornamentation should be organic, and that the Gothic form was not only the best national idiom but the panacea for the modern aesthetic malaise.

Ruskin's most enthusiastic colleague was William Morris, an architect and designer whose passions fueled the Arts and Crafts Movement and whose philosophy established the ethics of modern industrial design. Morris fervently rejected those forces that would separate art from everyday life and dedicated himself to fighting ugliness in all its forms. Believing that a society unable to produce good design had at its core a faulty ethical system, Morris developed a quasi-socialist philosophy. His system decreed that craftsmen-artists-designers would themselves take direct responsibility for their creations and thus restore the pride in work that had been violated by the anonymous production line. In their handcrafted nature, Morris's earliest furniture designs for his own home constituted his first protest against the machine aesthetic.

Distressed by the absence of British leadership in applied arts, Morris founded Morris, Marshall, Faulkner and Company (also known as Morris and Company) in 1861 in order to fabricate tastefully superior handcrafted furnishings for the mass consumer. Morris further sought to recreate a medieval arts and crafts environment, patterning his utopian ideals after those of the legendary "Merrie Olde England." In Morris's plan, workshops and guilds would be training grounds for the total artist, who would work with all mediums and forms, from architecture to typography.

Certain critics considered the Arts and Crafts Movement reactionary. Morris did sometimes encourage blind admiration for the antique, and he also condoned a certain snobbish intolerance for machinery. But he had a more conciliatory side as well. Aware of the latent promise of industry, he believed that in time its miracles of ingenuity would minimize the amount of time spent in unattractive labor.

Morris was a reformer, and Arts and Crafts was decidedly a reform movement—a struggle against the encroachment of industrialism on the workingman's way of life. The design pioneer Arthur H. Mackmurdo, who in 1882 founded the Century Guild (which marked a transition from Arts and Crafts to Art Nouveau), wrote that the movement was "not an aesthetic excursion; but a mighty upheaval of man's spiritual nature." As Nickolaus Pevsner observes, "What raises Morris as a reformer of design...is...that he recognized the indissoluble unity of an age and its social system.... Morris was the true prophet of the 20th Century, the father of the modern movement. We owe it to him that an ordinary man's dwelling house has once more become a subject of the architect's thought and a chair, a wallpaper, or a vase a worthy object of the artist's imagination.... Morris the artist may in the end not have been able to reach beyond the limitation of his century; Morris the man and thinker did."

Although some Arts and Crafts objects can be assigned to an individual, most represent the collective designs of the several loosely knit yet kindred communities based on Morris's precepts in England and the United States. Arts and Crafts quickly exerted influence as a decisive philosophical shift in Victorian aesthetics. Visually, the style remained consistent with the general Victorian preference for ornament, although it did wage war against the excessive Baroque and Romantic mannerisms of the age. Yet Arts and Crafts was not monolithic, running the gamut from its most characteristic primitive Gothic to Mackmurdo's asymmetrical floral designs, the Shaker-inspired simplicity of the American designer Gustav Stickley, the elegant ornamentalism of Louis Comfort Tiffany, and the early geometric stylings of Frank Lloyd Wright.

Despite some visual evidence to the contrary, Morris encouraged the return to simple figures, colors, and ornamental backgrounds. It was his emphasis on "decorative honesty," rather than his revivalist tendencies, that proved of lasting significance. From it arose the modern concept of the "total work of art," which inspired the various Arts and Crafts designers in England and America and later the Modernists on the Continent.

NOW·OPEN
AN·EXHIBITION·of
WALTER·CRANE'S
DESIGNS
AT·THE·FINE·ART
SOCIETY'S
148·NEW·BOND·S

47

THE CENTURY
GUILD

HOBBY HORSE
LONDON.
KEGAN PAUL, TRENCH AND CO:
I, PATERNOSTER SQUARE.

48

HILLYER·INSTI
TUTE·INDUS
TRIAL·AND
COMMERCIAL
EDUCATION
HARTFORD·Y·
M·C·A

SEASON·OF·1895
AND·1896·EVEN
ING·CLASSES·IN
MECHANICAL
DRAWING·PATTERN
·MAKING·BLACK
SMITHING··ELEC
TRICITY···SHORT
HAND·MATHEMAT
ICS·ETC·ETC··
FOR·CATALOGS·AND·PARTICULARS·
APLY·TO·THE·EDUCATIONAL·SECTY

49

JOHN
LANE'S
PVBLICATIONS
IN
BELLES-
LETTRES
FROM THE
BODLEY
HEAD

50

51

52

53

54

55

BRITISH

In an article published in an 1899 issue of *The International Studio,* Aymer Vallance said of Selwyn Image's design of *The Century Guild Hobby Horse:* "Never before had modern printing been treated as a serious art whose province was to embrace the whole process from the selection and spacing of the type and the position of the printed matter on the page, to the embellishment of the book with appropriate initials and other decorative ornaments." Renaissance printers had, of course, been no less concerned with typographic clarity and beauty; however, when compared with most early Victorian printing, the Arts and Crafts graphic style was indeed more handsome, if not curiously original. Influenced by Gothic manuscript illumination and wall tapestries, the floral and curvilinear motifs shown here suggest a new direction in graphic presentation, one that later contributed to Art Nouveau.

47. Designer unknown. *An Exhibition of Walter Crane's Designs.* Poster, c. 1895

48. Selwyn Image. *The Century Guild Hobby Horse.* Title page, 1884

49. Wilbur Macey Stone. *Hillyer Institute.* Poster, 1895

50. Aubrey Beardsley. *Belles-Lettres.* Page, c. 1896

51. Aubrey Beardsley. *The Studio.* Magazine cover, January 15, 1894. Courtesy Chris Mullen

52–55. Designers unknown. *The Studio.* Title pages from a competition exercise, c. 1888. Courtesy Chris Mullen

56. William Morris. *The Woodpecker.* Tapestry, 1885. William Morris Gallery, Walthamstow, England

56

33

57

58

BRITISH

From its inception, the handicraft revival was tinged with a Romantic antiquarianism. William Morris, who spent his whole life fighting ugliness, believed that Gothic was the best national idiom—an English art for England. *Gothic* is also the term applied to modern, sans-serif typefaces, those that reject classical Roman typography. As Morris defined it, despite its historical roots, Gothic was synonymous with change. Aubrey Beardsley's synthesis of the Gothic and the Romantic in the *Morte d'Arthur* typifies the imaginative strength of the new art. In Beardsley's work, naturalistic ornament served a formal rather than a simplistically decorative purpose. Morris further changed the basic printing practice of the late nineteenth century by returning it to the hands of artisans and craftsmen and by urging the development of a widespread English private-press movement. The pages produced by Morris's Kelmscott Press—influenced by incunabula and employing Gothic types and naturalistic motifs—were purposeful rejections of the rational and academic values of the Italian Renaissance. The lover of Renaissance typography will no doubt find the designs of Morris and his followers claustrophobic in their attempts to fill every inch of empty space with symbolic meaning, but in their time these designs opened a path to a new beauty.

57. Selwyn Image. *Jesus Hominum Salvator.* Book illustration, c. 1885

58. Edward Burne-Jones and William Morris. *Sigurd the Volsung.* Decorated page, with illustration by Burne-Jones and woodcut border by Morris, published by the Kelmscott Press, 1897

59. Aubrey Beardsley. *Morte d'Arthur.* Decorated page, 1893

60. Charles Ricketts. *Hero and Leander.* Title page, trial proof woodcut, 1894. Museum of Art, Rhode Island School of Design, Providence. Gift of Mrs. Gustave Radeke

61. Aubrey Beardsley. *Morte d'Arthur.* Page, 1893

62. Aubrey Beardsley. *Morte d'Arthur.* Frieze, 1893

63. Designer unknown. *The Book of Job.* Book cover, published by the Abbey Press, 1902

64. Gleeson White. *Sir Edward Burne-Jones, A Record and Review.* Design for book cover, from *The Studio,* 1894

65. Charles Ricketts. *The Ballad of Reading Gaol.* Artist's mark, 1898

66. Arthur H. Mackmurdo. *The Century Guild.* Artist's mark, 1884

67. C. R. Ashbee. *The Guild of Handicraft.* Artist's mark, date unknown

59

60

61

62

63

64

65

66

67

35

One morn, said the Cat to his Master, "I pray
You to go and to bathe in the river to-day;
The Marquis of Carabas, too, you must be,
And leave all the rest of the business to me."
Now, while the King down by the river passed by,
He heard dismal cries of—" Help! help! or he'll die!
The Marquis of Carabas drowns!—O my master!"
The King sent his guards to avert the disaster.
The Miller's son finds himself pulled out, and drest
In all that his Majesty had of the best;

69

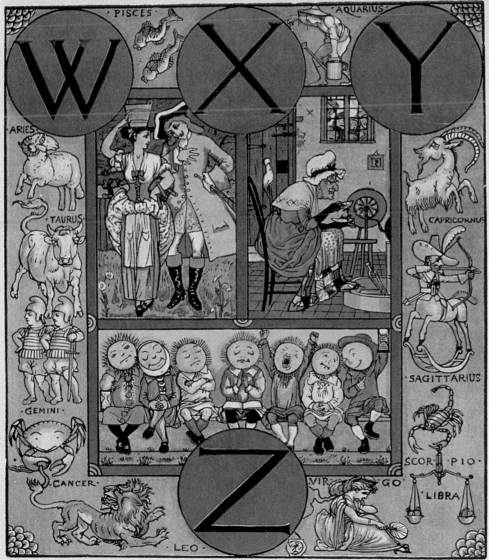

70

BRITISH

Various Arts and Crafts themes were elaborated as the style took hold in England and later on the Continent. William Morris's Gothic obsession was a major motif but only one aspect of a greater need to develop viable design standards. Owen Jones, who had designed the Egyptian, Roman, and Greek displays for the Great Exhibition of 1851, understood the need for the proper models on which to base aesthetically pleasing ornament. Jones compiled an international sampling of historical patterns and motifs in his popular *Grammar of Ornament,* which became a sourcebook for Arts and Crafts innovators. Among these was Arthur H. Mackmurdo, whose curvilinear patterns were a particularly noteworthy response to such exotic forms. Reprinted in many editions over the years, Jones's seminal work influenced designers even as late as the Art Deco era. The Arts and Crafts style also became a symbol of a certain liberalism and education, a heritage to which Walter Crane was a significant contributor. A socialist cartoonist as well as a designer of textiles, wallpaper, tiles, cards, and calendars, Crane left his most lasting mark as a children's book writer and illustrator. His series of inexpensive books were the first successful mass-market works in color for children. Crane's illustrations wed the influence of William Blake with that of Japanese woodblock prints. He was one of the first illustrators to acknowledge the relationship between illustration, typography, and page design.

68. Original Egyptian decorative designs. Page from *The Grammar of Ornament* by Owen Jones, 1856. Courtesy Chris Mullen

69. Walter Crane. *Puss in Boots.* Pages, date unknown. Courtesy Chris Mullen

70. Walter Crane. *The Alphabet of Old Friends.* Pages, date unknown. Courtesy Chris Mullen

71. Arthur H. Mackmurdo. Dining chair with fret back, 1881. William Morris Gallery, Walthamstow, England

71

37

AMERICAN

Gustav Stickley is credited with giving the Arts and Crafts style a uniquely American flavor. Stickley is best known for his functional, straight-line furniture in the Mission or Craftsman Style. He experimented with a guild system at his furniture plant in Syracuse, New York, and for thirteen years published and designed a periodical, *The Craftsman,* dedicated to the teachings of Ruskin and Morris. In his first issue, Stickley stated his goals: to "teach that beauty does not imply elaboration or ornament; to employ only those forms and materials which make for simplicity, individuality and dignity of effect." From 1890 to 1914, a spirit of adventure seized American printers, and the Arts and Crafts book represented a brief but intense episode in printing history. The influence of incunabula and medievalism is exemplified here by the designs of Daniel Berkley Updike and Walter Crane. An "aesthetic style," based on classical Roman typography, also grew in opposition to Arts and Crafts Romanticism. In other areas, American Arts and Crafts developed its own formal vocabulary. The Keramic Studio was founded as the voice of ceramicists, and Arts and Crafts guilds and workshops arose in many parts of the country around various strong individuals, including A. E. Mathews and Elbert Hubbard. Frank Lloyd Wright was also an early proponent of Arts and Crafts ideals, but lost fervor when he realized that the cursed machine was a necessary component in the future of American design. Outlasting its European counterparts, Arts and Crafts ended in America about 1914 as an "artsy-craftsy" middle-class style.

72. Gustav Stickley. Library table. Illustration from *The Craftsman,* c. 1901

73. Designer unknown. *Keramic Studio.* Magazine cover, December 1906. Everson Museum of Art, Syracuse, N.Y.

74. Gustav Stickley. *The Craftsman.* Magazine cover, 1901

75. Daniel Berkley Updike (designer) and Robert Anning Bell (illustrator). *Altar Book.* Decorative pages, 1896. Princeton University Library

76. Walter Crane. *Arts and Crafts.* Magazine cover, April 1893. Published by the Art Worker's Guild, Philadelphia

77. Designer unknown. Original designs used for the stenciling of walls and decoration, c. 1902. From *The Craftsman*

72

73

74

75

76

77

40

78. Henri de Toulouse-Lautrec. *Reine de Joie.* Poster, 1892. The Museum of Modern Art, New York. Gift of Mr. and Mrs. Richard Rodgers

Floreated madness, linear hysteria, strange decorative disease, stylistic free-for-all—such were the terms its contemporaries used to describe Art Nouveau, the first international design style. Dating from the 1880s to the outset of World War I, Art Nouveau was a rebellion against the entire Victorian sensibility, steeped as it was in the past. The exponents of the style fervently hoped to revolutionize every aspect of design in order to set a standard that would be compatible with the new age. For a relatively short period, Art Nouveau was, as one critic wrote, "one of the most imaginative innovations in the history of design."

Despite its name, Art Nouveau was born in England, the fountainhead of the European avant-garde at the time. It was a direct descendant of the Arts and Crafts Movement, specifically as practiced by Arthur H. Mackmurdo, who combined a penchant for Pre-Raphaelite Romantic symbolism with a pragmatic desire to reform design. A significant departure from the prevalent Gothicism, the cover of Mackmurdo's book *Wren's City Churches* (1883) formally employed Art Nouveau's characteristic organic, leafy motifs for the first time. Among the direct sources for the cover were Hokusai's woodblock prints and Blake's illustrations for "Songs of Innocence." Other English Art Nouveau progenitors include Aubrey Beardsley, who added a mystical quality to the new linear vocabulary, and C. F. A. Voysey, who helped bring English Art Nouveau to the Continent.

Caught between "art for art's sake" and functional aesthetics, Art Nouveau was an odd blend of art, artifice, and practicality. Like most things that insist on being totally new, it could not help reinterpreting the past: oriental art was seen afresh; Rococo art was borrowed to some degree; Celtic illuminated manuscripts were admired for their unity of design and their Romantic remoteness. The aesthetes among the Art Nouveau designers employed curvilinear and floral abstraction as a playful, yet generally functional, relief to conventional form. Yet, despite their professed revolutionary aims, they sometimes became immured in frivolous middle-class concerns. In fact, Art Nouveau designs obscured the surface of a structure just as often as the maligned Victorian ornamentation had.

Another faction of Art Nouveau practitioners, the so-called decadents, indulged wholeheartedly in the excesses of the style. In their fascination with mysticism, they developed a hierarchy of exotic goddesses and nymphets that were at once weird, fantastic, mysterious, esoteric, and decidedly kitsch.

Other Art Nouveau designers who saw the arts as servants of life sought ways to apply the lessons of modern technology to art. Interested more in the architectonic than the organic form, these rationalists generally concerned themselves with logical and geometric constructions. One of these, Lewis F. Day, stated: "Whether we like it or not, machinery, steam power and electricity…will have something to say about ornament of the future." Indeed, the more practical among these early Modernists thought that the machine could be used to disseminate beauty as well as progress or comfort throughout society. Art Nouveau did, in fact, become the first commercial art consistently used to enhance the beauty of industrial products.

With art books and magazines more available because of economical printing methods, the Art Nouveau revolution blossomed throughout the Continent. The first major stylistic upheaval in which antiquity was no longer the dominant influence, it became both a popular fashion and a bridge into the twentieth century. Savvy entrepreneurs in Europe and the United States—including Julius Meier-Graefe in Munich, Samuel Bing in Paris, Arthur L. Liberty in London, and Louis Comfort Tiffany in New York—proselytized, popularized, and, through relentless commercialism, eventually trivialized the new style.

While a common form language linked the various versions of Art Nouveau, the style developed differently in each country. In England, new simplified forms had dictated suitable decoration; in France, Le Style Moderne developed from a sense that decoration dictated form. The style came to Belgium in the early eighties, when Octave Maus established the Cercle des XX. Later Belgian developments included La Libre Esthetique, whose members espoused the whiplash linear style dominant in Brussels, and Victor Horta's "high Art Nouveau," marked by a hysterical linearism. During the mid-nineties, German Jugendstil (youth style) and, shortly afterward, the Austrian Secession were characterized by hard-edged, angular graphics, derived in part from northern printmaking techniques, and a typography decorative to the point of illegibility. The Secession was further influenced by Charles Rennie Mackintosh and the Glasgow School, whose rectilinear symmetry heralded the inevitable retreat from the purely decorative Art Nouveau style.

Although Art Nouveau was never really predominant in America, it was fashionable for a time. Tiffany's Fevrile glass, Louis Sullivan's Celtic architectural ornament, and Will Bradley's posters all drew upon Europe for inspiration. In Spain, the architect Antoni Gaudí and the exponents of Modernista saw the future graphically in terms of undulating surfaces and moving planes. In Italy, Stile Liberty never quite developed a national identity; the more original Novocento Style arose there at the turn of the century as the poet and politician Gabriele D'Annunzio called for a return to the Romantic past. In Holland, two influential Art Nouveau painters and poster artists, Jan Toorop and Johan Thorn Prikker, made sorties into the world of mystical symbolism.

By 1894, Henry Van de Velde (the Belgian architect and designer who founded the applied art school that became the Bauhaus) was the leading theorist of what he called "an art nouveau." He believed that good design was a social curative and wrote, "Ruskin and Morris chase ugliness out of man's heart, I out of his intellect." Van de Velde saw the new movement as a way for art and industry to derive a vision of the future together. Although the Art Nouveau decorative style was ultimately limited—and thus incapable of realizing such a vision—it did provide a curious stepping-stone that the Modernists would later employ to attain that future.

FRENCH/BELGIAN

The stage was set for *L'Art Moderne,* the name originally given to the new style coalescing in France and Belgium during the late nineteenth century. From the 1870s almost to the end of the century, Jules Chéret had enlivened Parisian streets with hundreds of his advertising posters featuring Rococo-inspired line and a brilliant color palette. By the 1890s, other illustrators of the *bon ton,* including Henri de Toulouse-Lautrec, Théophile Alexandre Steinlen, and Pierre Bonnard, joined the ranks of innovative street artists in advertising all types of events and products with posters that wed Japanese elegance, Symbolist mystery, and the Post-Impressionist vision. From England, Arthur H. Mackmurdo's botanical cover design for *Wren's City Churches* led to the emergence of the classic Art Nouveau graphic style. By the time it was elaborated in the posters of its most significant proponents, the Swiss Eugène Grasset and the Czech Alphonse Mucha (both émigrés to Paris), Art Nouveau had become a pan-European movement.

79. Arthur H. Mackmurdo. *Wren's City Churches.* Title page, published by G. Allen, 1883. The Mitchell Wolfson Jr. Collection of Decorative and Propaganda Arts, Miami

80. Privat Livemont. *La Réforme.* Poster, 1897. Musée de la Publicité, Paris

81. Henri Meunier. *Savon Swan.* Poster, c. 1899. Musée de la Publicité, Paris

82. Pierre Bonnard. *France-Champagne.* Poster, 1891. Cleveland Museum of Art. Mr. and Mrs. Lewis B. Williams Collection, Gift of Lewis B. Williams

83. Henri de Toulouse-Lautrec. Drawing of a woman, c. 1890

84. Jules Chéret. Drawing of a woman, c. 1895

85. Théophile Alexandre Steinlen. *Gil Blas.* Magazine cover, November 1893

79

80

81

82

83

84

85

86

87

88

89

90

FRENCH/BELGIAN

The late nineteenth-century revolution in French painting was fully appreciated by a relatively privileged few. René Martin, writing in *Le Figaro* in 1885, said that "there is far more talent shown in a poster than in many of the most discussed paintings in the salon," and by 1890 the Art Nouveau poster was the most popular form of mass art. Although the style had many guises, its most typical was the free-flowing organic form, based on floral abstraction and flat patterns, with a skipping or undulating rhythmic design. In its attempt to escape from formalism, Art Nouveau ended up with a perfect evocation of a natural form. Some thought the style would be the hope for a new tomorrow, others were sure it would result in cultural degeneracy. But, for the brief period during which it flourished, the Art Nouveau style served as a strong force in disseminating the applied arts to a mass audience.

86. Eugène Grasset. *Marque Georges Richard, Cycles & Automobiles.* Poster, 1899

87. Jean Miscelas Peske. *L'Estampe et l'Affiche.* Poster, 1898. Courtesy Posters Please, Inc., New York

88. Jean de Paléologue. *Fernand Clément & Cie.* Poster, 1894

89. Henri de Toulouse-Lautrec. *Jane Avril.* Poster, 1899

90. Henri de Toulouse-Lautrec. *Babylone d'Allemagne.* Poster, 1894. Kunstgewerbe-museum, Zurich

91. A. Turpain. *La Lumière.* Book cover, 1913. The Mitchell Wolfson Jr. Collection of Decorative and Propaganda Arts, Miami

91

93

94

FRENCH/BELGIAN

The Art Nouveau aesthetic marked virtually everything from buildings to furniture to glassware. The typefaces, borders, ornaments, and dingbats that characterized Art Nouveau printing accorded with the stylistic innovations of architects and designers such as Henri Guimard and Emile Gallé. Among the artists of *la belle époque* were some of the most original type designers, Georges Auriol, Alphonse Mucha, and Eugène Grasset, who created emblematic designs for leading Parisian typefoundries, like Deberny and Company, G. Peignot and Sons, and Robert Girard & Cie. All their new typefaces were heralded by specimen booklets, which also usually contained a wide selection of imaginative and stylish vignettes (or *clichés*), used to embellish the Art Nouveau page. Such design manuals as Mucha's *Combinaisons Ornementales* and *Documents Décoratifs* served as models from which the new trends could be advanced to printers throughout France.

92. Henri Guimard. Angled cupboard. From Nozal House, c. 1904–7. Musée de la Publicité, Paris

93. Alphonse Mucha. *Combinaisons Ornementales*. Cover of type specimen book, c. 1898

94. Alphonse Mucha. *Documents Décoratifs*. Cover of type specimen book, c. 1898

95. Various designers. Ornaments and silhouettes. Specimen from Fonderies Deberny & Peignot, 1910

96. Designer unknown. Cafe sign. Bronze, 1900. The Museum of Modern Art, New York. Gift of Joseph H. Heil

97. Designer unknown. Motifs and typography, c. 1900. *Top to bottom:* Auriol Italic; Kalligraphia; Wotan; Arnold Bocklin; Aegean

92

95

46

96

AABCDEFGHIJKLLMNOPQRSTTUVWXYZ

ABCDEFGHIJKLMNOPQRSTUVWXYZ

ABCDEFGHIJKLMNOPQRSTUVXYZ

ABCDEFGHIJKLMNOPQRSTUVWXYZ

ABCDEFGHIJKLMNOPQRSTTUVWXY

97

FRENCH/BELGIAN

Art Nouveau held such sway in the graphic arts that many contemporary artists and designers who did not otherwise consider themselves exponents of the style applied certain of its mannerisms to their work. Cartoonists in particular found that Art Nouveau traits helped them signal a contemporary look as distinguished from the more academic Beaux-Arts drawing tradition. The artists of *L'Assiette au Beurre* (The Butter Dish), which lasted from 1901 to 1912 and was one of France's most acerbic illustrated weeklies, often combined Art Nouveau exaggeration with the kind of elegant drawing of a Bonnard or Lautrec to help convey their caustic social and political messages. *L'Assiette au Beurre* in turn influenced the cartoon style of other French satiric and humor magazines, such as the nationalistic *La Baïonnette* and the lighthearted *Le Sourire.*

98. Thomaz Leal de Camara. *Visions!* Cover of *L'Assiette au Beurre,* satirizing British imperialism, 1903

99. Weiluc. *The Killers on the Roads.* Cover of *L'Assiette au Beurre,* on motorcar racing, 1902

100. Miklos Vadasz. *Princes Russes.* Cartoon from *L'Assiette au Beurre,* May 12, 1906

101. Dimitrios Galanis. *Love.* Cover of *L'Assiette au Beurre,* June 17, 1905

102. Dimitrios Galanis. Cartoon from *L'Assiette au Beurre,* commenting on French colonialism, 1902

103. Galantara. Cartoon from *L'Assiette au Beurre,* satirizing greed, 1901

104. Pierre Bonnard. *La Revue Blanche.* Poster, 1894. The Museum of Modern Art, New York

105. Marco de Gastyne. *La Baïonnette.* Magazine cover, 1917

106. Paul Iribe. *Le Sourire.* Magazine cover, 1903

98

99

100

101

102

103

104

105

106

FRENCH/BELGIAN

Jules Chéret created the most well known
posters of *la belle époque.* He was awarded the
nation's most prestigious award, the Légion
d'Honneur, "for creating a new branch of art by
applying art to commercial and industrial painting." Chéret opened the floodgates for scores of
other highly skilled decorators of the urban
streetscape, among them Emmanuel Orazi.
However, the most emblematic Art Nouveau
images are those of Alphonse Mucha, whose
Byzantine style characterized by idealized por-
traits of women framed by cherubs, palm leaves,
and mosaics helped to elevate advertising to a
fine art.

107. Alphonse Mucha. *Bières de la Meuse.*
Poster, 1897. Courtesy Posters Please, Inc., New
York

108. Alphonse Mucha. *Waverley Cycles.* Poster,
1898. Courtesy Posters Please, Inc., New York

109. Jules Chéret. *Ed. Sagot.* Poster, 1891.
Courtesy Posters Please, Inc., New York

110. Jules Chéret. *La Loïe Fuller.* Poster, 1893.
Courtesy Posters Please, Inc., New York

111. Emmanuel Orazi. *Contrexéville.* Poster,
1900. Courtesy Posters Please, Inc., New York

107

108

109

110

111

51

8. Jahrgang

Beiblatt des Simplicissimus

Nummer 8

München, den 19. Mai 1903 — Illustrierte Wochenschrift — Verlag von Albert Langen in München

Der „Simplicissimus" erscheint wöchentlich einmal. Bestellungen werden von allen Postämtern, Zeitungs-Expeditionen und Buchhandlungen entgegengenommen. Billige Ausgabe pro Nummer 15 Pf. ohne Frankatur, pro Quartal (13 Nummern) M. 1.80 (bei direkter Zusendung unter Kreuzband im Inland M. 2.25, im Ausland M. 2.45), pro Jahr M. 7.20 (bei direkter Zusendung im Inland M. 9.—, im Ausland M. 9.80).— Die Luxus-Ausgabe die mit besonderer Sorgfalt auf besserem Papier hergestellt wird, kostet pro Nummer 25 Pf. ohne Frankatur, pro Quartal M. 3.— (bei direkter Zusendung unter Kreuzband im Inland M. 3.75, in Rolle verpackt M. 5.—, im Ausland nur in Rolle M. 6.—), pro Jahr M. 12.— (bei direkter Zusendung im Inland M. 15.—, in Rolle verpackt M. 20.—, im Ausland nur in Rolle M. 24.—).

Zu spät

(Zeichnung von J. B. Engl)

„O mei, o mei, jezt haut sich der dumm' Bua an Daum'n ob weg'n der Militari. Dös is a Unglück, jezt bist a Krüpp'l und zu nix'n mehr z' brauch'n." — „Jessas ja, an dös hon i net denkt, jezt konn i nimmer raffa a."

113

JUGENDSTIL

Art Nouveau arrived a little later in Germany than in England, France, and Belgium, but it nevertheless became the dominant national style between 1896 and approximately 1909. Munich was the capital of Jugendstil (youth style), being the birthplace of the Munich Secession (which represented mystical and mythological strains in the decorative arts), the headquarters of the arts journal *Pan,* which championed the new art, and home to the style's major designers and leading applied-arts schools and galleries. With the founding in 1897 of the Vereinigten Werkstätten by Peter Behrens, Hermann Obrist, Richard Riemerschmid, and others under the influence of the theorist Henry Van de Velde, Jugendstil was applied to a wide range of products, furniture, and architecture. While Jugendstil was promoted in publications such as *Kunst und Handwerk, Dekorative Kunst,* and *Deutsche Kunst und Dekoration,* it was the trendsetting cultural weekly *Jugend,* founded by Georg Hirth in 1896, that gave Jugendstil its name. Also in the same year, Albert Langen began publishing his satirical weekly *Simplicissimus,* whose Jugendstil-inspired artists profoundly influenced the expressive look and acerbic content of cartoons and caricatures elsewhere in Europe.

112. Designers unknown. *Simplicissimus.* Page of advertisements, 1909

113. Franz Von Reznicek. *Die Frau in der Karikatur.* Cover of a book by Eduard Fuchs, 1906

114. Bruno Paul. Cartoon from *Simplicissimus.* 1904

115. Bruno Paul. *Simplicissimus Ausstellung.* Poster, 1906

114

115

JUGENDSTIL

Jugendstil developed into a distinctly German graphic vocabulary. Drawing on Germanic printmaking traditions and a certain Bavarian regimentation, Jugendstil was often more precise and hard-edged than its naturalist-oriented counterparts. Yet the style made allowances for its practitioners' individual approaches, as evidenced by the variety of methods, from the classical to the Romantic, seen on the illustrated covers of *Jugend*. Despite these individual mannerisms, the typical Jugendstil letter and image combination is unmistakable, whether employed as an advertisement for a restaurant, the cover of a novel, or a poster for an exhibition.

116. Arnost Hofbauer. *Topičův Salon.* Poster, 1898. Courtesy Posters Please, Inc., New York

117. Designer unknown. *Seltsame Geschichten (Curious Stories).* Book cover, 1905

118. M. Janselow. *Lustige Blätter.* Magazine cover, 1900

119. Hans Christiansen. *Jugend.* Magazine cover, 1899

120. Designer unknown. *Jugend.* Magazine cover, 1899

121. Designer unknown. *Jugend.* Magazine cover, 1900

122. Ludwig Lutz Ehrenberger. *Frz X. Thallmaier.* Poster, 1905. Courtesy Reinhold Brown Gallery, New York

116

117

118

119

120

121

122

ABCDEFGHIJKLMNOPQRSTUVWXYZ

ABCDEFGHIJKLMNOPQRSTUVWXYZ

ABCDEFGHIJKLMNOPQRSTUVWXY.

Steckenpferd-Lilienmilch-Seif

das beste tägliche Getränk

vanHouten's Cacao

ABCDEFGHIJKLMNOPQRSTUVWXYZ

ABCDEPFGHIJKLMNOPQRSTUVWXYZ

ABCDEFGHIJKLMNOPQRSTUVWXYZ

124

125

JUGENDSTIL

Jugendstil designers rejected traditional methods of typography in favor of unique display typefaces that worked harmoniously with the image. Such a choice is evident in the posters by Bruno Paul and Henry Van de Velde shown here, while the work by Johan Thorn Prikker (one of Holland's significant Art Nouveau proponents) shows an all-purpose use of a traditional Gothic lettering. One-of-a-kind brushed letters were used on posters and advertisements, and a few eccentric yet emblematic faces were devised as complete alphabets. The Germans actually produced the first Art Nouveau typeface, designed by Otto Eckmann for the Klingspor Typefoundry and sold to printers throughout Europe. Many of the odder, and often illegible, faces shown here were redrawn and used as novelty types decades later.

123. Designers unknown. Jugendstil typography and advertisements. *Top to bottom:* Carmen, c. 1900; Fantasia-Grotesque, c. 1900; Sezession, c. 1902; two advertisements from *Jugend,* 1907; Eckmann-Schrift, 1896; Siegfield, c. 1900; Herold Reklameschrift, 1904

124. Bruno Paul. *Kunst im Handwerk.* Exhibition poster for Arts in Crafts in Munich, 1901. Courtesy Fairleigh Dickinson University, Madison, N.J.

125. Henry Van de Velde. *Tropon.* Poster for a food company, 1897. Courtesy Fairleigh Dickinson University, Madison, N.J.

126. Johan Thorn Prikker. *Holländische Kunstausstellung.* Exhibition poster for the Kaiser Wilhelm Museum, 1903. Courtesy Fairleigh Dickinson University, Madison, N.J.

126

GLASGOW STYLE

Inspired by traditional Celtic ornament and Aubrey Beardsley's distinctive line, the Scotsman Charles Rennie Mackintosh developed a new visual language that became known as the Glasgow Style. Because of its initial use of botanical motifs during the early 1890s, the Glasgow Style is usually linked with Art Nouveau, but it was more precisely a rejection of such motifs in favor of more functional design. As Mario Amaya writes: "Mackintosh, with bold Scots directness and a rectilinear neatness seemed to offer a solution basing many of his designs on geometry, particularly the cube." The Glasgow Four (Mackintosh, his wife, Margaret Macdonald, and J. Herbert and Frances McNair) further influenced other designers working at the time in the Scottish capital. Their work as graphic, textile, and interior designers and as architects also fascinated the Austrian Secessionists, who found it an exciting alternative to floreated abstraction.

127. Charles Rennie Mackintosh. Clock, with six columns and domino figures, 1917–19. Courtesy Chris Mullen

128. Charles Rennie Mackintosh. High-backed ladder-back chair, 1902

129. M. G. Lightfoot. *Midsummer Night's Dream.* Book cover, date unknown. National Museums and Galleries on Merseyside, Walker Art Gallery, Liverpool

130. J. Herbert MacNair. *Liverpool Academy of Arts.* Poster, 1901. Merseyside County Art Galleries, Liverpool

131. J. Herbert McNair and Margaret and Frances Macdonald. *Glasgow Institute of the Fine Arts.* Poster, 1895. Library of Congress, Washington, D.C. Poster Collection

132. Jessie M. King. *The Arcadian.* Restaurant announcement, date unknown. Hunterian Art Gallery, University of Glasgow

133. Charles Rennie Mackintosh. *Stylized Flowers and Checkerwork.* Textile design, 1920. Hunterian Art Gallery, University of Glasgow, Mackintosh Collection

134. Charles Rennie Mackintosh. *Tulip Lattice.* Textile design, date unknown. Hunterian Art Gallery, University of Glasgow, Mackintosh Collection

129

127   128

130

131

132

133

134

135

136

137

138

139

140

VIENNA SECESSION

During the 1890s, the visual arts in Vienna were dominated by conservative academicians whose schools and societies refused to exhibit the new developments in European plastic and applied arts. Frustrated by unsuccessful attempts to expand the boundaries of their art and inspired by the Munich Secession's break with tradition, a group of young architects, painters, and graphic artists, including Josef Hoffmann, Joseph Olbrich, Gustav Klimt, and Koloman Moser in 1897 founded the Vereinigung Bildender Künstler Österreichs, better known as the Vienna Secession. As evidenced in their journal, *Ver Sacrum (Sacred Spring)*, the language of Sezessionstil was akin to that of Jugendstil with added personal touches of Pre-Raphaelitism, the antique, and the classical. Yet, as the designs of many of its exhibition posters show, certain members of the Secession rejected naturalistic tendencies in favor of Otto Wagner's purist straight line and Hoffmann's simplified geometry. In this regard, their work prefigured the functionalism of future Modernists.

135. Ferdinand Andri. *Secession.* Exhibition poster, date unknown. Collection Barry Friedman Ltd., New York

136. Ferdinand Hodler. *Ver Sacrum.* Exhibition poster, 1904. Kunstgewerbemuseum, Zurich

137. Koloman Moser. *Ver Sacrum.* Magazine cover, 1899

138. Koloman Moser. *Ver Sacrum.* Page, 1899

139. Designers unknown. *Ver Sacrum.* Advertisement page, 1899

140. Koloman Moser. *Ver Sacrum.* Magazine cover, 1899

VIENNA SECESSION

Despite their affinities with other contemporary styles, the Secessionists reaffirmed their artistic independence in their first issue of *Ver Sacrum:* "We desire an art not enslaved to foreigners. …The art from abroad should act upon us as an incentive to reflect upon ourselves; we want to recognize it, admire it, if it deserves our admiration; the only thing we don't want to do is imitate it." True to this statement, the Secessionist graphic style quickly evolved a distinctive personality, from the elegant classicism of Klimt's first exhibition poster to the group's unprecedented feats of typographic artistry.

141. Joseph Maria Olbrich. *Secession.* Catalogue cover showing the Secession Exhibition building, 1898–99. Collection Galerie Pabst, Munich

142. Alfred Roller. *Sixteenth Vienna Secession.* Exhibition poster, 1903. Kunstgewerbemuseum, Zurich

143. Koloman Moser. *Thirteenth Vienna Secession.* Exhibition poster, 1902. Graphische Sammlung Albertina, Vienna

144. Koloman Moser. *Frommes Kalendar.* Poster, 1899. Collection Barry Friedman Ltd., New York

145. Ferdinand Andri. *10th Exhibition of Vienna Secession.* Poster, c. 1901. Collection Reinhold Brown Gallery, New York

146. Gustav Klimt. *I. Kunstaustellung Secession.* Poster for the first Vienna Secession exhibition (before censorship), c. 1901. Courtesy Posters Please, Inc., New York

142

143

141

144

145

146

147

148

149

150

151

152

153

AMERICAN

By 1890, a new genre of advertising known as the art poster began to flower in America. Distinct from the typographically cluttered bills of the Victorian era, these were colorful, economically rendered posters usually sponsored by a publishing house to advertise a special issue of a magazine or newspaper or a new book. The master posterist Edward Penfield wrote, "I think the American Poster has opened a new school whose aim is simplicity and good composition." While *Harper's* used Penfield exclusively, other publishers employed such artists as Will Carqueville, Frank Hazenplug, Louis Rhead, and Maxfield Parrish. The firm of Stone and Kimball, American publishers of the English arts journal the *Yellow Book,* commissioned one poster from Lautrec, but their most notable were by Hazenplug and Will Bradley. Termed the American Beardsley, Bradley also designed covers for the influential trade journal *The Inland Printer* and his own magazine, *Bradley: His Book,* dedicated to the promotion of fine typography, design, paper, and printing. By the mid-nineties, the art poster had become so popular that manufacturers were promoting contests for the most original advertisements.

147. William L. Carqueville. *Lippincott's.* Poster, January 1895. Library of Congress, Washington, D.C. Poster Collection

148. Will Bradley. *Victor Bicycles.* Poster, 1896

149. Will Bradley. *The Inland Printer.* Poster, February 1895

150. Maxfield Parrish. *Midsummer Holiday.* Magazine cover for *The Century,* 1897

151. Frank Hazenplug. *The Chap-Book.* Poster for a literary magazine, 1896. Museum für Kunst und Gewerbe, Hamburg

152. Edward Penfield. *Harper's.* Poster, 1897. The Museum of Modern Art, New York

153. Louis Rhead. *Harper's Bazar.* Cover and back cover, 1894. Library of Congress, Washington, D.C. Poster Collection

154. Arthur Dow. *Modern Art.* Poster for a book published by Louis Prang, 1895. Library of Congress, Washington, D.C. Poster Collection

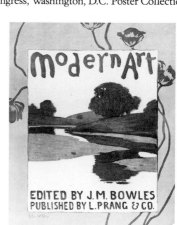

154

AMERICAN

By the turn of the century, Charles Dana Gibson could command $100,000 for one hundred black-and-white line drawings featuring his Gibson Girl. This graphic invention became a fashion rage and a boon to magazine circulation. Many other specialized illustrators and cartoonists shared Gibson's limelight—such was the commercial power of graphic art before radio or film. *Life* was called "the gentle satirist," criticizing yet also promoting the Gilded Age life-style through its smart writing, humorous graphic commentary, and delightful illustration. The Art Nouveau-inspired graphic styles of Clarence Coles Phillips and John Cecil Clay epitomized both the sophisticated bias of the magazine and the elegant graphic look of the day.

155. Charles Dana Gibson. Gibson girls. Sketches, c. 1902

156. John Cecil Clay. *Butterflies.* Magazine cover for *Life,* August 4, 1904

157. Coles Phillips. *Life.* Magazine cover, June 10, 1909

158. Coles Phillips. *Life.* Magazine cover, February 20, 1908

159. Coles Phillips. *Life.* Magazine cover, January 14, 1909

160. Coles Phillips. *Life.* Magazine cover, December 2, 1909

161. John Cecil Clay. *Harvesting.* Magazine cover for *Life,* October 5, 1905

162. Coles Phillips. *Light Consumes Coal, Save Light, Save Coal.* Poster, c. 1915–16. The Mitchell Wolfson Jr. Collection of Decorative and Propaganda Arts, Miami

157

156

158

159

155

160

161

164

165

166

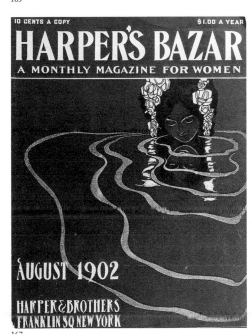

167

AMERICAN

Unlike European Art Nouveau designers, American graphic artists did not employ the style to change the spiritual, cultural, or political world. For them, the style was consistent with both the commercial and technological requisites of the age. *The Burr McIntosh Monthly* (the first American magazine to list an art director on its masthead) as well as the monthly *Harper's Bazar* employed anonymous cover artists who simply followed the dominant graphic trends. The General Electric trademark conforms to the prevailing modes of lettering yet has surprisingly and effectively passed the test of time, being just shy of one hundred years old and virtually in its original form. The advertising artist for the cereal cleverly designed the frame to look like an Art Nouveau motif, while the popular cartoonist Hy Mayer's personal style instinctively fits the period in which he worked. Only the monthly, *The Masses,* a Greenwich Village–based Socialist magazine, displays any of the ideological fervor of the European movements. But even this cover, inspired by Art Nouveau (or perhaps by *Simplicissimus),* is atypical since the magazine usually took a quasi-realistic, crayon-cartoon approach.

163. Will Hope. *The Masses.* Magazine cover, June 1916

164. Hy Mayer. *Rice & Hutchins Shoes.* Advertisement, 1900

165. *Shredded Wheat.* Advertisement in *Life* magazine, July 1905

166. Designer unknown. *The Burr McIntosh Monthly.* Magazine cover, March 1905

167. Designer unknown. *Harper's Bazar.* Magazine cover, August 1902

168. A. L. Rich. *GE.* Corporate trademark for General Electric, c. 1890 (A registered trademark of General Electric Company)

168

A

ITALIAN

Italy was not a major contributor to the legacy of
Art Nouveau and, in fact, it was the 1904
exhibition in Turin that made the world aware
that the style was on the wane. Much of Italian
Art Nouveau was derived from other nations'
artistic developments, like Pre-Raphaelitism and
Symbolism; Art Nouveau in Italy was even
called Stile Liberty, with reference to the
London emporium. Yet Italy's contributions
should not be entirely excluded. Italian Art
Nouveau was partly a geographical phenomenon:
the closer a region was to Austria, the greater the
Viennese influence and the more playful its
symbolic motifs. The Romantic poet and politician Gabriele D'Annunzio evolved a form of
literary Art Nouveau, which he later developed
into the reactionary Novocento Style, a celebration of Roman virtues and modernistic design.
The major practitioners of Italian Art Nouveau
are no less imaginative. Giovanni Mataloni and
Marcello Dudovich created eye-catching advertising with their personal yet contemporary
styles. Leonetto Cappiello, who earned his fame
in Italy and France, produced hundreds of exuberant lithographic posters and blended both
Art Nouveau and Art Deco in his style.

169. Giovanni Mataloni. *Incandescenza Lam-
pada con Reticella a Petrolio.* Poster for oil lamps
with incandescent mantles, 1896. The Mitchell
Wolfson Jr. Collection of Decorative and Propaganda Arts, Miami

170. Leonetto Cappiello. *Livorno, Stagione
Balneare.* Poster for a summer resort, 1901. The
Mitchell Wolfson Jr. Collection of Decorative
and Propaganda Arts, Miami

171. Marcello Dudovich. *Rassegna·Tecnica
dell'Esposizione Internazionale de Milano 1906.*
Poster, 1906. The Mitchell Wolfson Jr. Collection
of Decorative and Propaganda Arts, Miami

172. Marcello Dudovich. *Fisso l'Idea.* Poster,
1911. The Mitchell Wolfson Jr. Collection of
Decorative and Propaganda Arts, Miami

169

170

171

172

173. The Beggarstaff Brothers (James Pryde and William Nicholson). *Don Quixote.* Poster, 1896

By the close of the nineteenth century, industry had become an accepted fact of life. Even billowing smokestacks, once the harbingers of industrial evil, had become symbols of progress in advertising imagery. Yet, despite the increasing need for distinctive advertising, the antagonism between art and industry continued. As a rule, manufacturers and retailers were not interested in achieving superior design and printing for their advertising, being more concerned with selling their products in the most convenient and often the most garish manner. Businessmen dictated their preferences to visually unimaginative advertising agents; the agents would then job out commissions to printers, who in turn produced standardized layouts.

Graphic design did flourish in a few contexts, however. Certainly in France from the mid-1870s to 1890s, posters promoting cabarets, theater, circuses, music halls, and other cultural events dominated the streets and were immensely important decorations to the urban environment. In addition, some commercial packaging and advertising benefited from the skills of famous French artist-designers.

On the other hand, German designers did not generally collaborate with industry, as pointed out in 1910 by Dr. Hans Sachs, editor of *Das Plakat,* the respected international poster journal: "Here the old prejudices of the bourgeois against art and artists still reign. For the bourgeois manufacturer would no more think of having his products promoted by a 'flighty' artist...than an artist of this time would degrade his brush for such profane ends." At the close of the Victorian era, the aesthetic movements influenced by William Morris's prejudices against industry still dominated English design.

This state of affairs eventually changed, though in different ways in each of the industrialized nations. In Germany, advertisements remained drearily historical, despite exposure to French genius during the first major poster exhibit in 1894 in Hamburg. Yet at exactly the same time the commercial arts were beginning to flower in England through a unique approach to poster design. James Pryde and William

Nicholson, painters and brothers-in-law calling themselves the Beggarstaffs, opened a studio dedicated to revitalizing the art of the business-advertising poster. Their unadorned, Japanese-inspired designs made from simple pieces of cut colored paper communicated product information in the most economical yet powerful fashion. In an effort to interest manufacturers in their approach, the Beggarstaffs made dummy posters for generic products, such as "no-name soap" or "no-name coffee," which they offered for sale at trade expositions. Although they sold relatively few designs before returning to painting, they had considerable influence on what would become known as the "object" poster in Europe and America.

After 1900 the great artificial flower of Art Nouveau began to wither. Charles Rennie Mackintosh had already revived the square and Otto Wagner the straight line—both paving the way for more functional design. On May 19, 1903, the architect Josef Hoffmann, the banker Fritz Wärndorfer, and the designer Koloman Moser registered the name Die Wiener Werkstätte (The Vienna Workshops) for their new organization. Hoping to improve the aesthetics of all sorts of durable goods, from picture postcards to rugs and tea services, the Werkstätte built its ethic upon Wagner's idea of *gesamtkunstwerk* (the complete work of art). It developed into a series of workshops presided over by twelve "generalists," whose designs covered the entire field of applied art and were executed by more than thirty-six master craftsmen. Although it continued until 1932, well into the Modernist era, the Werkstätte was essentially a handicrafts guild. Its costly products were sold to a bourgeois clientele and, therefore, were only peripheral in bridging the gap between art and industry.

The bridge was completed in Berlin in 1907, when the architect Hermann Muthesius and his colleague, Harry Graf Kessler, founded the Deutscher Werkbund. This confederation of ideologically diverse architects and industrial and graphic designers—one critic termed it "an association of the most intimate enemies"—came together in order to find the best way to represent its work to

industry at home and abroad. Though modeled on Morris, the Werkbund was more than another version of Arts and Crafts: it realized that the most effective way to overcome the evils of industrialism was to cooperate with industry rather than to return to handicrafts. As one member described it, the Werkbund's purpose was "to overcome the alienation that had arisen between those who invent and those who carry out." Within these broad purposes, some sought to promote a particularly German quality in their work, while others hoped to solve the problems of contemporary social renewal.

Peter Behrens, architect, teacher, graphic designer, and one-time exponent of Art Nouveau, was among the most versatile of the Werkbund members. In 1907 Behrens was summoned to Berlin by Emil Rathenau, the enlightened president of Allgemeine Elektrizitäts-Gesellschaft (AEG), and presented with the task of formulating a uniform design style for AEG, not only for its graphics but for its buildings, interiors, and products as well. Behrens became the first corporate design director and succeeded in bringing the concept of *gesamtkunstwerk* into the machine age. The former Art Nouveau theorist Henry Van de Velde was equally significant to the Werkbund, in that his work also underwent a transition from symbolism to rationalism.

In the first years of contact between design and industry, the poster was the testing ground that demonstrated that collaboration was both possible and profitable. In 1896, Munich saw the birth of the Jugendstil poster, but after the turn of the century, Berlin, the center of commerce, became the home for the exciting movement known as Berliner Plakat or Plakatstil. It was the perspicacious printing agent Ernst Growald who was instrumental in persuading artists and merchants to work together. Of all the talented Berlin posterists, Lucian Bernhard was the first, in 1906, to veer away from decorative tendencies by focusing on one product image and bold yet minimal lettering. This approach, called the *sachplakat* or object poster, had a marked influence on international graphic style for decades to follow.

174

175

176

177

178

179

PLAKATSTIL

A loyal servant of business before the turn of the century, the poster reached its creative and communicative peak between 1900 and 1930. Thanks to communications directors like Peter Behrens at AEG, designer and industry became happily ensconced in a mutually beneficial relationship. Artists, printers, and publishers united to raise the poster to a high industrial art. To further this end, Dr. Hans Sachs founded the Friends of the Poster Society and its monthly organ, *Das Plakat,* which showcased the work of significant up-and-coming German posterists. Although other influential journals and annuals were published in Germany, Europe, and the United States, *Das Plakat,* with its finely printed covers, tip-ins, and fold-outs, gave its readers the most striking display of contemporary work. The Munich artist Ludwig Hohlwein, whose work evinced a lively yet tasteful use of type and image, was among the most important proponents of Plakatstil (poster style) worldwide.

174. Ludwig Hohlwein. *Marco Polo Tee.* Poster, 1910. Collection Reinhold Brown Gallery, New York

175. Ludwig Hohlwein. *Hermann Scherrer.* Poster, 1907. Collection Reinhold Brown Gallery, New York

176. J. D. Smith. *The Complete Sporting News, The New York Times.* Car card, 1925. Courtesy Fairleigh Dickinson University, Madison, N.J.

177. Walter Kampmann. *Das Plakat.* Magazine cover, 1921

178. Walter Schnackenberg. *Das Plakat.* Magazine cover, 1921

179. Pirchan. *Mitteilungen des Vereins Deutscher Reklamefachleute.* Poster, 1913. Courtesy Fairleigh Dickinson University, Madison, N.J.

180. Peter Behrens. *AEG (Allgemeine Elektrizitäts-Gesellschaft).* Trademark, 1908

180

PLAKATSTIL

Even in Berlin, where it was called the Berliner
Plakat, Plakatstil was a universal style without
direct links to any specific school or movement.
In fact, the only requisite for a successful poster
is that it attract attention immediately, given that
it must compete for the viewer's eye with many
other things on the street. The hallmarks of this
poster style were bold lettering, a simple central
image, and distinctive, eye-catching colors—in
short, an accessible message made aesthetically
pleasing. The examples here show a variety of
approaches to achieve one common result.

181. Burkhard Mangold. *Winter in Davos.*
Poster, 1914. Courtesy Posters Please, Inc.,
New York

182. F. G. Cooper. *Keep Cool Electrically.*
Poster, 1925

183. C. B. Falls. *Bert Williams.* Poster, date
unknown. Library of Congress, Washington,
D.C. Poster Collection

184. Willrab. *Problem.* Poster for cigarette
company, c. 1918

185. Robert Hardmeier. *Waschanstalt Zürich
AG.* Poster for a laundry firm, 1905. Kunstgewerbemuseum, Zurich

186. Louis Oppenheim. Self-promotional
advertisement from *Das Plakat,* 1919

181

182

183

184

185

186

188

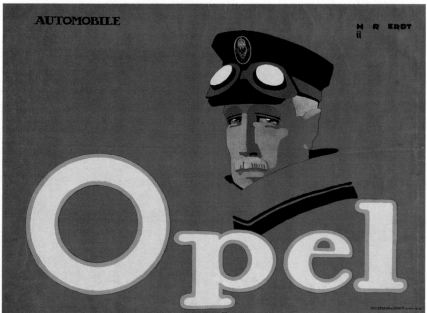

189

PLAKATSTIL

From an early age, Lucian Bernhard was a master of the *sachplakat* (object poster). In 1906, at sixteen, he created his famous poster for Priester Matches, which shows two simple red matches with yellow tips against a dark brown background and the word *Priester* in blue block letters dropped out of the background. This masterpiece of economy became the archetype for much subsequent advertising, such as Hans Rudi Erdt's poster for Opel automobiles. Before he left Berlin for New York in the 1920s, Bernhard had produced hundreds of similarly composed posters for major corporations, including those for Stiller Shoes and Adler Typewriter, as well as many logos and typefaces. Plakatstil held such sway that poster printers convinced advertisers to reduce their images to the size of postage stamps, which were then placed on envelopes and other items of mass distribution. With poster columns and hoardings on every street and advertising stamps on virtually anything portable, customers could not help but receive the advertisers' product messages.

187. Various designers. Advertising stamps, 1905–11

188. Lucian Bernhard. *Stiller Shoes.* Poster, 1908. Courtesy Reinhold Brown Gallery, New York

189. Lucian Bernhard. *Adler Typewriter.* Poster, 1908. Courtesy Reinhold Brown Gallery, New York

190. Hans Rudi Erdt. *Opel.* Poster, 1911. Courtesy Reinhold Brown Gallery, New York

190

WIENER WERKSTÄTTE

Josef Hoffmann and Koloman Moser earned enough recognition as Secessionists to propagate their ideas to a new generation of artists, but they lacked control over the means of their production. The founding of the Wiener Werkstätte in 1903 was, like Morris's Arts and Crafts movement, a means for these artists to wrest command of creation and distribution. Hoffmann described their goals as "to establish intimate contact between public, designer and craftsman, and to produce good, simple domestic requisites." The graphic arts bound the group together. Hoffmann's architecture had graphic rather than plastic values, and his love of simplicity and whiteness contributed to the evolution of Modernism. Many of the patterns created by the Werkstätte's graphic artists and reproduced in the magazine *Die Flache (The Surface)* were applied to textiles and other crafts. In 1907 the group initiated a collection of affordable postcards for sale through retail outlets. Werkstätte design is based on the use of the square and balances negative and positive space so that the pictorial weights of background and foreground are equalized. Original Gothic typefaces, geometric borders, and lettering that emulated handwriting characterized all their printed matter: geometry became more important than symbolism. Yet a love of filiform trifles persisted in Hoffmann's decorations for the Fledermaus nightclub and in the posters used to advertise its events.

191. Josef Hoffmann. Hoffmann chair, 1904

192. Moritz Jung. Postcard, 1908

193. Max Bernirschke. Decorative ornament, from *Die Flache*, 1903

194. Designer unknown. *Cabaret Fledermaus.* Poster, date unknown. Courtesy Galerie Pabst, Munich

195. Josef Bruckmuller. *Die Flache I.* Magazine cover, 1903

196. Moritz Jung. *Kinderspielwaren.* Specimen sheet from *Die Flache,* 1903

197. Moritz Jung. *Kinderspielwaren.* Specimen sheet from *Die Flache,* 1903

198. Oskar Kokoschka. *Kunstschau.* Exhibition poster, 1908. Collection Galerie Pabst, Munich

191

192

193

194

195

196

197

198

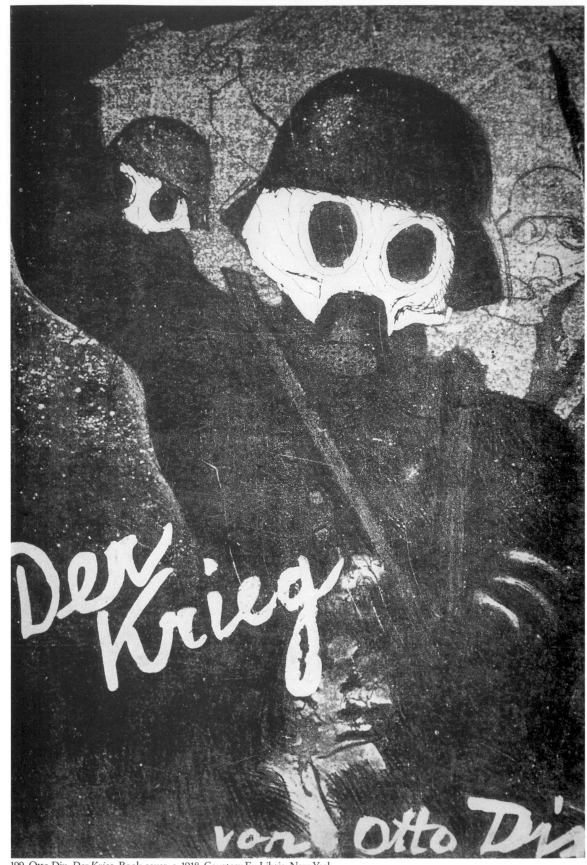

199. Otto Dix. *Der Krieg*. Book cover, c. 1918. Courtesy Ex Libris, New York

n the late nineteenth century, a new internationalism based on the belief that man had the ability to solve social problems through rational effort linked philosophers, scientists, and artists throughout Europe. Although Expressionism was born in Kaiser Wilhelm's Imperial Germany in 1905, there was nothing particularly German or imperial about it. While indebted to the Nordic tradition, its unorthodox visual language was more accurately a synthesis of pan-European trends: Jugendstil's black-and-white linear patterning, Impressionism's new scientific theories of vision, Fauvism's violent color palette, Van Gogh's and Gauguin's emotionality, Russian mysticism and spiritualism, and developments in Western science at the beginning of the new century. A personal calligraphy, based on an inner search for symbolism, replaced tired artistic conventions and soon emerged as a potent graphic art in Germany and abroad.

German Expressionism did not begin as an applied arts movement, nor was it allied with the industrial culture developing in Germany—although Expressionist architecture, film, theater, book illustration, and advertising design did eventually emerge. It began as a group of idealistic young men and women, previously excluded from the German arts establishment, became caught up in an international youth movement. The first group of Expressionists, called Die Brücke (The Bridge), formed in 1905; its members had studied architecture together at the Kunstgewerbeschule (arts and crafts school) in Dresden. Its most notable participants—including Erich Heckel, Ernst Ludwig Kirchner, Max Pechstein, Karl Schmidt-Rottluff, and Emil Nolde—embraced the idea that individualism was essential to artistic renewal. But being accustomed to the spiritual togetherness common in German universities at the time, they united into a brotherhood for strength against a hostile world.

Brücke artists believed painting had a greater value than architecture in the hierarchy of social usefulness. These "figurative" Expressionists turned away from objective reality so that their art might yield an inner, imaginative expression rather than an impression. Rejecting complete abstraction, they were rooted in the past by their emphasis on the human figure and their reliance on a humanistic Romanticism. Yet, at the same time, originality was a compulsion for them. Within the different traits of each individual's art, they generally favored Gothic expression and ignored the tenets of classical beauty, for to them pure expression had little to do with beauty. With hurricane-like speed, their periodicals, like the Berlin-based *Der Sturm* (The Storm), promulgated Expressionist ideas among the international arts community.

The second major Expressionist group, Der Blaue Reiter (The Blue Rider), was founded in 1912. Its leading proponents, the Russian Wassily Kandinsky and the Munich-born Franz Marc, cultivated the abstract as a universal source of symbols. These "abstract" Expressionists broke with optical reality in order to find a psychological basis for aesthetic pleasure. Their 1912 periodical, *Der Blaue Reiter Almanach,* championed the birth of a new spiritual epoch after the inevitable decline of nineteenth-century materialism.

Expressionism soon developed into a distinctive, primitive visual language. Its stark woodcuts and lithographs using very few but violent colors were characterized, according to the historian Helmut Rademacher, by "deformations, heightened intensity of expression and the treatment of reactions to psychic acts by an ecstatic pathos...." Influenced by the dominant style of caricature in acerbic satire magazines like *Simplicissimus* and *Jugend,* Expressionists distorted and elongated human figures and landscapes to create a mood of excitement within outlined and shaded forms. When employed as book or periodical illustrations, their images were rarely literal representations of texts but, rather, subjective evocations of an essence.

Before World War I, the urge for social change was expressed in largely metaphysical terms; political or cultural criticism was merely implied. During the war, some artists took prowar, nationalist positions, while others promulgated pacifist and cautionary messages. After Germany's defeat, with the abdication of the kaiser and the outset of the 1918 German revolution, many Expressionists became activists, allying themselves with left-wing parties to produce agitational posters, publications, and graphics. The Expressionist style defended the revolution, made calls to work and against strike-breaking, and even combated Bolshevism. In 1918, Dr. Adolph Behne, founder of the Arbeitsrat fur Kunst (Labor Office for Art), wrote about this new propagandistic trend: "They do not advertise for a firm but for an idea. They do not address themselves to a special public but to every sort of public....That is why they need to use new forms...." A month after the November revolution, the November-gruppe—including, among others, Pechstein, Oskar Kokoschka, Erich Mendelsohn, Otto Dix, and George Grosz—issued a battle call: "The future of art and the gravity of recent days compel us revolutionaries of the spirit (Cubists, Expressionists and Futurists) to union...." Although similar groups sprang up throughout Germany, feuds among pacifist, socialist, communist, and liberal factions made unity difficult.

The end of Expressionism came between 1920 and 1922. In the wake of the doomed Weimar Republic, the flame of political passion was extinguished. For artists, the incompatibility of their wishes and the political reality caused disenchantment with activism. It was also inevitable that the excitement of the novel and the unprecedented, which had given rise to German Expressionism, should lose its attraction once all facets of the style had been developed. A whole graphic repertoire of Expressionist forms, types, and color applications, created in the heat of feeling, was left to those who irresponsibly applied it to products as a stylistic veneer. An almost endless flood of artificial Expressionism debilitated the movement. With the coming to power of Adolf Hitler in 1933, Expressionist artists were denounced as degenerate, as "artistic pollution," and their legacy expunged from memory. Yet, even after World War II, Expressionist philosophy and graphic style continued to dramatically influence the practice of art and design.

200

201

203

202

204

205

GERMAN

The decorative trivialities of the Munich Secession provoked the Expressionist revolt. An inner search for personal symbolism—for a personal calligraphy—took the place of artistic conformity. The Expressionists believed that their art could be a force in the improvement of the human race. Having exposed the brutality of war, they went on to portray the harshness of German society in the postwar era. Examples here show the primitive woodcut style that distinguished the postwar Expressionists and became emblematic of the style as it took its place among other early Modernist movements.

200. Ernst Ludwig Kirchner. *Almanach auf des Jahr 1920.* Cover of almanac published by Fritz Gurlitt Verlag, 1920

201. Conrad Felixmüller. *Rettet Euch Menschen.* Woodcut, 1917

202. Conrad Felixmüller. *Der Kampf mit dem Engel (The Struggle with the Angel).* Title page, 1917

203. Ernst Ludwig Kirchner. *Umbra Vitae (Shadows of Life).* Page with woodcut illustrations from a book of poems by Georg Heym, 1924

204. Ernst Ludwig Kirchner. *Künstlergruppe Brücke.* Head piece, 1913

205. Emil Nolde. *Der Anbruch (A New Beginning).* Cover with woodcut illustration from a publication edited by Otto Schneider and J. B. Neumann in Berlin, January 1919

206. Hans Hoerl. *Die Aktion (The Action).* Cover of political publication, 1924

207. Franz Marc. *Der Sturm (The Storm).* Magazine cover, 1912

208. Conrad Felixmüller. *Der Weg (The Way).* Cover, with woodcut illustration, from a monthly periodical for Expressionist literature, art, and music, edited by Walter Blume, May/June 1919

206

207

208

GERMAN

Expressionism's final years, from 1918 to 1922, were a period of great excitement, fostered by the belief that artists could actually contribute to the shaping of a new society. Artists issued political manifestos and proclamations; journals were published with inspirational titles like *The Beginning, The New Germany,* and *Mankind;* and posters called for international reconciliation. Art made valuable contributions to the political spirit, and politics were at the core of all Expressionist endeavor, including cinema and theater. Ultimately falling prey to its own excesses, Expressionism was rejected by its own proponents. The Nazis vilified the Expressionists in their notorious *Degenerate Art* exhibit, thereby insuring that the style will forever be a symbol of protest and revolt.

209. Otto Freundlich. *Entartet "Kunst" Ausstellungsführer.* Cover of *Degenerate Art* exhibition catalogue, 1938

210. Oskar Kokoschka. *Nieder mit dem Bolschwismus (Down with Bolshevism).* Poster, 1919. The Museum of Modern Art, New York

211. Heinz Fuchs. *Arbeiter Hunger (Worker Hunger).* Poster, 1918–19. Courtesy Ex Libris, New York

212. Max Pechstein. *An die Laterne (To the Lamppost).* Poster, 1919. Staatliche Museen Preussischer Kulturbesitz, West Berlin, Kunstbibliothek mit Museum für Architektur, Modebild und Grafik-Design

213. Hans Poelzig. *Der Golem (The Golem).* Poster for the film based on the novel by Gustav Meyrink, 1920. The Museum of Modern Art, New York

214. Paul Leni. *Expressionismus und Film (Expressionism and Film).* Book cover, 1926. Courtesy Ex Libris, New York

215. Max Pechstein. *An Alle Künstler! (To All Artists!).* Poster, 1919

209

210

211

212

213

214

215

216. Herbert Bayer. *Section Allemande.* Poster, 1930. Staatliche Museen Preussischer Kulturbesitz, West Berlin, Kunstbibliothek

As pervasive as their influence is today, Modernist art and design were, from the outset, never completely accepted by the majority. The early Modernists encountered opposition from those believing their philosophies subversive, elitist, or both. What we call the Modernist era—roughly between 1908 (from the beginnings of Cubism) to 1933 (when Hitler came to power)—was a time of profound political, social, and cultural turmoil throughout the world. Various art forms, from architecture to film to typography, posed challenges to social systems made obsolete by rapidly changing machine age technologies. The different Modernist groups comprised activists who sought both to free art from its bourgeois ornamental superstructure and to influence the politics of contemporary life. Although the Futurist label was applied to only the Italians and the Russians, at the heart of the entire Modernist spirit was a forward-looking—and decidedly utopian —ethic. The most emblematic typeface of the age was even christened Futura.

The machine was the most cogent symbol of the Modernists' glorified, often sentimentalized, future, as Fernand Léger said, "The machine has altered the habitual look of things." To smash the old visual language and create a new one were the professed aims of the Modernist artist—aims expressed through abstract painting and sculpture, functional architecture, austere furnishings, and asymmetrical typography. The media were formidable tools: Modernism was propagated by highly publicized demonstrations and exhibitions as well as through numerous manifestos reprinted in avant-garde periodicals, almanacs, and newspapers, all having relatively wide distributions. The Modernist movement was not a monolith but rather a confluence of disparate groups and individuals who intersected at times to share ideas. While they all concurred with the desire to smash academic aestheticism, they rarely could reach consensus on the means to do so.

Cubism was the seminal experiment on which the form languages of the other movements were built. It marked the final break with reliance upon nature for subject matter and the complete rejection of decorative tendencies. As such, Cubism was despised by the bourgeoisie, yet eventually its surface mannerisms were borrowed by the day's leading fashion stylists. The Cubist practice of integrating random, collaged letterforms into paintings significantly influenced the free-form typography of subsequent movements.

Futurism, originally formulated by the Italian poet F. T. Marinetti in 1908, was the first to raise the Modernist banner on an international platform. This noisy proclamation of the Italian avant-garde curiously wed its theories of dynamic Modernism to militant patriotism. Being at once revolutionary and traditional, Futurism revealed the inconsistencies of living equally for the present and the future. Suprematism, developed by the Russian writer and painter Kasimir Malevich in 1913, synthesized Cubism and Futurism into an early geometric abstraction and added a metaphysical component. Suprematism found an opponent in Vladimir Tatlin's Constructivism, which sought to encompass all human spiritual, cognitive, and material activity. Originating in 1916 in Zurich and later continuing in Berlin, Dada was decidedly antiart and politically active. The Dutch De Stijl group, founded in 1917 by Theo van Doesburg, Piet Mondrian, and others, detached itself from Expressionist excesses in favor of a universal harmony devoid of emotional overtones

Although the plastic arts figured prominently in these movements, the applied arts were the ones to reach the broadest constituency. The first Modernist battles, like the progressive ones at the turn of the century, were waged against the industrialists, who controlled public taste and used it for their own functions and interests. A proper relationship between art and industry, Modernists believed, would dispel the hegemony of the industrialist. Through arts and crafts workshops in design schools such as the Bauhaus at Weimar and the Vkhutemas in Moscow, students were encouraged to produce utilitarian materials fit for everyday use. Reduced to their functional essence, these new products had no precedents in the decorative arts of the past. In theory at least, the masses, not the bourgeoisie, became the primary consumer.

The Modernist style was perhaps most immediately recognizable in a multitude of graphic communications: posters, brochures, books, handbills, and letterheads. The first substantial change occurred in typography. The classical symmetrical arrangements first erupted into Cubist, Futurist, and Dadaist typographic collage images, then evolved into the more disciplined, yet decidedly revolutionary, asymmetrical New Typography. Originating in Soviet Russia and Germany, the New Typography was quickly adopted in other centers of avant-garde activity, including Holland, Hungary, Czechoslovakia, and Poland, and was finally codified into a total revision of the rules of traditional commercial layout. Its principles were promulgated worldwide in philosophical essays and technical manuals by El Lissitzky, László Moholy-Nagy, Paul Renner, and its most devout (and rigid) adherent, Jan Tschichold. To these designers the rules of the old typography, practiced since the age of Gutenberg, violated the criterion of fitness for purpose in design.

The Polish advertising designer and painter Henryk Berlewi, who formed the Group of Abstract Constructive Art, wrote that advertising design "must rest on the same principles as prevail in modern industrial production." Logically, therefore, photography replaced realistic, decorative, or otherwise sentimentalized illustration. Photomontage, a completely mechanistic means of illustration, became an effective propaganda weapon and the most popular tool of the new graphic design. When used together, asymmetrical typography, geometric layout, and photographic illustration defined the radical new form language of Modernist design. Yet, as initial resistance to this powerful aesthetic turned into acceptance by commercial type foundries, printing firms, and advertising agencies, the honest Modernist characteristics were appropriated into Moderne, a bastardization of both the functional and the decorative approach.

FUTURISM

The task of redefining the spiritual and material world at the outset of the new century fell to those artistic pioneers who commanded the shock troops of Modernism. The first upheaval was led by the Italian writer, poet, and critic F. T. Marinetti, who in 1909 published the first Futurist manifesto as a call for artists to battle: "There can be no nostalgia! No pessimism! There's no turning back!" Marinetti espoused a permanent artistic and political revolution. Possessed by false patriotism, he believed that war would be a cleansing process. He rejected the bourgeois material values of the ruling class in favor of the emerging Fascism of Benito Mussolini. Marinetti and the poets, painters, and sculptors who embraced Futurism's "new religion of speed" mythologized the machine—first the automobile and later the airplane—as a totem of the modern spirit. The metal book shown here is a symbol of Futurism's affinity for the machine age. In Futurist graphics, this affinity was translated into a kinetic style marked by free-verse poetics and onomatopoeic noise; Cubist collages were an important influence typographically. For Marinetti, such works described in visual terms "the whirling world of steel, pride, fever and speed."

217. Filippo T. Marinetti. *Les Mots en Liberté Futuristes.* Book cover, 1919. Courtesy Ex Libris, New York

218. Filippo T. Marinetti. *Montagne + Vallate + Strade × Joffre (Mountains + Valleys + Streets × Joffre).* Book cover, Futurist manifesto, 1915. Courtesy Ex Libris, New York

219. Gino Severini. *Serpentine Dance.* Page from *Lacerba*, July 1, 1914. The Beinecke Rare Book and Manuscript Library, Yale University, New Haven, Conn.

220. Tullio D'Albisola. *Parole in Liberta Futuriste.* Metal cover for a book by Filippo T. Marinetti, 1932. Courtesy Ex Libris, New York

221. Filippo T. Marinetti. *Zang Tumb Tumb.* Book cover, 1912. Courtesy Ex Libris, New York

222. Filippo T. Marinetti. *Dizionario Aereo.* Book cover, date unknown. Courtesy Ex Libris, New York

217

218

219

220

221

222

223

224

225

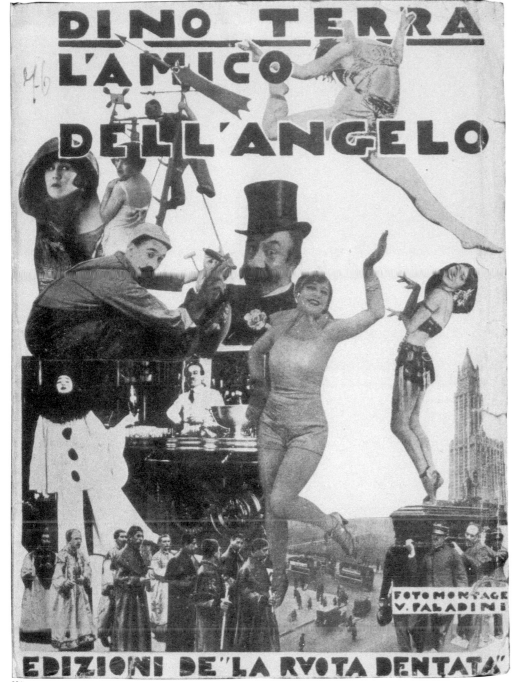

DINO TERRA
L'AMICO
DELL'ANGELO

FOTOMONTAGE
V. PALADINI

EDIZIONI DE "LA RVOTA DENTATA"

226

FUTURISM

Futurist graphic style derived from the theory
that the energy of the universe must be shown in
painting and graphics as dynamic sensation and,
further, that motion and light destroy the mate-
riality of solid bodies, continually transforming
reality. These theories required a new approach
to pictorial creation, which the painter Umberto
Boccioni identified in his *Manifesto of Futurist
Painting* as a means to construct "dynamic sensation," "lines of force," and "the battle of planes."
The newspaper, magazine, and book covers
shown here demonstrate how these principles
were applied to the graphic arts and also suggest
how the early Futurist experimentation with free
verse led to handmade book-objects and picture-
poems. The Futurist revolution then went on to
tackle the cinema, fashion, household objects,
and even the mails with the intention of renew-
ing all aspects of human life.

223. Designer unknown. *Futurismo.* Page
from Futurist publication, 1932. Courtesy Ex
Libris, New York

224. Designer unknown. *Futurismo.* Front
page, October 1933. Courtesy Ex Libris, New
York

225. Ivo Pannaggi. *Raun.* Book cover, 1932

226. V. Paladini. *Dino Terra, L'Amico
dell'Angelo.* Photomontage, 1927. Courtesy Ex
Libris, New York

227. Enrico Prampolini. *Broom.* Cover of an
international magazine of the arts, c. 1921. Courtesy Ex Libris, New York

228. Designer unknown. *Stile Futurista.* Book
cover, December 1934. Courtesy Ex Libris, New
York

229. Enrico Prampolini. *Vulcani.* Book cover,
date unknown. Courtesy Ex Libris, New York

227

STILE
FUTURISTA
ESTETICA DELLA MACCHINA
RIVISTA MENSILE · ARTE · VITA

ANNO I · N. 3 · DICEMBRE 1934 · XIII · C. C. CON LA POSTA · L. 5

228

OMAGGIO

F.T. MARINETTI
PRIGIONIERI
E
VULCANI
TEATRO
FUTURISTA

CASA EDITORIALE VECCHI
MILANO

229

FUTURISM

Fortunato Depero was indefatigable in his propagation of Futurist principles. He promoted the
art of the Futurist book, founded and directed
the machine-art magazine *Dinamo,* produced
Futurist radio programs, designed costumes
and furniture, opened the Casa d'Arte Futurista
in Italy and New York, and invented an
"onomalanguage," a free-word, free-sounding
expressive verbal rigmarole. Representing the so-
called second stage of Futurism (from 1919 to
about 1930), Depero was the individual most
responsible for putting the often inaccessible
Futurist theory into practice, particularly in the
service of business. His synthesis of dynamic and
expressionistic graphic forms was undeniably
original. Believing that product advertising
was the proper means by which to stimulate a
dialogue with the public, he took on assignments
for Campari, Magnesia San Pellegrino, and
Venus Pencils as well as for numerous magazines
and books. The historian Giorgio Ruggeri
writes: "In Depero one rediscovers applied
art…a heritage of so many new directions
in art."

230. Fortunato Depero. Theater costumes for
mechanical men, c. 1927

231. Fortunato Depero. *Depero Futurista.*
Bolted book cover for an exhibition catalogue,
1927

232. Fortunato Depero. *Dinamo.* Advertisement for a magazine, 1933. Museo Depero,
Rovereto, Italy

233. Fortunato Depero. *Magnesia S. Pellegrino.*
Poster, 1931. Museo Depero, Rovereto, Italy

234. Fortunato Depero. *Campari.* Advertisement, c. 1931

235. Fortunato Depero. *Bitter Cordial Campari.* Advertisement, c. 1923

231

230

232

233

bozzetto di padiglione   per la ditta **DAVIDE CAMPARI & C.**

234

235

236

237

VORTICISM

Vorticism, named by Ezra Pound in 1914 (from the vortex, the center of all energy), was one of Britain's most vehement avant-garde movements. Although linked by common artistic and philosophical threads to Marinetti's Futurism, Vorticism, as proposed by its leading spokesmen, Pound and Wyndham Lewis, differed from Futurism in some respects. It enthusiastically embraced Futurism as a revolutionary frame of mind while seeking to dissociate itself from Futurism as a visual style peculiar to a group of Italian artists, whose manifestos and spokesmen had made it the best publicized art movement on the Continent. Yet, the differences in form and practice between the two were actually often negligible. Lewis edited and designed the Vorticist's leading periodical, *Blast,* which, in keeping with the avant-garde spirit, was intended to shock—not only by its name but by its cover, size, and Gothic typography. It was printed in violent pink or puce, "the color of an acute sick-headache," said a critic. At best, its style conveyed a dogged aggressiveness as its writers tackled the issues of the day, hoping to destroy everything old and decadent in its path. *Coterie* was a less inflammatory Vorticist literary journal. E. McKnight Kauffer, an American expatriate who became a leading Modernist designer in Britain, created his first and most famous poster apparently under the influence of Lewis.

236. Wyndham Lewis. *Blast.* Cover for a Vorticist magazine, July 1915. Courtesy Ex Libris, New York

237. William Roberts. *Coterie.* Cover for a literary periodical, 1919. Courtesy Chris Mullen

238. E. McKnight Kauffer. *Flight of Birds.* Poster for the *Daily Herald,* 1919. Victoria and Albert Museum, The National Museum of Art and Design, London

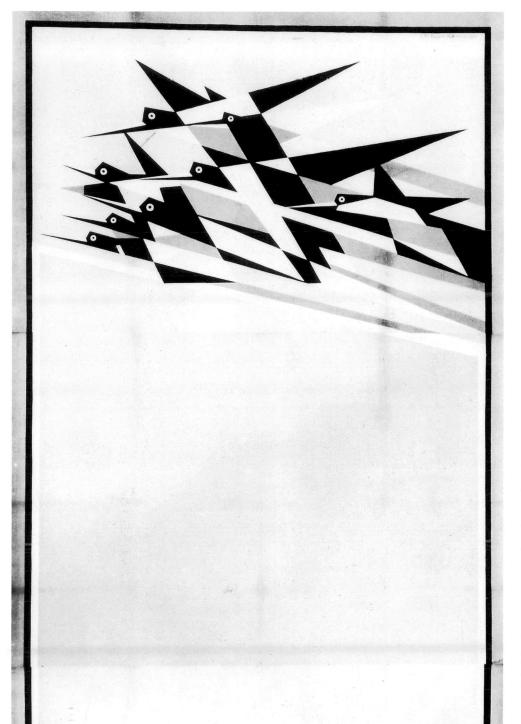

Soaring to Success !

DAILY HERALD

—the Early Bird.

238

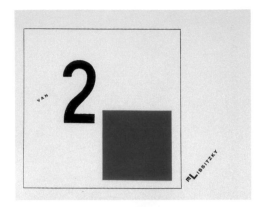

CONSTRUCTIVISM

Before Constructivism, there were several Russian prerevolutionary artistic experiments, including Cubo-Futurism, Rayonnism, and the mystical, nonobjective Suprematism of Kasimir Malevich. Developed by Vladimir Tatlin, Constructivism became an early Soviet youth movement, an artistic outlook that aimed to encompass the whole spiritual, cognitive, and material activity of man. By declaring themselves for the revolution, Constructivists expected to be able to introduce their own programs for the future. Lazar El Lissitzky sought to create a modern art that would take the viewer out of the traditional passive role and make him an active spectator. In fact, throughout the course of Russian art history (particularly with Russian Orthodox religious iconography), there runs a strong belief that art must have some redeeming social purpose, a purpose to be achieved by eliciting certain physical responses. Lissitzky's civil-war-era poster *Beat the Whites with the Red Wedge* not only tried to convince viewers of the legitimacy of the Bolshevik cause; it wanted them to vigorously strive for revolution. Under the influence of Suprematism, Lissitzky wrote that the square was "the source of all creative expression." His children's book *Of Two Squares* was a fable about the cooperation of a black and red square in dispersing chaos and establishing a new order.

239. El Lissitzky. *Of Two Squares.* Cover *(top left)* and pages from a children's book about the Russian Revolution and the triumph of Bolshevism, Dutch De Stijl Edition, 1922

240. El Lissitzky. *Beat the Whites with the Red Wedge.* Poster, 1920. Courtesy Szymon Bojko

239

CONSTRUCTIVISM

The Constructivists practiced their own brand of collectivism in which the individual and his work were subordinate to the group. More important than either their artistic innovation or political commitment was their fusion of the two into a single art reflecting their revolutionary times. In the minds of many, it was Constructivist typography that was most identified with the art of revolution. Yet the basic style (the result of individual work by, among others, Lissitzky, Alexander Rodchenko, Alexei Gan, Solomon Telingater, Gustav Klutsis, and Varvara Stepanova) developed in response to technological limitations and material shortages as well as from an understanding of Modernist theories. Lissitzky formulated his typographical design for Mayakovsky's book of polemical poems, *For the Voice,* on the idea of the "kinetics of succeeding pages," somewhat akin to the movement of film. Rodchenko believed that graphic design must be a coded sign, unambiguous, objectified, free from ornament. Gan and Telingater made typographical pictures that followed the demands of the texts being illustrated. Lettering was expected to function on both a substantive and an emotional level.

241. Gustav Klutsis. Photomontage for a special tribute to Lenin, 1924. Courtesy Szymon Bojko

242. El Lissitzky. *For the Voice.* Pages from a book of poems by Vladimir Mayakovsky, 1923. Courtesy Ex Libris, New York

243. Solomon Telingater. *The Word Belongs to Kirsanov.* Pages, 1930

244. El Lissitzky. *Broom.* Magazine cover, 1922. Courtesy Ex Libris, New York

245. Vladimir Mayakovsky and Alexander Rodchenko. *Give Pencils Which Are Good.* Poster for the Moscow Polygraphical Division, date unknown. Courtesy Ex Libris, New York

246. Alexander Rodchenko. *GUM (Government Universal Store).* Advertisement for watches, text by Vladimir Mayakovsky, 1923

241

242

243

244

245

246

CONSTRUCTIVISM

By 1921, the New Economic Policy was in place and the Soviet Union was on the path to economic normalcy and political stability, or so everyone hoped. About this time, Rodchenko, Tatlin, Stepanova, and other members of the INKHUK (Moscow's Institute for Artistic Culture) abandoned painting and sculpture for domestic design. What they called Productivism was their attempt to manufacture materials for everyday use—textiles, dishware, clothing, furniture, and so on—in a direct and efficient manner. Rodchenko, Stepanova, and others made advertising for commercial enterprises, like the GUM department store, as well as for theatrical and cultural events. Together with Mayakovsky, Rodchenko also formed an advertising partnership that created propaganda for nationalized commerce, education, and services. Calling themselves "advertising constructors," Mayakovsky wrote the poems and slogans and Rodchenko designed images that caught the eye with their strong geometry, bright color, and bold lettering.

247. Alexander Rodchenko. *Rezinotrest.* Poster for a rubber conglomerate, 1923. Courtesy Szymon Bojko

248. Alexander Rodchenko. *Three Mountains Beer.* Poster, 1923. Courtesy Ex Libris, New York

249. Alexander Rodchenko. *Baby Dummies.* Poster for the Rubber Trust promoting baby pacifiers, 1923. Courtesy Ex Libris, New York

250. Alexander Rodchenko. *Rezinotrest.* Poster promoting the production of galoshes for export, 1923. Courtesy Ex Libris, New York

251. Alexander Rodchenko. Poster urging Soviet citizens to become stockholders, 1923. Courtesy Ex Libris, New York

252. Varvara Stepanova. *Death of Tarelkin.* Theater poster, 1922. Courtesy Szymon Bojko

253. Alexander Rodchenko. Poster advertising Leningrad Publishing House, 1925. Courtesy Ex Libris, New York

247

248

249

250

251

252

253

254

255

256

257

258

259

260

CONSTRUCTIVISM

Anatoly Lunacharsky wrote, "If the revolution can give art its soul, then art can endow the revolution with speech." And despite Lenin's lack of confidence in the avant-garde, it was certainly the intention of many of its designers to create a proletarian art. Yet after Lenin's death in 1924 tolerance among Soviet leaders for the avant-garde began to wane. Despite some exuberant typographic work by the leading designers, many of the Soviet periodicals of the early 1920s were printed on gray paper with lackluster type. Collage and photomontage were the only graphic techniques that both the progressives and conservatives accepted as effective communications. Montage (from the French word *monter,* meaning to mount) developed simultaneously in the late teens in Germany and Russia. Photomontage, the making of a new image from two or more photographs, was, as Hannah Hoch wrote, "a tool to integrate objects in the world of machines and industry into the world of art." Montage as a film technique was also powerfully used in the Soviet cinema. The book jackets shown here suggest a trend in late Constructivist design away from "phonetic" typography to primarily "optical" expression.

254. Designer unknown. *From Easel to Machine.* Cover for a Constructivist manifesto, 1922. Courtesy Ex Libris, New York

255. El Lissitzky. *Rabbi.* Cover for the text of a play, 1922. Courtesy Ex Libris, New York

256. G. Bershadeskii. *The Flying Proletariat.* Cover for a book of poems, 1925. Courtesy Ex Libris, New York

257. Solomon Telingater. *At the Top of My Voice.* Photomontage book cover, 1931. Courtesy Ex Libris, New York

258. El Lissitzky. *Brigade of Artists.* Book cover, date unknown. Courtesy Ex Libris, New York

259. Designer unknown. *BOCC.* Book cover, date unknown. Courtesy Ex Libris, New York

260. Alexander Rodchenko and Vladimir Mayakovsky. *The Youth of Mayakovsky.* Book cover, 1931. Courtesy Ex Libris, New York

261. Officers of the Red army

261

105

CONSTRUCTIVISM

Soviet cinema was a truly revolutionary communications medium, as was the printed material used to promote it. Soviet film posters, which began to appear in quantity during the mid-twenties, were only somewhat influenced by typical Constructivist graphic design. The leading posterists, such as the Stenberg brothers and Semion Semionov, developed a distinctive style employing sans-serif type as a pictorial element and a combination of photomontage with a painted image. The Stenberg brothers worked within a highly sophisticated sense of two-dimensional space. Their images were on different planes that turn and slide one on top of another; space is suggested more by one's sense of vertigo than by traditional perspective. Of most interest was the Stenbergs' translation of the exclusively black and white films into vibrant, colorful posters. The color palette of all the posterists was quite unique amid the symbolic red and black colors of Constructivism. Yet the high quality of film posters, like that of the films themselves, lasted for only a brief time. By the early 1930s, the Stalinist ritual of harsh cultural criticism began to take its toll.

262. V. N. Lenin, c. 1919

263. Designer unknown. *My Destiny*. Movie poster, 1929. Courtesy Ex Libris, New York

264. Nikolai Prusakov and Grigory Borisov. *I Hurry to See the Khaz-Push*. Poster for an Armenian film, 1927. Courtesy Ex Libris, New York

265. Designer unknown. *Flying Luck*. Movie poster, c. 1928. Courtesy Ex Libris, New York

266. Designer unknown. *Symphony of the Donbas*. Movie poster, 1931. Courtesy Ex Libris, New York

267. Georgy and Vladimir Stenberg. *Charles Ray in the Movie* Punch. Poster, c. 1928. Courtesy Ex Libris, New York

268. Semion Semionov. *The Turkish Railway*. Movie poster, 1929. Courtesy Ex Libris, New York

269. Designer unknown. *The Knot*. Movie poster, c. 1927. Collection Reinhold Brown Gallery, New York

263

264

265

262

266

267

268

269

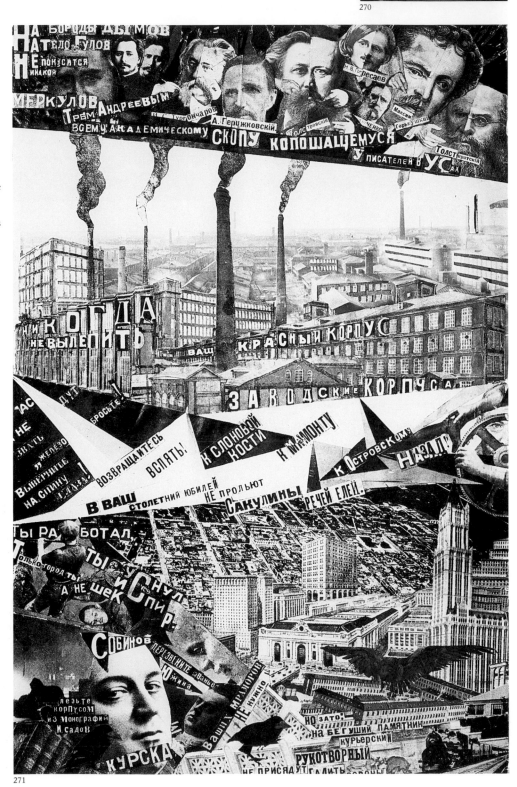

270

CONSTRUCTIVISM

Constructivism's theory and style were exported
to Europe through manifestos, periodicals, and
the personal efforts of its leading proponents.
Lissitzky, for example, spent a good deal of time
with Kurt Schwitters in Hanover, working on the
Dada periodical, *Merz,* and with Ilya Ehrenburg
in Berlin, publishing the Constructivist journal,
Objet. In 1922 the Polish painter and designer
Henryk Berlewi was inspired to create his
abstract Mechano-Faktura (mechanical art) constructions after hearing Lissitzky lecture in War-
saw. Two years later, he co-founded Reklama-
Mechano, an advertising agency whose work
came to best represent Polish Constructivism.
The Czech poet and artist Karel Teige adapted the
Constructivist language to the needs of his
nation's avant-garde. In Belgium, Fred Deltro
produced a series of caricatures of the ruling class
that were based on Constructivist-inspired geometry. The cover for the Dutch professional advertising magazine, *De Reklame,* shows how a typical
Lissitzky-like design can be used simply as a
decorative motif.

270. Designer unknown. *De Reclame.* Cover of
a Dutch advertising magazine, 1926. Courtesy
Fairleigh Dickinson University, Madison, N.J.

271. Juryi Roshkov. Photomontage for a
Vladimir Mayakovsky poem, 1925. Courtesy
Szymon Bojko

272. Henryk Berlewi. *Composition in Red and
Black (Mechano-Faktura Compositions).* Print,
1922. Courtesy Ex Libris, New York

273. Karel Teige. *Ma Buch (My Book).* Book
cover, 1922. Courtesy Ex Libris, New York

274. Fred Deltro. *Jeu de Massacre.* One of
twelve pochoirs for a book by Henri Barbusse
(Bruxelles Editions Socialistes), 1920. Courtesy
Fairleigh Dickinson University, Madison, N.J.

271

272

273

274

276

277

DE STIJL

De Stijl (The Style) was defined by the architect H. P. Berlage as "unity in plurality." Taking its name from a magazine edited from 1917 to 1931 by the Dutch painter, designer, and writer Theo van Doesburg, it was not a group in the usual sense. Most of those connected with De Stijl were associated only briefly and some of the most important never met at all. De Stijl concerned itself with developing a utopian style and spirit; it was not merely about the stylization of things. Anything emotional was taboo. All De Stijl design was based on the rectangle and the use of black, white, gray, and the primary colors, as evidenced in the graphic work of van Doesburg and Vilmos Huszar during World War I. After the war, many of the De Stijl artists went their separate ways, and van Doesburg replaced them with kindred artists from abroad, like El Lissitzky. The format and layout of his magazine also became purer and reductive, more in line with the internationalism of the New Typography.

   275. Gerrit Rietveld. *Red/Blue Chair,* 1918
   276. Vilmos Huszar. *De Stijl.* Magazine cover, 1917. Courtesy Ex Libris, New York
   277. Vilmos Huszar. *Miss Blanche Egyptian Cigarettes.* Poster, 1926
   278. Vilmos Huszar, *De Stijl.* Magazine cover, 1917. Courtesy Ex Libris, New York
   279. Theo van Doesburg. *Alphabet,* 1919
   280. László Moholy-Nagy and Theo van Doesburg. *Grundbegriffe der Neuen Gestaltenden Kunst.* Cover of a Bauhaus book, 1925. Courtesy Ex Libris, New York
   281. Piet Zwart. Logos for IOCO, 1922–23
   282. Vilmos Huszar. *Ex Libris Voor Lena de Roos.* Bookplate, 1922–24

MAANDBLAD VOOR DE MO-
DERNE BEELDENDE VAKKEN
REDACTIE THEO VAN DOES-
BURG MET MEDEWERKING
VAN VOORNAME BINNEN- EN
BUITENLANDSCHE KUNSTE-
NAARS. UITGAVE X. HARMS
TIEPEN TE DELFT IN 1917.

278

275

279

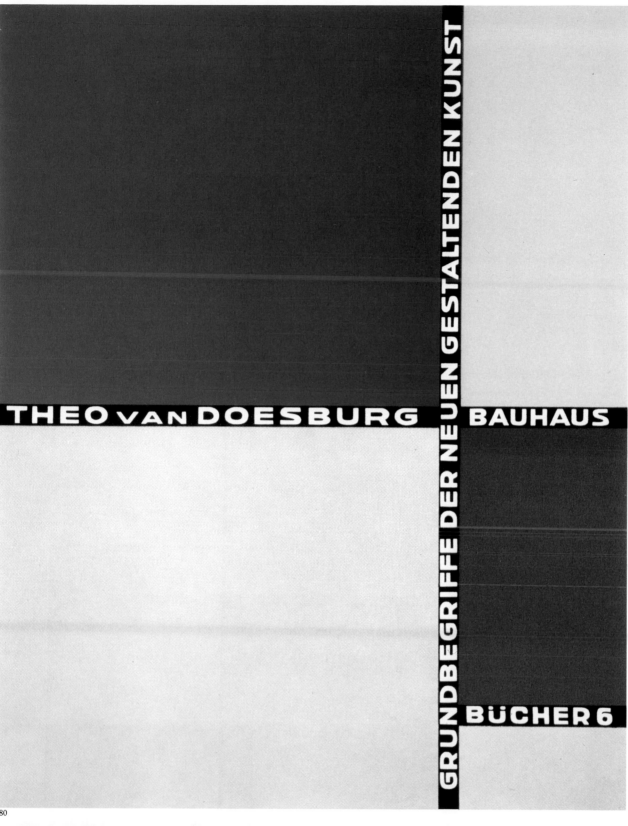

THEO van DOESBURG BAUHAUS

GRUNDBEGRIFFE DER NEUEN GESTALTENDEN KUNST

BÜCHER 6

280

281

282

IDEE UND AUFBAU DES STAATLICHEN BAUHAUSES WEIMAR VON WALTER GROPIUS

BAUHAUSVERLAG G.M.B.H. MÜNCHEN

283

284

286

285

287

288

BAUHAUS

By 1914 a reform movement had begun in Germany to change the method and quality of art education by combining the fine and applied arts into a single curriculum. The early Modernist Henry Van de Velde was placed in charge of the Weimar Kunstgewerbeschule, and Peter Behrens ran the Düsseldorf School of Arts and Crafts. In 1919 the architect Walter Gropius was appointed director of an institution that merged the Weimar Academy of Fine Art and the Weimar Kunstgewerbeschule. His first action was to reconstitute the school, to be called Das Staatliche Bauhaus, on the model of William Morris's Arts and Crafts workshops. Gropius was proudly anti-academic: his teachers were called *masters* and his students *apprentices* and *journeymen* to signify that the school was working in the real world. Workshops, not studios, provided the basis for Bauhaus teaching, in which craftsmen and fine artists would introduce students to the mysteries of creativity and help them achieve a formal language of their own. A preliminary course called *Vorkurs,* developed by Johannes Itten, was an introduction to all forms of art, as well as a testing ground for students. For its first four years, no official Bauhaus graphic style was evident. Shown here are various Bauhaus projects influenced by Expressionism, Dada, Constructivism, and De Stijl.

283. László Moholy-Nagy. *Idee und Aufbau des Staatlichen Bauhauses Weimar.* Book cover, c. 1923. Courtesy Ex Libris, New York

284. Oskar Schlemmer. Bauhaus logo, 1922. Courtesy Ex Libris, New York

285. Marcel Breuer. Steel chairs, 1926. Courtesy Ex Libris, New York

286. Johannes Itten. *Utopia.* Page from Bauhaus typographical book, 1921. Courtesy Ex Libris, New York

287. Herbert Bayer. *Staatliches Bauhaus in Weimar, 1919–1923.* Cover for the first Bauhaus exhibition catalogue, 1923. Courtesy Ex Libris, New York

288. Joost Schmidt. *Bauhaus.* Poster, 1923. Courtesy Ex Libris, New York

289. Margit Terry-Adler. *Utopia, Documente der Wirklichkeit I/II.* Book cover, 1921. Courtesy Ex Libris, New York

290. Joost Schmidt. *Weimar Bauhaus.* Book cover, 1924. Courtesy Ex Libris, New York

291. Walter Gropius (architect). Bauhaus School, Dessau

289

290

291

BAUHAUS

From the outset, Gropius believed that the Bauhaus should avoid imposing any particular style and that students should have the opportunity to develop their individuality. In distancing itself from the De Stijl ethic of a strictly defined geometric, impersonal style, the Bauhaus drifted toward a quasi-Expressionist style. When Theo van Doesburg came to teach at the Bauhaus, he encouraged Gropius to move in the direction of a more avant-garde Constructivism. The arrival of the Hungarian painter and designer László Moholy-Nagy furthered the interest in typography, printing, and photography and strengthened the Constructivist faction at the school. Although criticized for his methods, Moholy-Nagy prevailed in developing an asymmetrical typography that was both clear and convincing. When the Bauhaus was forced to move to Dessau, Gropius modified the curriculum and established a typography workshop, first under Herbert Bayer and then under Joost Schmidt (who changed the course title to *Commercial Art*). Among Bayer's many design contributions was his Universal Alphabet, which rejected all capital letters. By the late twenties, the Bauhaus style was the quintessence of functional graphic design.

292. Herbert Bayer. Sketch for an advertising sign, 1924. Courtesy Ex Libris, New York

293. Herbert Bayer. *Bauhaus-Ausstellung.* Postcard, 1923. Courtesy Ex Libris, New York

294. Ludwig Hirschfeld-Mack. *Farben Lichtspiele.* Advertisement, c. 1925. Courtesy Ex Libris, New York.

295. Herbert Bayer. *Einladung...zum Bart-Nasen-Herzensfest.* Party invitation, 1928. Courtesy Ex Libris, New York

296. Herbert Bayer. *Kandinsky's 60th.* Birthday poster, 1926. Kunstgewerbemuseum, Zurich

297. Joost Schmidt. *Yko.* Advertisement, 1924. Courtesy Ex Libris, New York

298. Herbert Bayer. Universal alphabet, 1925. Courtesy Ex Libris, New York

293

294

292

295

296

297

298

299

300

301

302

303

304

305

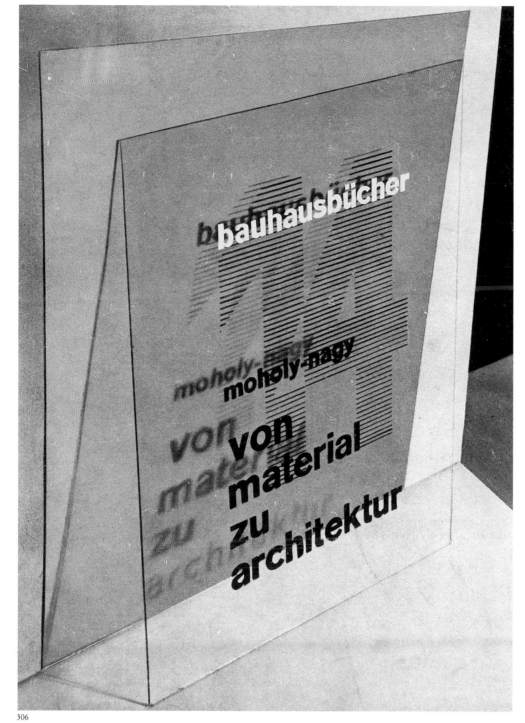

306

BAUHAUS

Soon after the Bauhaus moved to Dessau, it
became well known to the general public and,
thus, associated with a style—anything geometric, functional, or modern. Gropius himself
never ceased to deny the existence of a Bauhaus
style. Oskar Schlemmer said of this perceived
style that it "became a rejection of yesterday's
styles, a determination to be 'up-to-the-minute' at
all costs—this style can be found everywhere but
at the Bauhaus." Actually, the design of Bauhaus
materials was consistently determined by functional requisites, not by the obsession with style.
The essential features of all Bauhaus publications
were order, asymmetry, and a basic rectangular
grid structure. Decoration was limited to the use
of heavy rules, circles, and rectangles of type
metal. Photography and montage replaced realistic drawing as illustration. The sans-serif typeface was regarded as essential, and in 1925 Bayer's
proposal to drop capital letters from all printed
matter was accepted. Rather than conforming to a
style, Bauhaus objects may be more properly
described as having fitness of purpose.

299. László Moholy-Nagy. *Gropius Bauhaus
Bauten, Dessau (Bauhaus Book 12)*. Book jacket,
1930. Courtesy Ex Libris, New York

300. Joost Schmidt. *Offset 7*. Book jacket, 1926.
Courtesy Ex Libris, New York

301. László Moholy-Nagy. *Malerei, Fotografie,
Film (Painting, Photography, Film)*. Book jacket,
1925. Courtesy Ex Libris, New York

302. Herbert Bayer. *Kandinsky: Punkt und
Linie zu Fläche (Kandinsky: Point and Line on
Plane)*. Book jacket, 1926

303. Herbert Bayer. *Bauhaus*. Magazine cover,
1928. Courtesy Ex Libris, New York

304. Joost Schmidt and Xanti Schawinsky.
Bauhaus. Magazine cover, January 1929. Courtesy
Ex Libris, New York

305. Herbert Bayer. *Bauhaus, Dessau*. Book
cover, 1927. Courtesy Ex Libris, New York

306. László Moholy-Nagy. *Von Material zu
Architektur (Bauhaus Book 14)*. Book cover, 1929.
Courtesy Ex Libris, New York

NEW TYPOGRAPHY

The New Typography is most simply defined as a rejection of the classical rules of typographic symmetry. In a 1927 essay, El Lissitzky traces its development back to Marinetti's *parole in liberta,* Wyndham Lewis's layout for *Blast,* and the Dadaist photomontager John Heartfield's layout for the magazine *Neue Jugend.* El Lissitzky's typography was the first formal application of the new approach, and his sans-serif letterforms, limited range of primary colors, and geometricized forms were to become lasting clichés in advertising typography. Lissitzky was one of the first to absorb the lessons of modern art movements and apply them usefully to communications, and Moholy-Nagy, in turn, adapted Lissitzky's basic premises to his Bauhaus course. In 1924 Max Burchartz opened his advertising agency, Werbau, to work in the new style for industrial clients. In 1925 a young professor of typography from Leipzig, Jan Tschichold, who had no direct connection with the Bauhaus, collected and analyzed the significant examples of modern work in a special issue of *Typographische Mitteilungen* titled "Elementare Typographie." Three years later, Tschichold formulated and codified the fundamental principles of asymmetry in *Die Neue Typographie (The New Typography),* with which he sought to change the basic practices of the German printing industry. While asymmetric design afforded more variety and could be more readily accommodated to the new layout techniques, the type historian Herbert Spencer argues that "Tschichold's attempt to strictly codify modern typography...was neither necessary nor relevant." And thus, by its very nature, it contradicted the free spirit of modern typography.

307. Jan Tschichold. *Graphische Werbekunst.* Exhibition poster, 1926. Courtesy Ex Libris, New York

308. Anton Stankowski. *Hill auch in Witten!* Advertisement, 1925

309. Jan Tschichold. *Die Hose.* Movie poster, 1927. Courtesy Ex Libris, New York

310. Jan Tschichold. *Typographische Mitteilungen.* Magazine cover, 1925. Courtesy Ex Libris, New York

311. Max Burchartz. *Schubertfeier der Staedtischen Buehnen, Essen (Schubert Festival).* Poster, 1928. The Museum of Modern Art, New York. Gift of Philip Johnson

312. Jan Tschichold. *Laster der Menschheit (Lusts of Mankind).* Movie poster, 1926. Kunstgewerbemuseum, Zurich

313. Jan Tschichold. *Casanova.* Movie poster, 1927. Kunstgewerbemuseum, Zurich

314. Joost Schmidt. *Uher Type Foundry.* Page from type catalogue, 1932. Courtesy Ex Libris, New York

307

308

309

310

SCHUBERTFEIER
DER STÆDTISCHEN BUEHNEN ESSEN

1. TAG • MONTAG, DEN 19. NOV. 1928 • GROSSE AUSSTELLUNGSHALLE • 20 UHR

AM 100. TODESTAGE FRANZ SCHUBERTS

LAZARUS MUSIKALISCHES DRAMA
OPERNDIREKTOR RUDOLF SCHULZ-DORNBURG

2. TAG • DIENSTAG, DEN 20. NOVEMBER 1928 • OPERNHAUS • 19³⁰ UHR

TÄNZE UND BALLETTE
JENS KEITH

3. TAG • FREITAG, DEN 23. NOVEMBER 1928 • STÄDTISCHER SAALBAU • 20 UHR

SCHUBERT UND WIEN
GRETE WIESENTHAL-WIEN: WIENER TÄNZE
KAMMERSÄNGER WISSIAK-HANNOVER: ALTWIENER LIEDER
HANNA KIRBACH-OPERNHAUS ESSEN
STREICHQUARTETT LILY WEISS-WIEN

4. TAG • SONNTAG, DEN 25. NOV. 1928 • GROSSE AUSSTELLUNGSHALLE • 19 UHR

LAZARUS WIEDERHOLUNG

KARTENVERKAUF ZU ALLEN VERANSTALTUNGEN: KASSE DES OPERNHAUSES
VERKEHRSVEREIN IM HANDELSHOF • BUCHHANDLUNG O. SCHMEMANN, VIEHOFERSTRASSE 16
G. D. BAEDEKER, BURGSTRASSE 16 • BUCHHANDLUNG FREDEBEUL & KOENEN, KIBBELSTRASSE

ENTWURF BURCHARTZ-ESSEN • DRUCK F.W.ROHDEN-ESSEN

311

312

313

314

NEW TYPOGRAPHY

A fresh, new typography was badly needed that
would not depend on ready-made layouts and
would express the spirit, life, and visual sensibility of its day. And it was achieved in Czechoslovakia from the late twenties to early thirties. In
his years as design director for the Prague publishing house Druzstevni Prace, Ladislav Sutnar
practiced his own version of the New Typography
in a memorable series of book jackets for works
by Upton Sinclair and George Bernard Shaw. His
jacket for *Nejmenši Dům (Minimum Housing)* is a
masterpiece of simplicity and visual clarity. Sutnar
found photography the perfect medium for
reproducing reality and giving the reader a terse,
pointed message. His poster for an exhibition of
modern trade in the city of Brno employs a
dramatic collage of architectural and industrial
products in an animated counterpoint to the
economical typography. And Karel Teige's title
page for Konstantin Biebl's poem recalls the
typecase designs in Lissitzky's *For the Voice.*

315. Ladislav Sutnar. *Československo Brno 1929.*
Poster, 1929. Courtesy Ex Libris, New York

316. Karel Teige. *S Lodí Jež Dováží a Čaj a Kávu
(With the Ship Comes Tea and Coffee).* Title pages
from book of poetry by Konstantin Biebl, 1928.
Courtesy Ex Libris, New York

317. Zdeněk Rossmann (author and designer).
*Písmo a Fotografie v Reklamé (Lettering and Pho-
tography in Advertising).* Book jacket, 1938. Courtesy Ex Libris, New York

318. Ladislav Sutnar. *Nejmenši Dům (Minimum
Housing).* Book jacket, c. 1930–31. Courtesy Ex
Libris, New York

319. Ladislav Sutnar. *Poutlásky.* Book jacket for
Upton Sinclair novel, c. 1930. Courtesy Ex Libris,
New York

320. Ladislav Sutnar. *Drobnosti.* Book jacket
for George Bernard Shaw work, c. 1930. Courtesy
Ex Libris, New York

321. Ladislav Sutnar. *Obraceni Kapitana Brass-
bounda (Captain Brassbound's Conversion).* Book
jacket for George Bernard Shaw play, c. 1930.
Courtesy Ex Libris, New York

315

316

318

Zdeněk Rossmann

písmo a fotografie

v reklamě

317

319

320

321

121

o bydlení

322

žijeme 1931

323

žijeme 1931

324

8
ročník 2.
duben 1929
odeon
ReD

foto
film
typo

325

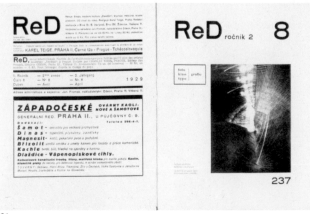

ReD ročník 2 8

237

326

327

NEW TYPOGRAPHY

The New Typography was inspired to some degree by a general degradation of typography, but it was also a response to new printing technologies that allowed designers to break free from the confines of the traditional typecase and curiously anticipated the later freedoms of phototypography. Tschichold's rigid rules were perhaps intended more for the untutored job printer, who required guidelines, than for those skilled and imaginative designers who already possessed communications skills. Shown here are examples of the New Typography that, though decidedly influenced by the spirit of Constructivism and De Stijl, nevertheless break the rules of earlier Modernist typography. The Czechoslovakian designer and art director Ladislav Sutnar demonstrates in the magazine covers for *O Bydlení (About Living)* and *Žijeme (For Life)* how a type and photo combination can signal a commitment to modern life. Karel Teige's cover and contents spread for *Red* suggest his affinity with the Bauhaus. And Yugoslav designer Ljubomir Micić plays with Constructivist forms on the covers of the arts journal *Zenit.*

322. Ladislav Sutnar, *O Bydlení (About Living).* Cover of an avant-garde interiors magazine, photomontage with typography, 1932. Courtesy Ex Libris, New York

323. Ladislav Sutnar. *Žijeme (For Life).* Cover for an "Illustrated Magazine of Modern Times," 1931. Courtesy Ex Libris, New York

324. Ladislav Sutnar. *Žijeme (For Life).* Magazine cover, 1931. Courtesy Ex Libris, New York

325. Karel Teige. *Red.* Magazine cover for a "Monthly of Modern Culture," 1929

326. Karel Teige. *Red.* Magazine pages, 1929. Courtesy Ex Libris, New York

327. Ljubomir Micić. *Zenit.* Cover of a magazine devoted to contemporaneous European art movements, 1924. Courtesy Ex Libris, New York

328. Ljubomir Micić. *Zenit.* Magazine cover, 1924. Courtesy Ex Libris, New York

328

123

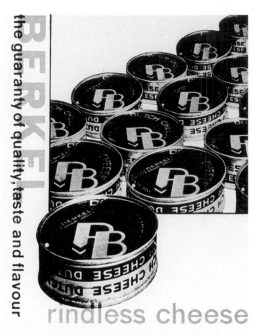

BERKEL
the guaranty of quality, taste and flavour

rindless cheese

329

330

331

332

333

NEW TYPOGRAPHY

Purified De Stijl typographics, emphasis on horizontal and vertical lines, use of the rectangle, and primary colors arranged in masses characterize the work of Piet Zwart and Paul Schuitema, the leading Dutch proponents of the New Typography. Zwart was one of the first in Holland to add photography to typographic elements, thus dramatically clarifying complicated messages. Schuitema followed suit and, by superimposing photographs in primary colors under typographic designs, was able to simulate cinematic motion. Both men applied their dynamic functionalism to business catalogues and advertisements for products and services as various as electrical wire, cables, cheese, broadcasting and paper companies, and the Dutch postal service (PTT), enlivening with typographic excitement some otherwise banal printed matter.

329. Paul Schuitema. *Rindless Cheese.* Advertisement for P. Van Berkel Ltd., date unknown. Courtesy Ex Libris, New York

330. Piet Zwart. *Hommage à une Jeune Fille.* A free-form typographic composition devised by the placement of elements from a typecase, 1925. Courtesy Ex Libris, New York

331. Piet Zwart. *Bruynzeel Architectural Products.* Catalogue spread, 1935. Courtesy Ex Libris, New York

332. Piet Zwart. *Papier.* Advertisement for Dutch cable manufacturing company, 1925

333. Piet Zwart. *Breakdown* Advertisement for NCW cable, c. 1925

334. Piet Zwart. *PCH.* Brochure for Broadcasting Station Scheveningen announcing ship-to-shore communication, 1928. Courtesy Ex Libris, New York

334

125

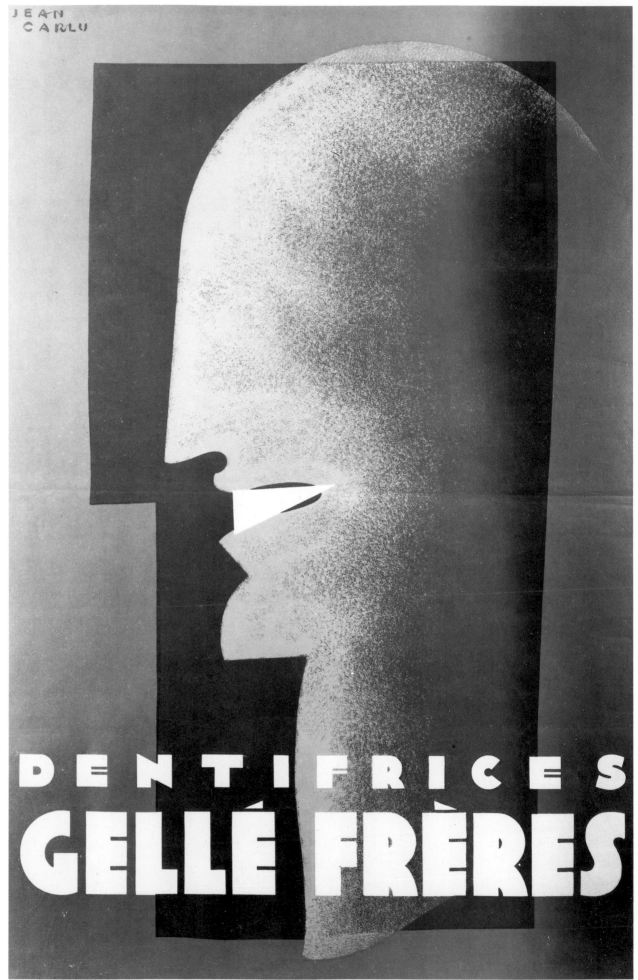

335. Jean Carlu. *Dentifrices Gellé Frères*. Poster for toothpaste, 1927. Musée de la Publicité, Paris

While Modernist designers struggled after World War I to transform society with their utopian ideals of function and fitness, Moderne or Modernistic design—a fashionable amalgam of the new reductive forms and the old decorative tendencies—was taking the consumer world by storm. In contrast to the perceived solemnities of the Modernist Bauhaus, these often frivolous and shocking manifestations of the Jazz Age were forged into a broad international style called Art Deco, later termed "the last of the total styles" by the historian Bevis Hillier.

Under different names in various countries, Art Deco universally affected architecture, furniture, clothing, and graphic arts between the world wars. As Art Nouveau began to wane, designers affiliated with the Société des Artistes Décorateurs realized that the middle class required another unthreatening style as an alternative to the increasingly abstract (and, for many, inaccessible) Modernism. Despite the prevailing Modernist philosophy, the compulsion of the European public for ornament persisted.

Art Deco was thus not retrogressive but responsive to contemporary wants. While, for instance, the couturier Paul Poiret despised Cubism, he found that certain of its elegant visual traits could be incorporated into a new decorative and luxurious style. The style also acknowledged and responded to the demands of industrial culture, including the availability of new materials such as plastics, ferroconcrete, and vita-glass. Geometric rather than asymmetric, rectilinear rather than linear, Art Deco was inspired by Art Nouveau, the Ballets Russes, North American and Aztec Indian art, and even by certain aspects of the Bauhaus. And, with the discovery in 1922 of Tutankhamen's tomb near Luxor, Art Deco ornament became a unique confluence of Egyptian ziggurats, sunbursts, and lightning bolts with a bit of the zigzag line of the Charleston added for good measure. With its Modernist characteristics, curious historical references, and controlled anarchy, it came to symbolize both efficient modern living and the elegant life-style. Art Deco reemphasized the end of traditional design, but unlike classical Modernism, it was founded on a mania for the new.

When the Exposition Internationale des Arts Décoratifs et Industriels Modernes opened in 1925, it covered two banks of the Seine and stood as a monument to both the excesses and the dichotomies of Art Deco. Most of the French exhibits, like E. J. Ruhlmann's furniture pavilion, were oppressively ornate when compared to the few decidedly Modernist structures, such as Konstantin Melnikov's angular glass Soviet pavilion and Le Corbusier's L'Esprit Nouveau. Exhibits from the Netherlands, Britain, and Austria evinced similar decorative obsessions. By the close of the exhibition, Art Deco's influence, like its ubiquitous sunray motif, fanned around the world.

Graphic design was practiced with the same frenzy as the other decorative arts. Art Deco's progressive yet unchallenging motifs provided not only an acceptable metaphor for the glory of machine-age culture but an effective code for consumerism as well. Advertising typography and layout acted as the primary communicators of the Art Deco graphic style. The official lettering on most signs and buildings at the 1925 exposition, Peignot, became one of the typographic emblems of the age. In addition, the elegant specimen sheets of Moderne display faces produced by type foundries served as paeans to the style. The French master advertising posterists, like A. M. Cassandre, Paul Colin, Jean Carlu, Charles Loupot, and Leonetto Cappiello, skillfully disseminated the Art Deco language to the public. In England, the American E. McKnight Kauffer imbued his advertisements and book jackets with Cubist and Futurist characteristics.

In 1929, the Parisian designer A. Tollmer published his book *Mise en Page,* which codified the Art Deco approach to layout. Subsequently translated into English, it became more universally used by advertising designers and printers than Jan Tschichold's *New Typography,* published the year before. Although the illustrations in *Mise en Page* are more anarchic and carnival-like than those in Tschichold's book, Tollmer's premise actually derives from the same Modernist typographic experiments. "Henceforth the art of layout is free of its bonds...," he wrote. "It must carry conviction of its own accord. The public must receive from it what in amorous terminology one might call 'the fatal dart.' In order...to obtain a freer variety of possible combinations, it became necessary to abandon the horizontal and vertical scheme...to develop an alternative...of obliques and curves. At this point we come to the modern technique, and more particularly to the technique of modern advertising."

As a pure style without ideology, Art Deco could be applied to any subject or theme. Its distinctive graphic look was identifiable regardless of national origin. And it was also nonpartisan: the Italian and German fascists applied it to their propaganda, as did the French communists, Spanish leftists, and British socialists. Its heroic and futuristic visual language was equally appropriate in the service of electrical appliances or despotic regimes.

International design magazines and annuals saturated the world market with Art Deco—in packaging, book and magazine design, and advertising. American advertisers balked at first at Art Deco's Modernist aspects but eventually responded to its combination of a rarefied esthetic quality with an up-to-date tempo. According to the historian Roland Marchand, during the 1926 New York Art Directors' annual exhibition, "Modern art forms were the predominant trend....The public seemed to want atmosphere, particularly in fantastic and eccentric forms."

Not all American design was based on such fantasies, however. The 1930s was the age of the industrial designer, who derived new Moderne forms from the science of aerodynamics. Late Deco's raybands and motion lines were not mere ornaments but symbols of Streamline technology. The Streamline era was inaugurated, celebrated, and ended at the 1939–40 New York World's Fair. The world was on the brink of war. Art Deco's international dominance soon petered out in the face of wartime austerity. The 1960s, another period of expanded consumerism, was to witness a nostalgic revival of the style.

FRENCH

As early as 1911, the stage had been set in Europe for a new decorative style. The Martine School of Decorative Art had been founded by Paul Poiret, and the Société des Artistes-Décorateurs were pursuing plans for an exhibition that would unite artist, manufacturer, and craftsman at a major decorative art exposition to be held in 1915. Owing to the war, however, the landmark Paris Exposition Internationale des Arts Décoratifs et Industriels Modernes did not take place until 1925. When it finally opened, the Expo was accused of demonstrating the vacuity of decoration for the sake of decoration, despite the presence of Le Corbusier's and Melinkov's Modernist pavilions. It was a triumph of Moderne over Modern, of design linked to art, not to the machine. The magazine-cover images shown here combined the decorative frenzy with Neo-classical and Cubist elements (and a touch of Modigliani). These ingredients made for a new stylized gesture, the hallmark of the Art Deco style.

336. Charles Loupot. *Exposition Internationale des Arts Décoratifs et Industriels Modernes.* Poster, 1925. The Mitchell Wolfson Jr. Collection of Decorative and Propaganda Arts, Miami

337. Designer unknown. *La Revue Ford.* Magazine cover, 1927

338. Georges Lapape. *Vogue.* Magazine cover, October 15, 1924. Courtesy *Vogue,* The Condé Nast Publications Inc.

339. Bolin. *Vogue.* Magazine cover, November 1, 1926. Courtesy *Vogue,* The Condé Nast Publications Inc.

340. Eduardo Benito. *Vogue.* Magazine cover, May 1, 1926. Courtesy *Vogue,* The Condé Nast Publications Inc.

341. Eduardo Benito. *Vogue.* Magazine cover, October 15, 1927. Courtesy *Vogue,* The Condé Nast Publications Inc.

337

336

338

339

340

341

342

343

344

345

FRENCH

Despite Modernism's efforts to simplify design, the urge to decorate and be decorated was not dead, never having been totally renounced by the middle class, whose creature comforts demanded ornament of some kind. Art Deco was a symbolically appropriate style for this purpose, since it made overt references to luxury and extravagance. The influential French fashion designers catered to such demands not only in their clothing design but also in their packaging. The perfumer Coty, for example, commissioned the craftsman René Lalique to produce ornate labels for his bottles. Parisian department stores like Les Grands Magasins, Galeries Lafayette, and Au Bon Marché gave special attention to those products in all departments—from cosmetics to liquors to tobaccos—that evoked the *au courant* spirit.

342. Designer unknown. Fan advertising champagne, date unknown. Courtesy John and Margaret Martinez

343. Designer unknown. *Cocktail Grand Luxe.* Advertisement card, 1932

344. Designer unknown. *Campeones.* Cigarette package, c. 1928. Courtesy Rikuyo-sha Publishing, Inc., Tokyo

345. Designer unknown. *Rhum.* Package design, c. 1928. Courtesy Rikuyo-sha Publishing, Inc., Tokyo

346. Designer unknown. Face powder box, c. 1930. Courtesy Rikuyo-sha Publishing, Inc., Tokyo

347. Designer unknown. Face powder box, c. 1930. Courtesy Rikuyo-sha Publishing, Inc., Tokyo

346

347

FRENCH

Modern and Moderne eventually came to co-exist as stylistic alternatives. In the 1930s, however, the austerity of Modernism interested only an intellectual minority, and the preference for things "modernistic" was considerably more far-reaching. Art Deco was, in fact, one of the first mass-produced styles to find acceptance with most consumers. Moderne styling became a popular graphic idiom. Following the fashion illustration of the day, posterists created works that gave the era its own unique graphic language, one that was decorative and anti-Impressionistic. Typefoundries promoted novelty display typefaces through richly illustrated specimen sheets and periodicals. The most influential of these was Deberny & Peignot's *Divertissements Typographiques,* which spotlighted the two most emblematic types of the epoch, Peignot and Bifur, both designed by A. M. Cassandre.

348. A. M. Cassandre. *Deberny & Peignot.* Advertisement on a delivery truck, 1925

349. Designer unknown. Toy truck, with advertisement for St. Raphaël wine, date unknown

350. René Vincent. *Les Automobiles Georges Irat.* Poster, 1923. Courtesy Posters Please, Inc., New York

351. Paolo Garretto. *Amilcar.* Poster, 1929. Courtesy Posters Please, Inc., New York

352. Designer unknown. *Arts & Decoration.* Advertisement pages from a periodical, 1928

353. Leonetto Cappiello. *Lampe Osmine.* Poster, 1920. Mitchell Wolfson Jr. Collection of Decorative and Propaganda Arts, Miami

354. Designer unknown. *Flit Soldier.* Three-dimensional advertisement, c. 1930

350

348

349

351

352

353

354

355

356

357

FRENCH

Paris was the wellspring of the contemporary poster during the nineteenth century and also its capital between the wars. Not tied to any one movement, the leading French graphic designers drew inspiration from various sources. Georges Barbier owed his style both to oriental art and to the scenic design of Diaghilev's Ballets Russes, the spectacle that revolutionized the European dance world. Influenced by Leonetto Cappiello's virtuosity, the Frenchmen A. M. Cassandre (Adolphe Jean-Marie Mouron) and Jean Carlu and the Swiss Charles Loupout and Paul Colin became the most significant posterists associated with the Art Deco era. They embraced Cubist and Constructivist trends yet transcended their clichés, thereby revolutionizing the poster and dominating French advertising.

355. A. M. Cassandre. *L'Intransigeant.* Poster for the newspaper, 1925. Courtesy Reinhold Brown Gallery, New York

356. Jean Carlu. *Disques Odéon.* Poster for records, 1929. Gewerbemuseum, Basel, Museum für Gestaltung

357. A. M. Cassandre. *Grand Sport.* Poster, 1925. Courtesy Reinhold Brown Gallery, New York

358. A. M. Cassandre. *Wagon-Bar.* Railway poster, 1932. Courtesy Reinhold Brown Gallery, New York

359. Georges Barbier. *Paulette Duval/Vaceslav Svoboda.* Poster, 1920. Courtesy Posters Please, Inc., New York

360. Designer unknown. *Encyclopédie des Arts Décoratifs et Industriels Modernes.* Twelve-volume set of encyclopedias on Paris Art Deco, 1925. The Mitchell Wolfson Jr. Collection of Decorative and Propaganda Arts, Miami

360

358

359

135

GERMAN

In no other country was the struggle for style more important than in Germany. That that nation gave the highest value to style as a mode of expression was evidenced, for example, by its development of Expressionism and its assimilation of Bauhaus modes as a national style. Commercial designers between the wars thus had a rich Modernist tradition from which to develop a distinctly German strain of Art Deco. Karl Schulpig, one of the top trademark designers, successfully combined Bauhausian geometry and Expressionistic iconography in much of his work. Schulz-Neudamm's poster for Fritz Lang's film *Metropolis* was an appropriately decorative rendering of a Futurist theme. Rectilinear form prevailed in most German illustration.

361. Karl Schulpig. Self-promotional advertisement, 1925

362. Schulz-Neudamm. *Metropolis.* Film poster, 1926. The Museum of Modern Art, New York. Gift of Universum-Film Aktiengesellschaft

363. Herzig. *Tanztee und Tonfilm.* Cover of a song book, 1928

364. Designer unknown. *Georg Gerson.* Promotional advertisement for printing and advertising firm, 1923

361

362

363

364

INTERNATIONALE MONATSHEFTE FÜR BAUKUNST · RAUMKUNST · WERKKUNST

DIE PYRAMIDE

SIEBEN STÄBE · VERLAGS- UND DRUCKEREI-GESELLSCHAFT M·B·H· BERLIN-ZEHLENDORF

FERNSPR = ZEHLENDORF

NR. 3007 · POSTSCHECK-

KONTO = BERLIN 33607

BANK-KONTO = DARMSTÄDTER

U. NATIONALBANK, FILIALE

BERLIN-LICHTERFELDE-W.

365

AUTORISIERTE OPEL-VERTRETUNG

GENERAL-VERTRETUNG ERNST MAG

FÜR BERLIN UND PROVINZ BRANDENBURG

LUDWIG FLATAU

AUTOMOBILE · MOTORRÄDER · WASSERFAHRZEUGE

REPARATURWERKSTATT · ZUBEHÖR ·

ERSATZTEILLAGER · TANKSTELLE

FERNSPR = WESTEND 2253

BERLIN-

CHARLOTTENBURG 5

KAISERDAMM 105

366

KONRAD BEICHT

ARCHITEKT B·D·A

HOCHBAU UND INNENAUSSTATTUNG

BANK = DRESDNER BANK, FILIALE LIEGNITZ

POSTSCHECK-KONTO = BRESLAU NR. 35073

BÜRO UND WOHNUNG = FERNSPRECHER 3225

ATELIER = FERNSPRECHER 3225

367

368

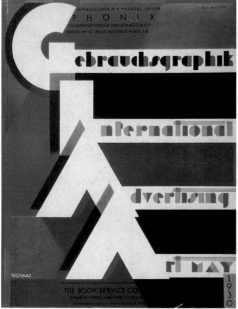

369

GERMAN

The German professional design and advertising magazines, notably *Die Reklame* and *Gebrauchsgraphik,* promoted various, and sometimes seemingly contradictory, definitions of modernity. Hence, they presented Bauhausian graphic motifs as appropriate for all kinds of advertising and editorial layout; to the purists, such a linking of the Bauhaus with Art Deco was sacrilegious. But for those who believed that the Bauhaus method was the future of commercial design, the widespread acceptance by non-Bauhaus designers and printers of its Modernist motifs should have been cause for celebration.

365. Paul Pfund. *Die Pyramide.* Letterhead design for a monthly art magazine, c. 1929

366. Paul Pfund. *Ludwig Flatau.* Letterhead design for an auto dealer, c. 1929

367. Paul Pfund. *Konrod Beicht, Architekt.* Letterhead design for an architect, 1929

368. Designer unknown. *Buchdruckerei der Union Deutsche Verlagsgesellschaft, Stuttgart.* Advertisement for a printing firm from *Das Plakat,* 1919

369. Leonard. *Gebrauchsgraphik.* Magazine cover, 1930

SWISS

A haven for those fleeing the war, neutral Switzerland continued to develop its exemplary advertising style (Werbestil), giving special emphasis to the poster. Swiss artists had been exposed earlier to the movements and styles flowering elsewhere in Europe, yet it was not until the late twenties, as poster historian Alain Weill writes, "that the Swiss poster developed in decisive fashion, to create a typically Swiss style. This style is doubtless the assimilation of two opposing influences: France on one side, Germany on the other." Among those who visited Paris was Herbert Matter, who studied with Fernand Légér and Amédée Ozenfant and worked briefly for Deberny & Peignot. Matter's *PKZ* poster epitomizes the pictorial simplicity of this era. Other Swiss posterists studied in Berlin under the German master O. H. W. Hadank; among those who studied in Munich was Otto Bamberger, who originated the "object poster" in Switzerland.

370. Designer unknown. *Cigarettes Sato.* Poster, 1933. Kunstgewerbemuseum, Zurich

371. Reno. *Serodent, La Santé des Dents.* Poster, 1932. Kunstgewerbemuseum, Zurich

372. Herbert Matter. *PKZ.* Poster, 1928. Österreichisches Museum für Angewandte Kunst, Die Neue Sammlung, Vienna

370

371

WOLFSBERG ZÜRICH

MOTOR COMPTOIR ZÜRICH 1932
AUTO HALLE 4.–7.
LETZIGRABEN MÄRZ

374

375

376

SWISS

The Deco era was known for its sleek, fast automobiles. Along with planes and ships, they were the most potent and prized symbols of modernity. The Swiss, especially, conducted a love affair with the car, and many of their finest and most characteristically Art Deco posters were devoted to motorcar races and exhibitions.

373. Otto Baumberger. *Motor Comptoir Zürich*. Poster, 1932. Kunstgewerbemuseum, Zurich

374. Designer unknown. *Genève*. Poster, 1936. Kunstgewerbemuseum, Zurich

375. Kaspar Ernst Graf. *Grand Prix Suisse, Automobile, Berne*. Poster, 1934. Kunstgewerbemuseum, Zurich

376. Noel Fontanet. *Automobil-Ausstellung*. Exhibition poster, 1930. Kunstgewerbemuseum, Zurich

377

378

379

380

381

382

EASTERN EUROPEAN

Other forms of Art Deco emerged in the various European capitals. Deco was the dominant visual code between the wars, and it was impossible to pick up a graphic design magazine or annual during this time and not find at least one of its characteristic traits—undulating geometric patterns, airbrushed raybands, decorative sunbursts, and so on. In a special 1930 issue of the German printers' journal *Archiv* dedicated to Hungarian Modernism, there appears Robert Bereny's poster showing a haughty gent smoking Modiano cigarettes, a masterpiece of witty Deco styling. About his work Bereny said, "The poster should be painterly, for the simple reason that, psychologically speaking, the human being regards everything that is painted as painterly." Advertisements here by the Austrian poster masters Julius Klinger, the partners Cosl and Frey, and Emil Preetorius typify the German reductivist Deco style. And the poster for LOPP by an unknown Polish designer underscores the universality of Art Deco.

377. Robert Bereny. *Modiano.* Poster for cigarettes and cigarette paper, 1928

378. Julius Klinger. *Wasserkraft-Elektrizitäts.* Poster for an Austrian hydroelectric utility, 1922

379. Cosl-Frey. Self-promotional poster for design studio, c. 1930. Courtesy Fairleigh Dickinson University, Madison, N.J.

380. Julius Klinger. *Spessl.* Poster, 1923. Courtesy Fairleigh Dickinson University, Madison, N.J.

381. Emil Preetorius. *Kathreiner Weine.* Austrian poster, date unknown. Courtesy Fairleigh Dickinson University, Madison, N.J.

382. Designer unknown. *LOPP.* Polish poster for an aviation company, date unknown. Courtesy Fairleigh Dickinson University, Madison, N.J.

BIBLIOTECHINA DELLE LANE MARZOTTO

LE CONQUISTE DELL'AVIAZIONE

N.° 23
LE CONQUISTE DELL'AVIAZIONE

384

IL CAPO SQUADRA BALILLA

385

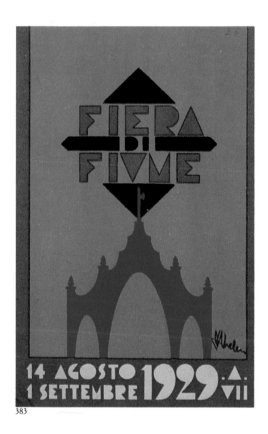

FIERA DI FIVME

14 AGOSTO 1929 · A ·
1 SETTEMBRE · VII

383

VIª MOSTRA MERCATO

50% RIDUZIONI FERROVIARIE

RIGOBALDI

ENIT

1936 ANNO XIV

DELL' ARTIGIANATO FIRENZE 26 APRILE ... 9 MAGGIO

386

387

ITALIAN

The Italian pavilion at the 1925 Paris exposition was decked out in antique Roman appointments consistent with D'Annunzio's rhetoric about the glorious Italian past. Only a single room displayed innovative design: Marinetti's exhibit of three Futurists, Balla, Boccioni, and Depero, who had not succumbed to the Novecento reaction. Italian decorative art between the wars was an odd coupling of both Modernist and classical conceits. Italian art, unlike its counterpart in Germany, thrived under Fascism. Yet Futurism, despite Mussolini's sanction, lost much of its vitality when used as the regime's propaganda tool. A Futurist-inspired, decorative style of illustration, layout, and typography eventually dominated Italian commercial design before the war.

383. Designer unknown. *Fiera di Fiume.* Postcard, 1929. The Mitchell Wolfson Jr. Collection of Decorative and Propaganda Arts, Miami

384. Designer unknown. *Le Conquiste dell' Aviazione.* Pamphlet cover, 1928

385. Designer unknown. *Italian Fascist Youth Battalion Handbook.* Cover, 1929

386. Giovanni Riccobaldi. *Via Mostra Mercato dell'Artigianato, Firenze.* Postcard, 1936. The Mitchell Wolfson Jr. Collection of Decorative and Propaganda Arts, Miami

387. Designer unknown. *Gioventi Fascista.* Magazine cover, 1933

388. Designer unknown. *Roma Chicago New York Roma.* Poster, 1933. The Mitchell Wolfson Jr. Collection of Decorative and Propaganda Arts, Miami

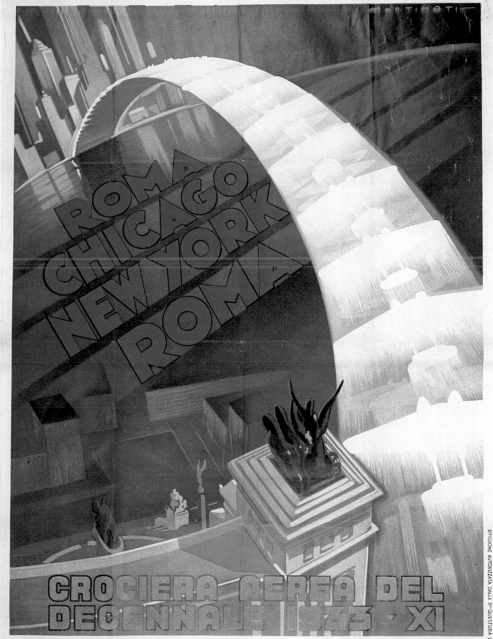

388

ITALIAN

Mussolini liked to call Italian artists, architects, and industrialists his "producers." They were indeed arms of the party, for their products were consistently used to represent the new order. However, not all graphic design of the period showed the *fasci* or Mussolini as central motifs. From before World War I, Italian industry and business had successfully employed the talents of graphic designers like Federico Seneca, whose distinctive posters for Buitoni products, Perugina chocolates, and Modiano cigarettes made him one of the most sought-after posterists of the era. Venna's cover for *Gran Bazar* demonstrates a typical use of the Deco-style cartoon in advertising and editorial illustration.

389. Federico Seneca. *Buitoni.* Poster, 1927. Courtesy Steven Guarnaccia

390. Lucio Venna. *Carnevale (Gran Bazar).* Magazine cover, 1930

391. Antonio Seguini. *Modiano: I Campionato Interprovinciale Radiomotociclistico per Giovani Fascisti.* Poster, 1933. Fotografie Industriali e Pubblicitarie Documentari Cinematografici, Civici Musei Udine

392. Designer unknown. *Calendario.* Title page from a commemorative calendar of Fascist military campaigns, 1934

389

390

391

392

ENGLISH

About 1919, English design, which had been deeply committed to decorativism for almost a century, emerged from the Victorian era to embrace a functionalism consistent with the needs of contemporary industry. Particularly in the fields of architecture and industrial design, Britain soon became a model of modern industrial production. By the 1925 exposition, decorative design, influenced by Modernist art and practiced by Duncan Grant and Vanessa Bell, came in for a reappraisal. E. McKnight Kauffer imbued his graphic designs (as well as his murals, textiles, and carpets) with forms similar to those of Le Corbusier and Léger. In 1930, Aldous Huxley, who often wrote on matters of typography and design, stated in *The Studio*: "The contemporary style has evolved out of the harsh artistic puritanism of a Cubism which, in its first violent reaction against prettiness, would suffer nothing but straight lines and angles, into something more ripe and humane, for which there is yet no convenient name." The book jackets and posters here reveal many of the formal concerns with color, geometry, and pattern that constituted the English Art Deco vocabulary.

393. Tom Purvis. *East Coast by Liner*. Poster, 1935. Courtesy Chris Mullen

394. Halliwell. *Speed Your Message*. Poster, 1931. The Mitchell Wolfson Jr. Collection of Decorative and Propaganda Arts, Miami

395. E. McKnight Kauffer. *BBC Handbook*. Book jacket, 1929. Courtesy Chris Mullen

396. Wallace and Tiernan. *The Year Book of the London School of Printing and Kindred Trades*. Book cover, 1929. The Mitchell Wolfson Jr. Collection of Decorative and Propaganda Arts, Miami

397. E. McKnight Kauffer. *You Can Be Sure of Shell*. Poster, 1934. Courtesy Chris Mullen

396

397

ENGLISH

With the founding in 1919 of the British Institute of Industrial Arts and the Design and Industrial Association, British art and industry conclusively joined forces. Graphic designers actively participated in this relationship, contributing to significant advertising campaigns for manufacturers and services, including the London Underground, the four national railway corporations, and Shell–Mex and B.P. oil companies. The designer most responsible for advancing the British graphic style of the Deco era was Frank Pick. In directing the advertising for the London subways, Pick understood the need for a cohesive design system. In addition to architectural systematization, he had the subway map redesigned and commissioned a unique alphabet from Edward Johnson, who designed an early sans-serif alphabet that was soon adopted in different forms by Modernists throughout the world. Pick also commissioned Kauffer's Cubist-inspired posters of the early twenties, which made people appreciate modern art almost despite themselves. The Shell Company, whose advertising was directed by Jack Baddington, treated the public to an ever-changing display of posters on the sides of its delivery trucks.

398. A. Rogers. *Speed.* Poster, 1930. London Transport Museum

399. Ashley Eldrid Havinden. *Den Neuen Plymouth.* Poster (German version of English original), 1929. Courtesy Posters Please, Inc., New York

400. Dora Batty. *R.A.F. Display—Colindale Station.* Poster, 1932. London Transport Museum

401. Designer unknown. *Curtiss Flying Service.* Poster, c. 1929. Courtesy Santoro Collection, London

398

399

400

401

402

403

404

405

406

407

AMERICAN

Writing in 1933, the American interior designer Donald Deskey defined the style that had taken his country by storm: "From the chaotic situation arising out of an era of prosperity without precedent for decoration, produced by Expo '25 …a style emerged…or, better still…a common denominator—the modernist style. I believe this term is a pure Americanism. It originated from the hysteria created by Expo and serves to denote the kind of work produced in the period 1925–29 which has no connection with anything produced previously.…The clichés of the past were exchanged for an ill-digested present-day formula. Self-styled designers blindly applied ornament to the surface of form—in itself badly planned. Their ornamental syntax consisted almost entirely of…the zigzag, the triangle, fawn-like curves.…In the meantime the really modern style was defined in other than modernist terms and was only concerned with outside appearances and the surface of things." For Deskey and others, Art Deco was the style of the age but also its scourge.

402. Designer unknown. *High Voltage Railway Electrification.* Sculptural inlaid panel designed for the Westinghouse Pavilion, Chicago World's Fair, 1933. The Mitchell Wolfson Jr. Collection of Decorative and Propaganda Arts, Miami

403. Designer unknown. *General Electric— Mazda Lamps.* Advertising display for lightbulbs, 1925. The Mitchell Wolfson Jr. Collection of Decorative and Propaganda Arts, Miami

404. Designer unknown. *Conoco Magazine.* Cover, May/June 1932

405. Frank Lloyd Wright. Adhesive seal, small paper bag, and trade card for V. C. Morris Store, 1942. The Mitchell Wolfson Jr. Collection of Decorative and Propaganda Arts, Miami

406. Charles Chappel. *Contact.* Advertisement from specimen book, 1930

407. Designer unknown. *Contact.* Advertisement from specimen book, 1930

AMERICAN

Also known as Jazz Modern, the Zig Zag Style, Depression Moderne, and Manhattan Modern, American Art Deco was fed by revivals of North American Indian, Aztec, and Egyptian art. Deco artists sought to create a style that combined simplicity with dynamism. Even during the worst period of economic depression, the style was associated with glamor, luxury, and extravagance. Motifs such as greyhounds, pyramids, obelisks, lightning bolts, and sunrays put the stamp of modernity on everything from oceanliners to jewelry boxes. As Jeffrey Meikle writes, Deco motifs also suggest the "staccato rhythm of the assembly line." Graphic stylists like Merle Armitage and Fortunato Amato created print environments that could induce the consumer to buy a product—whether magazine, book, or toaster—because it was modern.

408. Fortunato Amato. *Stage.* Magazine cover, September 1937

409. Merle Armitage. *George Gershwin.* Title pages of book, 1938

410. Clarence Hornung. Logo for A. I. Friedman, c. 1938

411. Julius J. Stern. *Stella.* Trademark, 1937

412. Designer unknown. *Reveille.* Trademark, 1936

413. Designer unknown. *Barkon Lighting.* Trademark, 1937

414. Designer unknown. *RCA.* Trademark for Radio Corporation of America, 1928

415. Designer unknown. Decorative display types, from *Commercial Art Advertising Layout,* c. 1928

416. Designer unknown. Advertisements for *Town & Country,* employing contemporary geometric ornament, c. 1928

408

409

410

411 STELLA

R·E·V·E·I·L·L·E

412

BARKON LIGHTING

413

RCA

414

415

HARPER'S BAZAAR

MARCH 1st 1938

AMERICAN FASHIONS

A.M. CASSANDRE

15 FR. IN PARIS   50 CENTS   2/6 IN LONDON

417

418

419

420

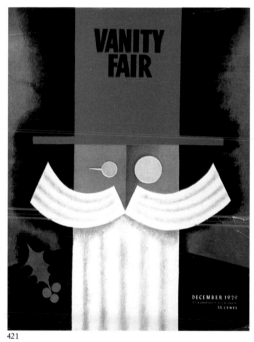

421

AMERICAN

John Dos Passos characterized the American decorative style as "the shop-window world of Fifth Avenue." City of the Empire State and Chrysler buildings, New York was the Deco capital of America. And the covers of the magazines published in New York were like its shop-windows, complete with fanciful, dreamlike, and symbolic decorative illustration. New York was also the mecca for modernistic European artists. The posterist A. M. Cassandre came from Paris to design covers for *Harper's Bazaar,* as did Paolo Garretto, who worked regularly for *Fortune, The New Yorker,* and *Vanity Fair,* and M. F. Agah, who landed the prestigious art directorship at *Vanity Fair.*

417. A. M. Cassandre. *Harper's Bazaar.* Magazine cover, March 1, 1938

418. John Held, Jr. *Life.* Magazine cover, June 24, 1926

419. Paolo Garretto. *Fortune.* Magazine cover, February 1932

420. Designer unknown. *Film Fun.* Magazine cover, 1925

421. M. F. Agah. *Vanity Fair.* Magazine cover, December 1929

422. Georges Schreiber. *Manhattan Melody.* Vase, 1951. The Mitchell Wolfson Jr. Collection of Decorative and Propaganda Arts, Miami

422

159

STREAMLINE

Streamlining was more than a distinctly American modern style, it was the metaphor of a new epoch. The marriage of art, industry, and science, it was passionately practiced by a new profession of industrial designers, who applied themselves to the aerodynamic redesign of all sorts of machinery, from airplanes to pencil sharpeners. Though its look related to Art Deco, its trappings were not just surface trivialities; while symbolizing an age of speed, it also proclaimed great optimism. Americans learned about modern design through the ephemera of streamlined commercial culture, specifically its advertising. One of the leading proponents of Streamlining, Walter Dorwin Teague, said the graphic style embraced "Beaux Arts principles, moderne qualities, billboard art, and industrial styling." The billboard designs here demonstrate the streamlining of graphic art.

423. H. M. A. Strauss. Schematic for patent registration for electric food mixer, 1938. Courtesy Eric Baker

424. J. C. Leyendecker. *Jantzen Swimsuits.* Billboard advertisement, date unknown. Courtesy Fairleigh Dickinson University, Madison, N.J.

425. Designer unknown. *Lipton's Tea.* Billboard advertisement, date unknown. Courtesy Fairleigh Dickinson University, Madison, N.J.

426. Designer unknown. *Lafayette Radio.* Billboard advertisement, 1936. Courtesy Fairleigh Dickinson University, Madison, N.J.

427. Otis Shepard. *Wrigley's Spearmint Gum.* Billboard advertisement, 1936. Courtesy Fairleigh Dickinson University, Madison, N.J.

428. Alexey Brodovitch. *Schaum Beer.* Proposal for a billboard, 1933

429. Otis Shepard. *Platz Dark Beer.* Proposal for a billboard, 1935

423

424

425

426

427

428

429

RURAL ELECTRIFICATION ADMINISTRATION
U. S. DEPARTMENT OF AGRICULTURE

KEEP YOUR TEETH CLEAN

431

WORK with CARE

432

America's answer!

PRODUCTION

JEAN CARLU

DIVISION OF INFORMATION
OFFICE FOR EMERGENCY MANAGEMENT

433

STREAMLINE

During the late thirties, with America still feeling the tragic effects of the Depression, the government's Works Progress Administration commissioned graphic designers to produce posters and other informational graphics for the public good. Artists and small studios around the country created (many anonymously) hundreds of WPA posters encouraging literacy, personal hygiene, and good habits in the workplace. Many of these posters were stylistically influenced by the European Modernists (particularly those artists forced by the Fascists to emigrate to the United States) and by the machine aesthetic, popularized in exhibitions like the one at New York's Museum of Modern Art. Lester Beall created a series of posters for the Rural Electrification Administration intended as reminders that the Department of Agriculture is always working for the citizenry. His use of photography and strong, symbolic color is reminiscent of work done at the Bauhaus. In 1941, Jean Carlu was commissioned by Charles Coiner, Vice President of N. W. Ayer, to render a defense poster, with memorable results.

430. Lester Beall. *Rural Electrification Administration*. Poster, 1937. Library of Congress, Washington, D.C. Poster Collection

431. Designer unknown. *Keep Your Teeth Clean*. WPA poster, 1936. Library of Congress, Washington, D.C. Poster Collection

432. Robert Muchley. *Work with Care*. WPA poster, 1936. Library of Congress, Washington, D.C. Poster Collection

433. Jean Carlu. *America's Answer! Production*. Poster, 1941. Library of Congress, Washington, D.C. Poster Collection

434. Josef Albers. *Machine Art*. Exhibition poster for the Museum of Modern Art, 1927. Courtesy Ex Libris, New York

MUSEUM OF MODERN ART
MACHINE ART

434

436

STREAMLINE

"A Century of Progress," the 1933 Chicago World's Fair, was the first American exposition extensively devised by industrial designers. It announced the new machine age in all its futuristic majesty. Yet it was the 1939–1940 New York World's Fair, "The World of Tomorrow," that epitomized the designer's utopia. Walter Dorwin Teague, Norman Bel Geddes, Henry Dreyfuss, and Raymond Loewy (all graphic designers at one time) designed the major pavilions that testified to the more efficient, prosperous, and beautiful America of the future. The Trylon and Perisphere, devised by architects Wallace K. Harrison and J. André Fouilhoux, was the centerpiece of the fair and symbol of this future. Nembhard N. Culin's poster advertising the fair is typical of the Streamline graphic style. The future was a common leitmotif for many illustrators and designers working at the time, as evidenced by the catalogue and magazine covers shown here.

435. Jim Nash. *Mobilgas.* Trademark, 1933

436. Leo Rackow. *A.C.F. (American Car and Foundry Company).* Catalogue cover, 1938. The Mitchell Wolfson Jr. Collection of Decorative and Propaganda Arts, Miami

437. Designer unknown. *Popular Science.* Magazine cover, 1938

438. Hugh Ferriss. *Creative Art.* Magazine cover, August 1931

439. Charles Egri. *PM.* Magazine cover, February/March 1939

440. Designer unknown. *Science and Mechanics.* Magazine cover, September 1932

441. Nembhard N. Culin. *The New York World's Fair in 1939.* Poster, 1939. The Mitchell Wolfson Jr. Collection of Decorative and Propaganda Arts, Miami

442. Designer unknown. Trylon and Perisphere salt-and-pepper shakers, 1939

435

437

438

439

440

441

442

443

444

445

DUTCH

It is difficult to pinpoint a specifically Dutch Art Deco style. P. A. H. Hofman's poster for the Utrecht Industries Fair conforms most clearly to the Deco formula. The other examples do not fall neatly into one category, but since they are decidedly influenced by Modern precedents, might be considered Art Deco. The magazine *Wendingen (Upheaval),* edited by H. Th. Wijdeveld after World War I, was a champion of eclectic modernity when compared with the asceticism of a De Stijl journal. The magazine cover by Samuel Schwartz shows a Surrealist current popular in Dutch advertising posters at the time. The cover for the annual promotional piece for G. H. Bührmann's papermill, *Papiermolen,* was apparently designed to represent the dominant trend.

443. Samuel L. Schwartz. *Wendingen.* Cover of a magazine of early twentieth-century design and architecture, c. 1931. Courtesy Fairleigh Dickinson University, Madison, N.J.

444. Designer unknown. *Papiermolen.* Cover for a paper promotion, 1933

445. P. A. H. Hofman. *Industries Fair, Utrecht, Holland.* Poster, 1930. The Mitchell Wolfson Jr. Collection of Decorative and Propaganda Arts, Miami

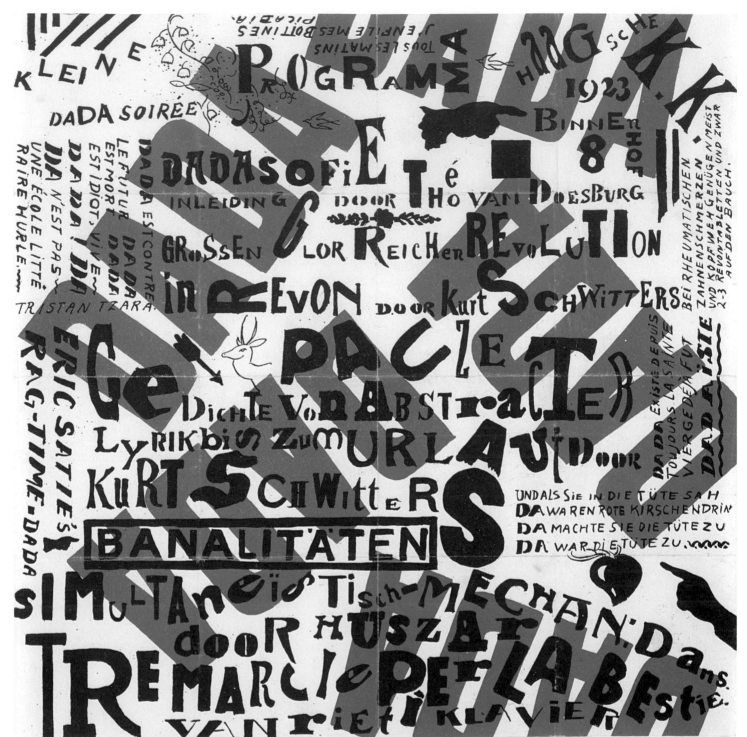

446. Kurt Schwitters and Theo van Doesburg. *Kleine Dada Soirée.* Poster for Dada event, 1922. Courtesy Reinhold Brown Gallery, New York

ada means nothing," declared the Romanian-born poet Tristan Tzara, yet the term was to become highly charged. Dadaists rejected all forms of bourgeois art, including those, like Expressionism, once deemed revolutionary but later neutered, they felt, by middle-class acceptance. Dada was invented by a German refugee, the philosopher-poet Hugo Ball, and his companion, Emmy Hennings, in 1916 in neutral Zurich at the height of World War I. The two were joined, in Zurich and in New York, by other émigré artists who had found safe haven from the horrors of a war they blamed on the decadence of Western civilization. Dadaists scorned the idea that art was the highest form of human expression and sought to destroy the traditional barriers within artistic endeavor: the poet became a typographer, the painter a poet. While they rejected all theory and most types of organization, Dadaists developed a unique syntax and vocabulary in poetry, theater, and graphic design.

Between 1916 and 1918, the Zurich Dadaists were involved at the Cabaret Voltaire with a series of outrageous antiart happenings, reported on by Ball, Richard Huelsenbeck, Jean Arp, and Sophie Täuber-Arp in the Dada review named after the cafe. As organized by Tzara, the Dada evenings were influenced by the outlandish showmanship of the Italian Futurists. Concurrently in New York, Dada leaders Marcel Duchamp and Francis Picabia concerned themselves with revealing, and hastening, the aesthetic decomposition of Western art. (Duchamp's scandalous "ready-mades" had foreshadowed his later Dadaist concoctions.) Dada also developed a stronghold in Paris, where it evolved during the mid-twenties into Surrealism, described by the art historian Lucy Lippard as "housebroken Dada."

Immediately after the war, many of the exiles, the majority of whom were German, returned to Berlin to carry on a decidedly politicized Dada. Expressionism, which had begun by bringing Germans so many welcome truths, had become something of an official national style; aimed at inwardness, abstraction,

the renunciation of all objectivity, it was the natural enemy of Dada. In Berlin, Huelsenbeck joined forces with the painter Raoul Hausmann, the satirist George Grosz, and the brothers Wieland Herzfelde and John Heartfield, to turn Dada into a sharper weapon of attack against both the old and new ruling orders. During his first lecture on Dada in 1918, Huelsenbeck stated the Dada position: "For the first time Dadaism poses no longer in an aesthetic manner before life. It lacerates all the great words: ethic, culture, 'interiorisation,' which are only covers for weak muscles." In a polemic titled *Art Is in Danger,* Grosz stated, "If we artists were the expression of anything at all, then we were the expression of the ferment of dissatisfaction and unrest." His group soon shed the last remnants of Dada's pretense to art in favor of agitation in the service of the Spartacist, and later the communist, cause.

In its revulsion from the duplicitous Social Democratic Party then ruling the ill-fated Weimar Republic, Dada declared a satiric shadow government. Its members adopted official-sounding titles like *Oberdada, Welt-Dada, Dadaosopher,* and *Propagandada* and published parodistic manifestoes and pamphlets like *What Is Dadaism and What Does It Want in Germany?* (1919). Yet, despite its rhetoric, one could argue that Dada's real loyalty was not to politics but rather to Dada itself—a decidedly logical concept in the Dada scheme of things.

A distinct Dadaist graphic style evolved from combining the random methods of Cubist *collés* and Futurist *parole a liberta* with the efficiency and economy of mechanical-reproduction techniques. Widely scattered and mixed typography characterized the numerous Berlin Dada periodicals, while the Zurich magazines or Picabia's *391* had more crammed, jumbled pages. Dada's anarchic layouts capitalized on the contrast between a page of type and a single word stamped across it like a slogan or on words boldly isolated as in cheap posters and advertisements—all as far removed as possible from elegance and good taste.

Simultaneously employed in Berlin and Moscow, the most lasting Dada innovation was photomontage. Heartfield (the art director and co-founder with Grosz and Herzfelde of the publishing house the Malik Verlag) pioneered this mechanical art and was its most exemplary practitioner, but Hausmann also took credit for its discovery. "On the wall of almost every house was a colored lithograph depicting the image of a grenadier...," Hausmann wrote about his revelation. "To make this military memento more personal a photographic portrait of a soldier had been used in place of the head. This was a stroke of lightning, one could...make paintings entirely composed of cut out photographs....I began to realize this new vision by using photographs from magazines...[and] decided to call these works photomontages. This term translated our aversion to playing artists, and considering ourselves as engineers...from that came our preference for overalls." Less aesthetically concerned than other Dadaists, Heartfield made montage political postcards that said in image what was prohibited in words by government censors.

Germany had two other, comparatively apolitical Dada groups. In Cologne, Max Ernst, Theodor Baargeld, and Jean Arp fomented trouble in the unorthodox reviews *Der Ventilator* and *Die Schammade.* In Hanover, Kurt Schwitters conducted a one-man movement, parallel and sometimes merging with Dada, called Merz. A poet, painter, typographer, and advertising-design consultant, Schwitters published his stylistically influential review, *Merz,* from 1923 to 1932. Its design, drawing inspiration from El Lissitzky's Constructivism and Van Doesburg's De Stijl, was more geometric than that of the Berlin journals.

Dada's extreme ribaldry and irreverence seduced disaffected artists for only a brief time. After 1922, with Germany in social, political, and economic chaos, many of Dada's proponents moved either inward toward Surrealism or outward toward Constructivism and the New Objectivity. Although they drifted away from the Dada style, Grosz and Heartfield continued to produce trenchant political commentary until the Nazis put an end to their efforts and they left Germany.

447

448

Although certain stylistic traits immediately identify a Dada painting or graphic work, the styles of the individual artists were more various, being influenced by Expressionism, machine imagery, and geometric abstraction. Dada, moreover, owes its typographic concoctions to Marinetti's *parole in liberta,* and indeed much of its theatrics were borrowed from the Futurists. Shown here is a sampling from the stacks of Dada literature issued from the Dada capitals: Zurich, Berlin, Cologne, Hanover, Paris, and New York. While the first two issues of the Zurich periodical *Dada* are conventional in appearance, by *Dada 3* Tristan Tzara, the editor, has introduced the organized chaos that typifies Dada's graphic expression. The cover of *Der Dada,* designed with dismembered type taken from newspapers and official organs, suggests contempt for officialdom. *Mecano,* edited by Theo van Doesburg and published in 1922, was something of a supplement to *De Stijl.* Adopting Dada graphic characteristics, it counted among its missions poking fun at the solemnities of the Bauhaus. *Merz* began publishing irregularly in 1923 as the organ of Kurt Schwitters's one-man movement and, unlike other Dada periodicals, was eventually designed according to the principles of the New Typography. Schwitters devoted complete issues to advertising and typography. The *Dada Siegt!* poster announcing a 1920 Cologne exhibit is typical of Dada's deliberate rejection of the traditional rules of typography.

447. Designer unknown. *Dada.* Pages from magazine edited by Tristan Tzara, c. 1917–21. Courtesy Ex Libris, New York

448. Marcel Janco. *Dada 3.* Magazine cover, with woodcut illustration, 1918. Courtesy Ex Libris, New York

449. Raoul Hausmann. *Der Dada.* Cover for the German Dadaist publication, 1919. Courtesy Ex Libris, New York

450. Theo van Doesburg. *Mecano.* Cover of Dutch Dada magazine publishing experimental poetry and typography, c. 1922. Courtesy Ex Libris, New York

451. Kurt Schwitters. Letterhead for *Merz,* c. 1923. Courtesy Ex Libris, New York

452. Max Ernst/Johannes Baargeld. *Dada Siegt!* Poster, 1920. Courtesy Reinhold Brown Gallery, New York

453. Kurt Schwitters. *Merz 4.* Magazine cover, 1923. Courtesy Ex Libris, New York

454. Kurt Schwitters. *Merz.* Magazine pages, 1923. Courtesy Ex Libris, New York

449

450

451

453

454

455

456

457

458

459

Many Dada happenings took place in nightclubs and cabarets like Zurich's Cabaret Voltaire and Berlin's Club Dada. The nightclub Schall und Rauch became a meeting place for the Berlin Dadaists; George Grosz designed many of its theatrical sets and, with other members, including Hannah Hoch, created covers for its house organ and program. Owing to the fierce factional struggles in the German government, Berlin Dadaists were more politically involved than those in other cities. John Heartfield's avowedly left-wing *Die Neue Jugend,* an outlet for early Dada manifestos, was disguised as a prospectus for a Grosz portfolio to avoid the strict censorship of newspapers. Heartfield perfected the technique of photomontage as a polemical tool. Kurt Schwitters, who was less interested in politics, became a design consultant and was able to fine-tune his typography through *Merz.* In three issues devoted to the "fairy tale," he developed *Die Scheuche (The Scarecrow),* illustrated with type forms, which owes much to Lissitzky's *Of Two Squares.*

455. P. Erkens. *Schall und Rauch.* Cover illustration for a cabaret program/magazine, November 1920

456. Hannah Hoch. *Schall und Rauch.* Cover illustration for a cabaret program/magazine, April 1920

457. John Heartfield. *Im Zeichen der Rationalisierung.* Photomontage, political poster, 1927

458. John Heartfield. *Neue Jugend.* Front page of a left-wing monthly publication, published by Der Malik Verlag, June 1917

459. George Grosz. *Schall und Rauch.* Cover illustration for a cabaret program/magazine, March 1920

460. Kathe Steinitz, Kurt Schwitters, and Theo van Doesburg. *Die Scheuche (The Scarecrow).* Cover for children's book, 1925. Courtesy Ex Libris, New York

461. Kathe Steinitz, Kurt Schwitters, and Theo van Doesburg. *Die Scheuche (The Scarecrow).* Pages from a children's book, 1925. Courtesy Ex Libris, New York

460

461

In 1917, George Grosz, John Heartfield, and
Weiland Herzfelde founded the Malik Verlag in
order to publish Communist periodicals, manifestos, and portfolios as well as low-priced novels
of social interest. Following *Die Neue Jugend,* the
trio collaborated on a series of small journals,
which regularly changed names due to government banning orders. In the Dada tradition, the
first one, *Jedermann Sein Eigner Fussball (Every
Man His Own Football,* one issue only), includes
Heartfield's first attempt at satirical montage,
showing a fan with the heads of government
superimposed and asking the question, "Who is
the most beautiful?" *Die Pliete (Bankrupt)* is less
Dada-oriented in its emphasis on continued
social struggle and violent political revolution;
one of its covers features a conventional cartoon
showing Noske, the chief of Weimar security
forces, after he violently suppressed a workers'
protest demonstration. The trio used their journals to attack the concept of an art that had no
relevance whatsoever to the working class. Malik
continued to publish books after the demise of
Dada in the early twenties, with Heartfield as its
art director devoted to perfecting the montage
technique for jacket designs. He also became a
frequent contributor to the *Arbeiter Illustrierten
Zeitung (AIZ),* the Communist workers' newspaper, for which he did his most powerful anti-
Fascist montage/cartoons.

462. John Heartfield. *Jedermann Sein Eigner
Fussball (Every Man His Own Football).* Publica-
tion cover, February 1919. Fairleigh Dickinson
University, Madison, N.J.

463. John Heartfield. *AIZ (Workers' Illustrated
Times).* Photomontage cover, c. 1930

464. George Grosz and John Heartfield. *Die
Pliete (Bankrupt).* Illustrated magazine/news-
paper cover, 1919.

465. John Heartfield. *Drei Welten: Gesammelte
Erzählungen.* Jacket for book by Isaac Babel,
1931. Courtesy Fairleigh Dickinson University,
Madison, N.J.

466. John Heartfield. *Deutschland, Deutsch-
land Über Alles (Germany, Germany, Above All
Others).* Jacket for book by Kurt Tucholsky, 1929.
Courtesy Fairleigh Dickinson University,
Madison, N.J.

467. John Heartfield. *Das Geld Schreibt.* Jacket
for book by Upton Sinclair, 1930. Courtesy Fairleigh Dickinson University, Madison, N.J.

468. John Heartfield. *Petroleum.* Jacket for
book by Upton Sinclair, 1927. Courtesy Fairleigh
Dickinson University, Madison, N.J.

462

463

464

465

467

466

468

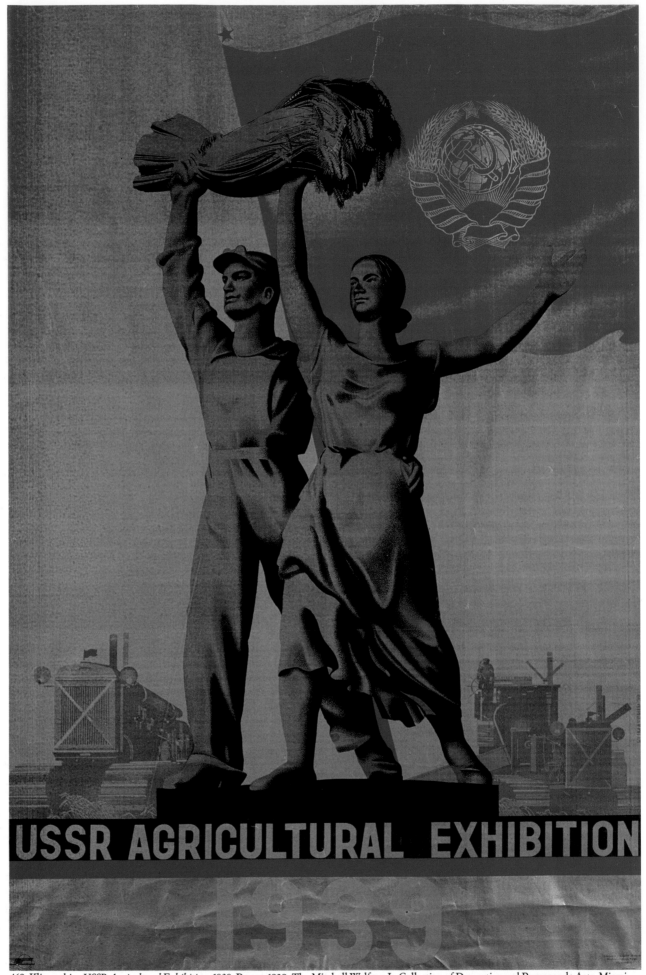

469. Klimaschin. *USSR Agricultural Exhibition, 1939.* Poster, 1939. The Mitchell Wolfson Jr. Collection of Decorative and Propaganda Arts, Miami

lthough avant-garde Soviet artists were enthusiastic in propagating the revolution, Lenin
had little confidence that their
abstract visual language could
communicate effectively with a predominantly illiterate population. He also sus-
pected that the young, trailblazing
Constructivists and Productivists had a
hidden aesthetic agenda that superseded
the needs of the infant government. Lenin
had his own agenda: he wanted to shock
the Russian people out of their back-
wardness. Fervently believing that their
new art would accomplish this goal, the
revolutionary artists argued that advanced
artistic ideas reflected advanced political
ideas. From 1918 to 1922, under the aus-
pices of Anatoly Lunacharsky, modern
Soviet graphic design applied its daring
experiments in the service of social
change. But as the revolution became set
on an increasingly conservative course,
those leaders who disapproved of progressive art forced its practitioners to abandon
their methods in favor of less radical
approaches. By the time Stalin came to
power, many of those who still refused to
sacrifice their ideals were either pressured
into exile or met worse fates at home.

Nevertheless, Stalin appreciated the
power of the image in a country where
such a large percentage of the population
was illiterate. He understood that folk art
was a ready-made communications tool,
although he rejected its traditional, often
religious subject matter. Posters became a
direct medium for educating the peasant
in almost every aspect of daily life—from
the efficacy of bathing, to instructions on
how to drive a tractor, to warnings against
laziness, intoxication, and waste. A somewhat jaundiced article in a 1931 issue of
Fortune refers to the posters' "bold
splashes of color [that] appeal to a people
who see only drabness in their daily life.
[The posters'] naivete commends them
more strongly to men and women who,
like children and savages, love to look at
similar pictures."

In 1932 the Communist Party abolished
the remaining cultural organizations in
which Modernists were members and
instead set up monolithic unions of Soviet
writers, architects, composers, and artists
who conformed to official art forms. In
1934 a new doctrine called Socialist Realism, devised by Stalin and Maxim Gorky,
was presented at the first Soviet Writers'
Congress. Socialist Realism rejected formalism, along with the plastic arts and
design, deeming them "the bourgeois
influences on art." Idealized scenes of
leaders and workers replaced more
abstract images, while staid typographic
treatments forced out the dynamic, asymmetrical layouts of the New Typography.
Though figurative painting was most preferred, photography and montage were
acceptable and continued to be practiced
by artists like Alexander Rodchenko.

The repressive Soviet regime was not
the only one to feel enmity against the
European avant-garde and its perceived
elitism. Since the end of World War I,
Modernist artists and designers in Germany had supported left-wing political
organizations against the oligarchy, the
old-guard militarists, and Adolf Hitler's
National Socialist party. In 1929 the Nazi
ideologist Alfred Rosenberg founded the
Militant League for German Culture to
combat avant-garde influences. Upon
coming to power in 1933, Hitler exacted
his revenge by expunging all actual and
symbolic traces of his artist enemies. He
even outlawed modern sans-serif typefaces in favor of the medieval German
Fraktur (eventually, realizing Fraktur's
problems of legibility, he declared that
Fraktur should be outlawed as a Jewish
invention). In 1937, at the opening of his
infamous *Degenerate Art* exhibition at the
newly built House of German Art, Hitler
railed that "works of art that cannot be
understood but need a swollen set of
instructions to prove their right to exist
and find their way to neurotics who are
receptive to such stupid . . . nonsense will
no longer openly reach the German
nation. . . . With the opening of this exhibition has come the end of artistic lunacy
and with it the artistic pollution of our
people."

Hitler and Joseph Goebbels, the cun-
ning Nazi Minister of Propaganda,
replaced Modernist art with classically
heroic, Romantic depictions of the Aryan
Superman or with equally overbearing
images in a more realistic style (which
were not too formally different from those
of Soviet Socialist Realism). The propaganda poster actually played a greater role
in the Nazis' rise to power than is generally realized: when the radio was shut off,
the cinema dark, and the political meet-
ings over, the poster still stood on every
street corner. One master of the agitational political poster, the artist Mjölnir,
was given the Teutonic honorific of Reich
Plenipotentiary for Artistic Formulation.
Even Ludwig Hohlwein, one of the virtu-
osos of the objective style in poster design,
became a treasured propagandist for his
keen ability to portray Aryan beauty.

Much of the early Italian fascist printed
propaganda used Futurist and Art Deco
styles to advertise Mussolini's cult of personality; on the other hand, most compa-
rable German ephemera were unadorned,
stark, and monumental, more consistent
with other Nazi visual motifs. Hitler had
formed the opinion that the masses were
malleable, either already corrupt or corrupt-
ible. There was no place in his propaganda
for a qualifying clause and, therefore,
nothing was left to interpretation. He
wrote, "The more radical and inciting my
propaganda was, the more it frightened
off weaklings and irresolute characters
and prevented their pushing into the first
nucleus of the [Nazi] organization."

The heroic style was not exclusively a
tool of dictatorships—during the Spanish
Civil War, both the fascist insurgents and
the supporters of the Popular Front effectively imbued their printed propaganda
with heroic imagery. And not all heroic
imagery has been used in the service of
politics. Advertising and editorial illustration in Western industrial democracies
has often employed romantic realism as a
timeworn means of enhancing a product
or idea in the consumer's eye. Yet heroic
realism has never really been elevated to a
national style in Western democracies,
except during wartime, and then only for
very specific needs. Even during World
War II, Modernist approaches brought to
the United States and England by European immigrants characterized certain
wartime propaganda, thus planting the
seeds of postwar graphic endeavor. Heroic
realism as an official graphic style still prevails in Soviet countries.

177

DEUTSCHE LUFTHANSA

Werbung 50/III. 36. 13000. Gedruckt in Deutschland.

470

When it finally came, the decision as to what was true Soviet revolutionary art did not favor the avant-garde. Stalin's imposition of his Socialist Realism decrees in 1932 suppressed most of Russia's most creative and committed artists. Although a few, like Alexander Rodchenko, continued to create propaganda consistent with the official style, many others were forbidden to practice their art. Stalin effectively revived academic painting, which one critic called the "worst academics in the world," and established a sanctioned graphic language that left nothing to the imagination. For Hitler the avant-garde symbolized Bolshevism and the debasement of *Kultur.* By 1933, virtually all traces of modern German design were eliminated from public view and replaced by Teutonic models from the past.

470. Ludwig Holwein. *Deutsche Lufthansa.* Poster, 1936. Library of Congress, Washington, D.C. Poster Collection

471. Victor Borisovich Koretski. *Hello, Great Soviet Union.* Poster, photomontage, c. 1960

472. Ludwig Holwein. *Sammelt Euch im NS Reichskreigerbund.* Postcard, c. 1940

473. Victor Borisovich Koretski. *We Want Peace.* Poster, photomontage, c. 1945

474 Victor Borisovich Koretski. *Peace, Friend ship, Solidarity, No to Fascism.* Poster, c. 1978

ПРИВЕТ
ВЕЛИКОМУ
СОЮЗУ ССР!

471

472

473

НЕТ-ФАШИЗМУ!

474

476

Since war demands extraordinary sacrifice, it is often as difficult to arouse people to fight as it is to win a battle strategically. War is a difficult theme to abstract, and therefore realism is the logical and most effective means to visually sell a war. Yet the realism must not portray the savage horrors of war but rather an idealized truth. The task of illustrators in the wartime United States, Spain, and elsewhere was to mythologize through paint. The Chinese brand of Heroic Realism (usually produced as poster or book illustration by collectives of artists and printers) was employed for both political haranguing and commercial advertising, but always conveyed a message with the least possible ambiguity.

475. Illustrator unknown. *Daring Detective.* Magazine cover, May 1938

476. Herrn. *Salvad la Producción (Safeguard Production).* Poster for the General Union of Workers during the Spanish Civil War, 1938

477. Designer unknown. *To Have and to Hold.* Propaganda poster for U.S. war bonds, 1944

478. Designer unknown. *Win a Good Harvest—Increase Grain Production.* Chinese poster printed at Shanghai People's Publishing House, 1973

479. Designer unknown. *Resolutely Support the Anti-imperialist Struggles of the People of Asia, Africa and Latin America.* Political poster, 1960

475

477

478

Resolutely Support the Anti-imperialist Struggles of the People of Asia, Africa and Latin America.
Soutenir fermement la lutte anti-impérialiste des peuples d'Asie, d'Afrique et d'Amérique latine
Firme apoyo a la lucha antiimperialista de los pueblos de Asia, Africa y América Latina

480. Herbert Matter. *Pontresina*. Travel poster, 1936. Kunstgewerbemuseum, Zurich

Despite its detractors, classical Modernism exerted an immense influence on advertising and graphic design in most consumer societies immediately before and following World War II. Its iconoclastic practitioners developed a functional vocabulary that was supported by certain mainstream critics and eventually adopted by many important corporations. Some progressive government agencies even commissioned Modernist designers for various communications projects—from railway signage in Britain to postal information in Holland to wartime survival manuals in the United States. Art Deco notwithstanding, functionalism in design retained currency in those nations which, although hard hit by economic crises, relied on an industrial renaissance for renewed prosperity. While the repressive decrees of Stalin and Hitler ensured an abrupt end to Modernism in most of Europe, the industrial enterprise on which the style was predicated continued and would continue for decades to follow. Machine age graphic design was destined to endure—although somewhat altered by the new communications requirements of business in the postwar era.

In the United States, where Modernist techniques were not at first warmly accepted by conservative advertisers, marketing surveys surprisingly concluded that consumers equated Modernist design with what one style manual at the time called "the promise of the future." The American advertising pioneer, Ernest Caulkins, who championed the idea that advertising should be an equal marriage of text and image, extolled the virtues of Modernism, stating that it "offered the opportunity of expressing the inexpressible…expressing not so much a motor car, but speed; not so much a gown, but style." Simplicity was the designer's watchword, and style, therefore, would not be presented through wordy texts or literal pictures but through the association of a product with the most appropriate graphic forms.

In Late Modern, classical Modernist techniques were popularly accepted and widely applied, but the dogma associated with the orthodox schools and movements was jettisoned. Late Modern encompasses a number of distinct stylistic periods, spanning more than fifty years. The first period—immediately following Stalin's and Hitler's initial repressions of Modernist art in the early 1930s—witnessed a diaspora of Modernists, at first to the Eastern European countries and then to England, Switzerland, and the United States, where they profoundly affected prevailing design theory and practice. The second period, after the war, was one of business realignment in which emerging international corporations, needing identity systems and strategic communications, fostered a new rationalist design approach in the International Style. Then, beginning in the mid-1950s and continuing to the present, a revived interest in the design styles of the *fin de siècle* and in the artifacts of material prosperity made itself felt in contemporary layout and typography for magazines, advertising, and posters. Concurrently, advancements in photographic and computer technologies applied to typography and printing began to change not only the look but the methodology of graphic design.

The kindred spirits in the postwar design centers (London, Chicago, New York, Zurich, Basel, Ulm, Stuttgart) all began with the same prewar methods in developing their new styles. Yet Late Modern is not about conformity. Its stylistic diversity arose as much from the rejection of unworkable or unappealing ideas as from the development of new ones. Moreover—with another devastating world war over and the promised "World of Tomorrow" finally at hand—designers sought with great purpose to make styles that responded to the character of their time, although there was scant international consensus on what this was. It was viewed quite differently, for example, by the Swiss designers Max Bill, Josef Müller-Brockmann, and Armin Hofmann—who saw graphic design as systematized and architecturally constructed on a grid—and by the New York–based principals of Push Pin Studios, who preferred a provocative interplay of historical styles and forms.

Although classical Modernist designers often had utopian goals, Late Modernists held conflicting opinions about such universal aims. The period was, perhaps, more one of personal reevaluation than overriding public concern. Jan Tschichold, for instance, renounced the Prussian rigidity of the rules set forth in his Modernist bible, *New Typography,* in favor of a return to classical typography and symmetry. Other notable postwar designers, among them, Paul Rand, Alvin Lustig, Alexey Brodovitch, and Lester Beall, took certain truths from Modernism and incorporated them into distinctly personal languages. Rand's identity systems and collateral materials for major American corporations like IBM and Westinghouse are imbued with his distinctive wit and logic yet totally devoid of personal indulgences. Brodovitch's design for *Harper's Bazaar* was an outstanding example of personal style and taste in a mass-market magazine.

Narrative illustration was also redefined in the Late Modern period. Often used in a literal, unimaginative manner for editorial or advertising purposes, figurative illustration was generally regarded as a sentimental throwback to the past. While orthodox Modernists rejected narrative completely in favor of what Muller-Brockmann called the "objective illustration" of photography and photomontage, others found new means of integrating figure drawing with design in the style of turn-of-the-century posterists. Most notable among these were the Polish poster artists who, influenced by the Symbolists and Surrealists, developed a painterly graphic style with a lexicon of powerful, eerie images. The Poles, in turn, inspired the American psychedelic artists of the sixties, who went on to invent a new style of illustration by pairing comic-strip and historical references with East Indian motifs.

Japanese design is a highly imaginative synthesis of the most compelling Late Modern Western forms with traditional Japanese ones, abetted by an abundance of high-tech materials with which to visualize the future. Japan's distinctive Late Modern style has had a significant impact on the eighties' Post-Modern and New Wave designs.

183

SWISS

The Swiss object poster was distinct from the Berlin *sachplakat* in that the Swiss replaced the reductive flatness of the typical German image with a boldly rendered lithographic design. Known for his hyperrealism, Niklaus Stoecklin became a leader of what one historian calls "illustrative advertising design," in which the drawn or painted image includes the sole product identification, without any other type or lettering. Posters here by the illustrators Charles Kuhn and Herbert Leupin followed in this objective tradition. Influenced by the early phototypographic designs of the German-born Anton Stankowski, Herbert Matter created startling photomontage travel posters that defined a new style called object photography. During the thirties, Walter Herdeg designed all the publicity for the St. Moritz resort, using photomontage and hand-colored photography. In 1944, Herdeg founded *Graphis*, the Zurich-based design magazine that championed a renewed internationalism in the applied arts.

    481. Charles Kuhn. *Taxi Winterhalder.* Poster, 1937. Kunstgewerbemuseum, Zurich

    482. Niklaus Stoecklin. *PKZ.* Poster, 1934. Kunstgewerbemuseum, Zurich

    483. Niklaus Stoecklin. *Binaca.* Poster, 1934

    484. Walter Herdeg. *Graphis.* Magazine cover, 1947

    485. Herbert Leupin. *Steinfels.* Poster for soap, c. 1944

481

482

483

484

485

A

ENGLISH

Frank Pick, London Transport's innovative creative director, set and maintained a standard of artistic achievement unprecedented in England before the mid-twenties. In his desire to raise the level of efficiency and safety of London's Underground, Pick sought out the most up-to-date artforms (like Man Ray's delightfully futuristic poster) to leave a positive impression on the commuting public. Advertising pioneers like Pick and his successor, William Crawford, deserve credit for opening the public's mind not only to the virtues of the service they promoted but also to the modern design vocabulary. Their efforts allowed E. McKnight Kauffer, F. H. K. Henrion, and Tom Eckersley, among others, to improve the quality of print communications and, by extension, of the entire visual landscape. Describing this new methodology, Ashley Havinden writes, "The modern point of view …is to design *inside out,* as opposed to the traditional, which is a tendency to impose a preconceived solution to a problem by designing from the *outside in.*"

486. Frank Pick and Edward Johnston. *London Underground.* Trademark for London Transport, 1920

487. Man Ray. *Keeps London Going.* Poster for London Transport, 1932. The Museum of Modern Art, New York. Gift of Bernard Davis

488. F. H. K. Henrion. *Here Comes the Sun.* Poster, 1948. Courtesy the designer

489. E. McKnight Kauffer. *Empire Telegrams.* Poster for telegrams, 1941

490. Tom Eckersley. *Graphis 31.* Cover of magazine edited and art-directed by Walter Herdeg, 1950. Courtesy the designer

486

-KEEPS LONDON GOING

487

488

489

490

491

492

493

494

495

Despite the shift in emphasis from advertising commercial products to promulgating war-related messages, World War II expanded opportunities for British advertising designers. In the poster field, the government realized that the conventional strident patriotic and cautionary messages would not have sufficient urgency to attract the public's attention. The Ministry of Information therefore commissioned some of the leading Modernists, including Abram Games, Tom Eckersley, and F. H. K. Henrion, to produce a series of decidedly contemporary designs. These designers often combined painting and collage to transmit the government's life-saving injunctions clearly and effectively. Perhaps the most important use of good design by the Ministry of Information was their development of the public exhibition as a potent technique of social communication. Such exhibitions ranged from small shows to full-scale displays of posters and other visual aids, employed to inform and educate the public about Britain's various war needs.

491. E. McKnight Kauffer. *Britain at War.* Cover for The Museum of Modern Art exhibition catalogue, 1941

492. Abram Games. *Your Britain, Fight for It Now.* Poster for the War Office, 1943. Courtesy the designer

493. Abram Games. *Join the ATS.* Poster for the War Office, 1941. Courtesy the designer

494. Tom Eckersley. *Saving Is Everybody's War Job.* Poster for the Post Office Savings Bank of England, 1943. Courtesy the designer

495. Abram Games. *The Emergency Blood Transfusion Service Needs Blood Donors.* Poster for the War Office, c. 1942. Library of Congress, Washington, D.C. Poster Collection

As a design element, shape has a coordinating function. Observe the skeletal aeroplane frame shown below—this and thousands of component parts are contained in the relatively simple form of the final flying whole. A similar example of coordination is that of a watch, whose familiar shape serves as a container of a complex interior. Thus the use of shape for coordination is a basic principle of industrial design. The application of this principle to the design of a printed double spread is seen in the use of shapes, like frames, boxes or panels, to coordinate various information elements—words, photographs, drawings, diagrams. In the exhibition design on the opposite page, shapes in the form of frame and panels again coordinate small parts within larger units. Similarly, these two facing pages themselves coordinate various elements in their disposition within white space.

shape for coordination

501

502

AMERICAN

In a 1941 issue of *PM* magazine, László Moholy-Nagy wrote somewhat disappointedly about American design: "The Constructivist movement in Europe originated in countries with undeveloped industry.... The message about American organization, production processes, life standards, created a Utopian picture in the mind of these young European artists. Their imaginative picture of America governed their thinking and their work. They admired exactness and precision...the skyscraper, the highways, the immense span of bridges....They tried to be the children of a new age as they believed Americans to be.

"When I came to this country I was greatly surprised to find that we Europeans were, to a certain extent, more American than the Americans. I found that our imagination went too far. [The Americans] created their high civilization by instinct, introducing invention after invention into their daily routine. However, they did not attach any philosophy to it as we did in Europe. For them the nostalgia remained for the good old traditional art.

"...It took me a long time to understand the Victorian dwellings and the imitations of Colonial architecture or the old-fashioned advertising. Fortunately I soon saw that a new generation was rising with the potentiality and discipline of that America imagined by us in Europe."

Among these young Americans, wrote Moholy-Nagy, Paul Rand was "one of the best and most capable representatives." These members of the first wave of American Modernists were influenced by other recent European émigrés besides Moholy-Nagy, including the Hungarian Gyorgy Kepes, the Czechoslovak Ladislav Sutnar, and Bauhaus master Herbert Bayer. Joining Rand were Lester Beall, who was dubbed the Midwest Modernist, and Alex Steinweiss, a New Yorker who pioneered in album-cover design.

496. Gyorgy Kepes. *What Is Modern Painting?* Exhibition catalogue cover for The Museum of Modern Art, 1952. Courtesy the designer

497. Alex Steinweiss. *AD.* Cover of professional magazine, 1941. Courtesy the designer

498. Isamu Noguchi. *View.* Cover of Surrealist art magazine, 1946

499, 500. Ladislav Sutnar. *Design and Paper.* Cover and inside pages for promotional brochure for the Marquardt Paper Co., 1941

501. Lester Beall. *Modern Pioneers in Peoria.* Pages from a promotional brochure for a printer, 1935

502. Paul Rand. *Direction.* Magazine cover, April 1940. Courtesy the designer

AMERICAN

The United States Office of War Information employed a large staff of book and magazine designers during World War II to design cautionary and patriotic posters, survival manuals, news magazines for overseas distribution, and hundreds of other pieces of wartime propaganda. Young American Modernists had a unique opportunity to prove the viability of the new design, specifically as contrasted to the Heroic Realism of other countries' graphics. In 1942, the Austrian émigré Joseph Binder won first prize in a Museum of Modern Art competition for his iconographic recruitment poster for the United States Army Air Corps. N. W. Ayer and Son's art director, Leo Lionni, created a series of dynamic posters intended to motivate defense plant workers. In the 1930s Walter P. Paepcke, the president of Container Corporation of America, had become an early patron of Modernist design; during the war, CCA's art director, Egbert Jacobsen, commissioned designs from leading émigré and American Modernists, including Herbert Matter, Herbert Bayer, and Jean Carlu, for the company's advertising campaigns focusing on its war efforts and products. Autocar Corporation, which supplied armored trucks to the army, commissioned Paul Rand to produce a striking (and curiously timeless) visual record of its war production.

503. Ralph Eckerstrom. *CCA.* Trademark for Container Corporation of America, 1957

504. Leo Lionni. *Keep 'Em Rolling!* Poster, 1941. The Museum of Modern Art, New York. Gift of the Office for Emergency Management

505. Leo Lionni. *Container Corporation of America.* Poster, 1942. Courtesy the designer

506. Joseph Binder. *Air Corps U.S. Army.* Poster, 1941. The Museum of Modern Art, New York. Gift of the designer

507. Herbert Matter. *Container Corporation of America.* Poster, 1943. Courtesy Ex Libris, New York

508. Paul Rand. *Mechanized Mules of Victory.* Cover and pages of a truck catalogue for Autocar Corporation, 1942. Courtesy the designer

504

505

506

507

503

victory
in the
driver's
seat...

for victory

The U. S. Army has called upon Autocar to build big, powerful vehicles...speedy vehicles, for hauling a precious human cargo of American soldiers...sturdy impregnable vehicles, to safeguard that cargo... fighting vehicles, to conquer the forces of ill-will. Autocar immediately entered this as order Number 1 on its books, and made the order-of-the-day "production"! For the duration of the emergency Victory is in the driver's seat at Autocar, guiding an all-out effort that refuses to recognize the "impossible".

From its very inception in 1897 every Autocar activity has trained the Company for its vital role in the war program. For 45 years without interruption it has manufactured motor vehicles exclusively, concentrating in the last decade on heavy-duty trucks of 5 tons or over. For 45 years Autocar has pioneered the way, developing many history-making "firsts" in the industry: the first porcelain spark-plug; the first American shaft-driven automobile; the first double reduction gear drive; the first

circulating oil system. For 45 years Autocar insistence on mechanical perfection has wrought a tradition of precision that is honored by every one of its master workers. These are achievements that only time can win. The harvest of these years, of this vast experience, is at the service of our government. Autocar is meeting its tremendous responsibility to national defense by putting its 45 years' experience to work in helping to build for America a motorized armada such as the world has never seen.

Autocar was among the first in 1940 to receive Defense orders. Today those orders have grown to a huge backlog of many millions representing a sum proportionately higher than Autocar's already high share of the heavy-duty market and, therefore, high tribute to the quality of its product. Autocar is now producing diversified types of military vehicles: an anti-tank vehicle; Personnel Carrier; Scout Car; and Troop Carrier. Highlights from one of these assembly lines are illustrated on the following pages:

Enemy bullets shot from the usual small weapons are not likely to pierce the heavy armor plate of this body, assembled in Autocar's plant. So that delay might not pierce Autocar's high production schedule, the company perfected this special body-assembly line in the same new two-story building that houses the chassis assembly. The two assembly lines ...chassis on the first floor and body on the second ... travel their own Autocar-engineered routes to one junction where they are joined into a Rolling Fortress.

The men who work on the vitals of these vehicles are unexcelled in their mechanical skill. Their hands move with the swiftness and sureness of a surgeon's, darting decisively from tool box to point of work. Armed with tremendous resources of skill and experience, the army of men at Autocar wages a relentless and victorious war against time. These men are in the front ranks in the battle of production. They are doing all in their power to supply America with an ever mounting number of military trucks.

What the artisans of Autocar production are doing now for America's military forces they have done countless times for American industry. They have built every kind of hauling vehicle from the light delivery truck to huge motorized transports for oil and gasoline. Now, for their Number 1 customer, Uncle Sam, they have increased their plant by 93,000 square feet and have added 1,500 employees to the staff, all within little more than a year's time. They permit nothing to stand in the way of production for victory.

Military strategy need not restrict the use of these vehicles to modern, smooth highways. The tractor treads used in place of rear wheels will carry them swiftly over uneven terrain...they never lose their grip. Caterpillar-like, they climb out of the deepest holes. Teamed with the rolling front bumper they keep our motorized infantry moving resistlessly forward. Despite their huge weight and powerful armor, these Autocar manufactured vehicles can cover ground at a speed of 50 miles an hour.

To save time, Autocar, the only heavy-duty truck company to do so, ingeniously combines the body and chassis assembly lines under one roof. The assembly routes were engineered and coordinated by Autocar experts so that the armor-plated body is completed simultaneously with the chassis, at a spot directly above the location of the latter. Strong cables then lower the body over the chassis, and experts set to work to fit the two major sections together with waste time and excess motion completely eliminated.

Thirty times a day a completed military truck leaves the Autocar assembly line ready to roll into action. Among these is the powerful anti-tank weapon pictured on this page. Mounted on this vehicle, in addition to a machine gun, is a tank-smashing .75 mm gun. Autocar is the only company assembling these units that actually handles the installation of the guns. These superb rolling weapons of defense were engineered by the Autocar Company, working in close collaboration with government Ordnance engineers.

In executing its supreme obligation to our country, Autocar has strengthened its position for operations in post-emergency America. The heightened facilities added in behalf of defense, will be necessary to fulfill a commercial demand that had been steadily mounting before the emergency. When the war is won and liberty is secure, the stage will be set at Autocar to steer its products of peace and free enterprise to every corner of our great nation... in numbers greater than ever before in its history.

509

510

511

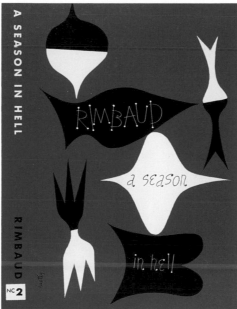

512

513

AMERICAN

With the war over, graphic designers returned to the business of selling commercial products and ideas with a host of modern methods now fully integrated into the advertising and publishing industries. Ashley Havinden in his book *Advertising and the Artist* characterizes this modern aesthetic: "The aim of the good designer is never to show off his erudition or his modernity. He must never intrude a personal or private preoccupation with any design form. His sole intention is to put whatever talents he has for inventive construction, simplicity and understanding of the medium to…the service of expressing the idea, or complex of ideas, with utmost clarity, force and conviction." Combining European ideas of abstraction, dynamism, and asymmetry with a particularly American directness, the new design provided a viable alternative to the blatant and often vulgar style of mass-market design. Among its most successful practitioners were E. McKnight Kauffer, Mathew Leibowitz, Bradbury Thompson, John Follis, Alvin Lustig, and Herbert Matter.

509. E. McKnight Kauffer. *Keep It Under Your Stetson.* Advertisement in *Life* magazine, 1947

510. Mathew Leibowitz. *Male Torso.* Brochure cover for Sharp & Dohme, c. 1945

511. Bradbury Thompson. *Westvaco Inspirations 152.* Inside spread, 1952. Courtesy the designer

512. John Follis. *Arts & Architecture.* Magazine cover, December 1949. Courtesy the designer

513. Alvin Lustig. *A Season in Hell.* Jacket for a book by Arthur Rimbaud, 1945. Courtesy of Elaine Lustig Cohen, Ex Libris, New York

514. Herbert Matter. *Fortune.* Magazine cover, July 1948

514

SWISS INTERNATIONAL STYLE

Their country's neutrality enabled Swiss graphic designers to continue their work during the war. Max Bill, a former Bauhaus student and a pioneer of the Swiss style, based his methodology on Constructivism. His colleague Josef Müller-Brockmann describes the process: "Copy and a picture are arranged and related in accordance with objective and functional criteria. The areas are sensitively organized with an assured touch in mathematical proportions, and due attention is paid to the rules of typography." After the war, Bill became director of the influential Hochschule für Gestaltung in Ulm, and his rationalist design ethic spread throughout Europe. The Swiss School, or International Style of Typography, was further elaborated by younger designers, from Zurich and Basel, like Müller-Brockmann, Richard P. Lohse, Hans Neuburg, Carlo L. Vivarelli, and Karl Gerstner, all of whom saw design as a vital means of communicating objective facts. Object photography, sans-serif typography, lack of ornamentation, and strict composition on the basis of the grid system are characteristic of this style. Although its inventor is not known, the grid became the most significant design tool of the postwar era. Used for prospectuses, brochures, books, and exhibition catalogues, it was perfectly adaptable to the requirements of international business. The periodical *Neue Grafik (New Graphic Design),* founded in 1958 by Lohse, Müller-Brockmann, Vivarelli, and Neuburg, reported on, analyzed, and championed this systematic approach.

515. Josef Müller-Brockmann. *Beethoven.* Concert poster, 1955. Courtesy the designer

516. *Neue Grafik 9.* Magazine cover of an international review of graphic design, March 1961. Edited by Richard P. Lohse, Josef Müller-Brockmann, Hans Neuburg, Carlo L. Vivarelli. Courtesy Josef Müller-Brockmann

517. Karl Gerstner. *You, Too, Are Liberal.* Poster, 1956. Courtesy Moore College of Art, Philadelphia. Goldie Paley Gallery

518. Max Bill. *Kunsthaus Zürich.* Exhibition poster, 1936. Kunstgewerbemuseum, Zurich

519. Carlo L. Vivarelli. *Für das Alter (For the Elderly).* Poster, 1949. Kunstgewerbemuseum, Zurich

520. Fridolin Muller. *Für das Alter (For the Elderly).* Poster, 1964. Courtesy Moore College of Art, Philadelphia. Goldie Paley Gallery

521. Various designers. Entries in a trademark design competition for Electrolux, from *Neue Grafik 13,* 1962. Permission of Josef Müller-Brockmann

515

516

517

518

519

520

521

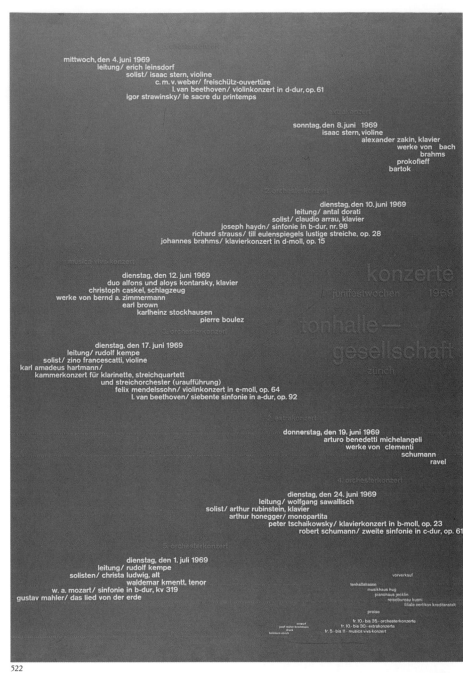

mittwoch, den 4. juni 1969
leitung/ erich leinsdorf
solist/ isaac stern, violine
c. m. v. weber/ freischütz-ouvertüre
l. van beethoven/ violinkonzert in d-dur, op. 61
igor strawinsky/ le sacre du printemps

sonntag, den 8. juni 1969
isaac stern, violine
alexander zakin, klavier
werke von bach
brahms
prokofieff
bartok

dienstag, den 10. juni 1969
leitung/ antal dorati
solist/ claudio arrau, klavier
joseph haydn/ sinfonie in b-dur, nr. 98
richard strauss/ till eulenspiegels lustige streiche, op. 28
johannes brahms/ klavierkonzert in d-moll, op. 15

dienstag, den 12. juni 1969
duo alfons und aloys kontarsky, klavier
christoph caskel, schlagzeug
werke von bernd a. zimmermann
earl brown
karlheinz stockhausen
pierre boulez

dienstag, den 17. juni 1969
leitung/ rudolf kempe
solist/ zino francescatti, violine
karl amadeus hartmann/
kammerkonzert für klarinette, streichquartett
und streichorchester (uraufführung)
felix mendelssohn/ violinkonzert in e-moll, op. 64
l. van beethoven/ siebente sinfonie in a-dur, op. 92

donnerstag, den 19. juni 1969
arturo benedetti michelangeli
werke von clementi
schumann
ravel

dienstag, den 24. juni 1969
leitung/ wolfgang sawallisch
solist/ arthur rubinstein, klavier
arthur honegger/ monopartita
peter tschaikowsky/ klavierkonzert in b-moll, op. 23
robert schumann/ zweite sinfonie in c-dur, op. 61

dienstag, den 1. juli 1969
leitung/ rudolf kempe
solisten/ christa ludwig, alt
waldemar kmentt, tenor
w. a. mozart/ sinfonie in b-dur, kv 319
gustav mahler/ das lied von der erde

konzerte
junifestwochen 1969

tonhalle—
gesellschaft
zürich

vorverkauf

tonhallekasse
musikhaus hug
pianohaus jecklin
reisebureau kuoni
filiale oerlikon kreditanstalt

preise

fr. 10.- bis 35.- orchesterkonzerte
fr. 10.- bis 30.- extrakonzerte
fr. 5.- bis 11.- musica viva-konzert

522

523

524

525

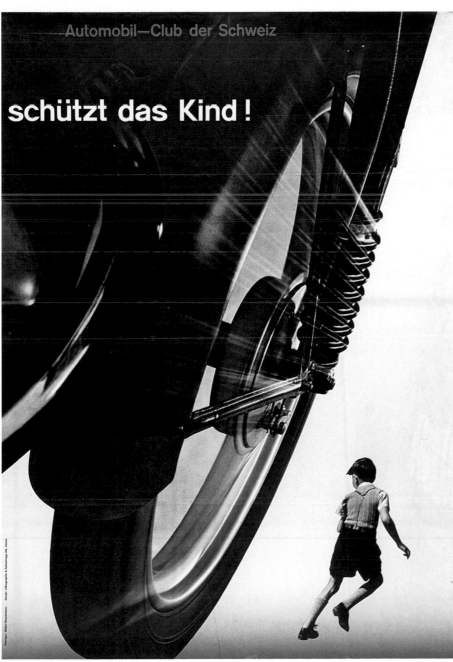

526

SWISS INTERNATIONAL STYLE

The Swiss design philosophy is actually propagated through two major schools, one in Zurich, the other in Basel. Josef Müller-Brockmann typifies the former's approach, Armin Hofmann the latter's. According to Kenneth Hiebert, a Basel School alumnus, that school's methodology derives from the idea that "abstract structure is the vehicle for communication. It relies on an analysis that rigorously questions and accounts for all parts of a message. The act of searching for an appropriate structure forces the designer to make the most basic inquiry about a message, to isolate its primary essence from considerations of surface style." Communication, not seduction, is Basel's primary goal, one that dictates the need for symbols appropriate to the content of the message. Ideally, the method results in a metaphor and message that have universal appeal. As Hiebert writes, the Swiss School is concerned that design be more than "a frivolous cluttering of the environment."

522. Armin Hofmann. *Konzerte Tonhalle–Gesellschaft.* Concert poster, 1969. Courtesy the designer

523. Armin Hofmann. *Basel Municipal Theater.* Poster, 1963. Courtesy the designer

524. Josef Müller-Brockmann. *Weniger Lärm (Less Noise).* Poster against noise pollution, 1960. Courtesy the designer

525. Armin Hofmann. *Kunsthalle Basel.* Exhibition poster, 1958. Courtesy the designer

526. Josef Müller-Brockmann. *Schützt das Kind! (Protect the Child!).* Poster for the Swiss automobile club, 1955. Courtesy the designer

CORPORATE STYLE

By the early 1950s, television and computers had begun to usher in the Information Age, and the more refined term *corporate communications* replaced the somewhat pedestrian *commercial art.* The job of the corporate communications designer was to create and maintain consistent identities and advertising campaigns. Those American designers schooled in or influenced by European Modernism had created a distinctive period methodology. Free from many of the dogmatic European strictures, their work shared certain common traits like unadorned, economical graphics and kinetic photographic accents.

527. William Golden. *CBS.* Trademark, 1951

528. Paul Rand. *IBM.* Trademark, 1956

529. Brownjohn, Chermayeff and Geismar Associates. *About U.S.: Experimental Typography by American Designers.* Pages from a booklet produced for the Composing Room, 1960

530. Gene Federico. *Woman's Day.* Advertisement for the magazine, 1953. Courtesy the designer

531. Rudolph De Harak. *The Siege of Leningrad.* Book cover, 1963. Courtesy the designer

532. Lou Dorfsman. *The Rocket's Red Glare.* Advertisement for CBS television, appearing in *The New York Times,* 1962. Courtesy the designer

533. Louis Silverstein. *Where Else but New York? Where Else but The New York Times?* Promotional advertisement, c. 1962. Courtesy the designer

534. Alexey Brodovitch. *Portfolio.* Cover for a graphic arts magazine, 1951. Permission Frank Zachary

535. Saul Bass. *Anatomy of a Murder.* Movie poster, 1959. Courtesy the designer

529

530

527

528

531

532

THE
ROCKET'S
RED
GLARE...

CBS◉2

Where else but The New York Times?

533

534

535

201

536

537

538

539

540

541

REVIVAL

In the mid-1950s, certain designers and illustrators discovered an alternative to classical Modernism when they began to reprise vintage graphic approaches in a move that prefigured Post-Modernism. Previously considered obsolete and therefore thrown into the wastebin of popular culture, primitive painting, Victoriana, Art Nouveau, and Art Deco graphic motifs were taken up again as fresh sources of inspiration. Painterly and drawn images were reunited with typography as a total design. In addition, the revival of nineteenth-century wood types and the subsequent reissues of early twentieth-century display faces on film contributed to a renewed enthusiasm among designers for retro forms. While not suited for multinational business communications, the usually playful application of historical mannerisms was perfect for certain editorial and book designs, record albums, cultural posters, and packaging.

536. Paul Davis. *Plunkitt of Tammany Hall.* Illustration for book jacket, 1962. Courtesy the designer

537. David Lance Goines. *Chez Panisse.* Poster, 1973. Courtesy the designer

538. Seymour Chwast. *The Sensational Houdini.* Poster, 1973. Courtesy the designer

539. Milton Glaser. *Geometric Landscape.* Poster for Stuttgart bank, 1975. Courtesy the designer

540. Otto Storch. *Rings on Her Fingers.* Pages from *McCall's* magazine, 1961. Courtesy *McCall's* magazine

541. Barry Zaid. *Mata Hari.* Drawings published in *The Push Pin Graphic,* 1973. Courtesy the designer

542. Milton Glaser. *Holiday.* Magazine cover, 1967. Courtesy the designer

542

ECLECTIC

By the 1960s, a design consciousness had become ingrained in every commerce-oriented, industrial society. With the proliferation of design schools, greater access to phototechnologies, and such a big store of graphic design approaches to choose from, no one style dominated. Although the leading individual stylists were copied, the lack of any guiding spiritual, political, or aesthetic force encouraged the eclectic sensibility, in works as diverse as James McMullan's realist watercolors and R. Crumb's irreverent comic strips. Herb Lubalin, with his so-called "smashed-type" and provocative word/image concoctions, exerted a huge influence, not only on American advertising and editorial design but on schools in Eastern Europe, where copies of *Avant Garde* and other publications featuring his work were rare and expensive. Also influential were art directors Henry Wolf and Willi Fleckhaus, who masterfully orchestrated both the look and contents of their respective magazines. And in London, Pentagram Studios developed a freewheeling approach to corporate and commercial communications and imbued otherwise pedestrian business communications with a characteristic wry wit, as in their alphabet employing found objects.

543. Herb Lubalin. *Avant Garde.* Magazine cover, January 1968. Courtesy Tony DiSpigna

544. James McMullan. *Paul Desmond: Late Lament.* Album cover, 1987. Courtesy the designer

545. R. Crumb (artist), Bob Cato and John Berg (art directors). *Cheap Thrills.* Album cover for Big Brother & The Holding Company (Columbia Records), 1968. Courtesy the artist

546. Michael Salisbury. *West.* Magazine cover for Sunday supplement of the *Los Angeles Times,* December 26, 1971. Courtesy the designer

547. Mervyn Kurlansky. Alphabet using found studio objects, designed for a special issue on typography for Preston Polytechnic's own design publication, 1977. Courtesy Pentagram, London

548. Henry Wolf. *Show.* Magazine cover, February 1964. Courtesy the designer

549. Willi Fleckhaus. *Twen.* Magazine contents page, 1970. Courtesy Bob Ciano

543

544

545

546

547

548

549

POLISH

The contemporary Polish school of posters arose after World War II as a spirited attempt to rebuild the wartorn nation. Without television, with few radios, and short on newspapers, the new Communist government recognized the power of posters as a form of communication and instituted a state-supported agency to commission and publish them on a broad spectrum of themes. Although some were political and educational, most announced cultural events. Film posters were the first fertile ground in which the distinctly bizarre Polish style flowered. Scenes from the film were rarely shown; instead, the artists captured the film's essence, often through visual metaphor. Cultural posters became a significant outlet for individual artistic expression, as artists aimed to establish their own artistic styles and identities. Rather than a coherent movement, the Polish school was a wildly diverse community of painters and graphic designers.

550. Franciszek Starowieyski. *Oni (They)*. Theatre poster, c. 1983. Courtesy the designer

551. Jan Lenica. *Lebensbilder-Zeitbilder*. Poster for an opening exhibition of the Postermuseum in Essen, West Germany, 1984. Courtesy the designer

552. Roman Cieslewicz. *Liberté-Wolnosc (Polish Liberty)*. Political poster, 1981. Courtesy the designer

553. Andrzej Pagowski and Krystyna Hofmann. *Wojna Swiatow (The War of the Worlds)*. Film poster, 1982. Courtesy the designers

554. Andrzej Czeczot. *Szewcy (Shoemakers)*. Poster for a play by Witkacy, 1985. Courtesy the designer

550

551

552

553

554

555

556

557

558

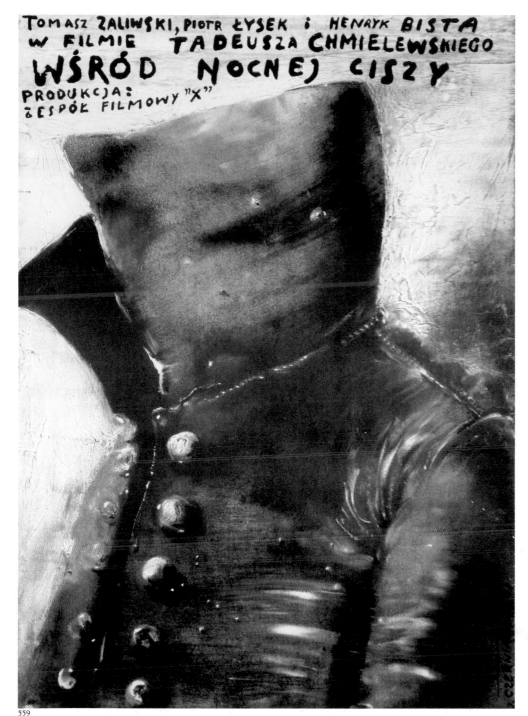

559

POLISH

The 1950s through the 1970s are regarded by critics as the golden age of Polish posters. While considered advertising art, the Polish work was unlike anything ever seen in Western commerce. Its typically strange, idiosyncratic world view developed through innovative applications of Western styles like Art Nouveau, Surrealism, and Pop Art. Unencumbered by the rules of Western design, Polish designers used painting, photography, and hand-lettering in unprecedented, often discordant, combinations. Among the leading stylists were Franciszek Starowieyski, who built upon the Surrealist vocabulary, and Jan Lenica, whose haunting imagery drew upon Jugendstil. The proliferation of design clichés eventually contributed to a creative malaise in the late seventies. When the Solidarity Movement emerged in the early eighties, the need for exciting visual communications was briefly reestablished.

555. Franciszek Starowieyski. *Breda*. Poster, c. 1984. Courtesy the designer

556. Edward Dwurnik. *Teatr Narodowy (National Theater)*. Poster, c. 1985. Courtesy the designer

557. Mieczyslaw Gorowski. *Z Kolekcji Krzysztofa Dydo (From the Collection of Christopher Dydo)*. Poster, 1983. Courtesy the designer

558. Leszek Drzewinski. *Punkty za Pochodzenie (Point of Origin)*. Antiwar poster, 1985. Courtesy the designer

559. Jerzy Czerniawski. *Wśród Nocnej Ciszy (Stillness of Night)*. Poster, c. 1984. Courtesy the designer

561

PSYCHEDELIC

For a very brief period, Psychedelia was an honest reflection of the 1960s American youth culture; then it was usurped as a marketable fashion by trendsetters in the merchandising business. Curiously, Psychedelia is best defined by Otto Wagner's term *gesamtkunstwerk* (the total work of art), for it connotes the hippie movement's return to communal living, its attempts at arts and crafts production, and its union of art, music, and literature. In its purest form, the Psychedelic style was applied to the design of newspapers, broadsides, posters, clothing, jewelry, furniture, and automobiles (many of its early proponents in California decorated hot rods for a living before turning to rock and roll). Psychedelia was a visual code; those who could pierce the layers of symbolism to read the message, either with the naked eye or with the aid of hallucinogens, became members of the "underground" family. Although Psychedelia reused Austrian Secessionist lettering, Art Nouveau ornament, East Indian symbols, and Victorian typography, its drug-inspired palette and comic-book iconography mark it as a distinctly American graphic style. The most innovative Psychedelic artists were the underground cartoonists Wes Wilson, Rick Griffin, Stanley Mouse, and Victor Moscoso, who all together produced hundreds of posters for West Coast rock concerts.

560. Gerald Holtom. Nuclear disarmament symbol, 1956

561. David King and Roger Law. *The Jimi Hendrix Experience / Axis: Bold as Love.* Record album cover, 1967

562. Wes Wilson. *The Association: Concert at the Fillmore Auditorium.* Concert poster, 1966. Courtesy the designer

563. Wes Wilson. *The Byrds at the Fillmore.* Poster, 1967

564. Victor Moscoso. *The Miller Blues Band.* Concert poster, 1966. Courtesy the designer

565. Victor Moscoso. *Otis Rush.* Concert poster, 1967. Courtesy the designer

566. Victor Moscoso. *Big Brother & the Holding Company.* Concert poster, 1967. Courtesy the designer

560

562

563

564

565

566

567

ALPHA PSYCHEDELITYPE

PSYCHEDELITYPES!

568

569

570

571

5   6   7

PSYCHEDELIC

A capital of the beat movement in the fifties, San Francisco was also the birthplace of the hippie and Psychedelic movements. Yet variants of the Psychedelic style spread throughout the United States and eventually Europe. During the late sixties, John Van Hamersveld, whose graphic style varied from typographical illustration to fluid cartoon imagery, was an inventive proponent in Los Angeles. Since Psychedelic image making could be rather simple (hand-lettering, for instance, required only a rapidograph) and printing costs were low (the split-fountain color technique needed only one pass through a press), Psychedelic posters were ubiquitous. In Seattle, called "a city of posters" by one critic, a prolific community of poster and handbill artists established itself. New York City was known for its underground newspapers and the original Psychedelicatessen, while other centers of Psychedelic activity were found in Atlanta, Chicago, and Dallas. One contributing factor to Psychedelia's demise was Photolettering Inc.'s issuance in 1969 of its Psychedelitype catalogue, which made it possible for anyone to set type in a Psychedelic style.

567. John Van Hamersveld. *Psychedelic Solutions.* Drawing, 1969. Courtesy the designer

568. Designer unknown. *Psychedelitypes!* Alphabets from Photolettering Inc., 1969

569. Designer unknown. *Buffalo Springfield.* Concert poster, 1967. Courtesy Art Chantry

570. Tom Robbins and Ray Collins. *Loving Sunday.* Poster for a love-in, 1967. Courtesy Art Chantry

571. John R. Moenring. *Donovan.* Concert poster, 1962. Courtesy Art Chantry

572. Wes Wilson. *Buffalo Springfield/Steve Miller Blues Band.* Concert poster, 1967. Library of Congress. Washington, D.C. Poster Collection

573. Rick Griffin. *The Oracle.* Magazine cover, 1968

572

573

JAPANESE

Influenced by the European avant-garde, a concurrent Modernist movement began in Tokyo around 1910 but was squelched in the mid-thirties, during Japan's age of militarism. It took nearly two more decades before that spirit could be recovered. As the channel for influence shifted from Europe to the United States, historian James Fraser noted that "in the post–World War II period, Japanese graphic design has given as much as it has absorbed." In his capacity as managing director of the Japan Design Center in 1960, Yusaka Kamekura brought Japan's innovative new designers together with its booming postwar industry, and the results were remarkable. Tadanori Yokoo broke from the International Style to pursue a more intuitive and anarchic approach that emphasized the Japanese fascination with past, present, and future cultural icons, both Eastern and Western.

574. Kenji Itoh. *Kataoka Bussan Co., Ltd.* Package design for tea, 1986. Courtesy the designer

575. Takashi Nomura (designer) and Seitaro Kuroda (illustrator). *Mosquito on the 10th Floor.* Film poster, 1982. Courtesy Keisuke Nagatomo

576. Shigeo Okamoto. *Life and Pottery.* Poster for the 21st Pottery Test and Research Center Exhibition, 1986. Courtesy the designer

577. Tadanori Yokoo. *Science Fiction Movies.* Film festival poster, 1975. Courtesy the designer

578. Tadanori Yokoo. *The Wonders of Life on Earth.* Poster for a book by Isamu Kurita, 1965. Courtesy the designer

579. Tadanori Yokoo. *John Silver.* Theater poster, 1967. Courtesy the designer

575

576

574

577

578

581

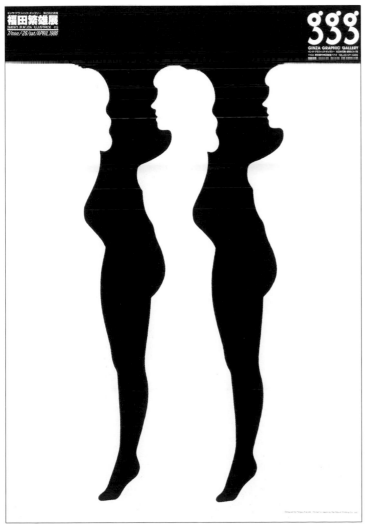

582

JAPANESE

The 1970 Osaka World Exposition, with seventy-
six participating countries, marked a turning
point for Japanese designers. Associating with so
many foreign visitors stimulated them to reex-
amine their own cultural roots and to apply
them to their architecture, arts and crafts, and
graphic design. Although most contemporary
Japanese advertising designers adopted Western
images from Pop Art, comic strips, television,
and film, they transformed them into evocations
of the emerging contemporary, high-tech Japanese society. In moving from an essentially
Constructivist- and Bauhaus-inspired methodology to a more culturally eclectic visual lexicon, Japanese designers prefigured New Wave
and Post-Modern tendencies in America and
Europe. This change of emphasis did not occur
in an organized manner, however, but separately
evolved in the work of individual designers.
Prominent among Japan's leading individualists
is Shigeo Fukuda. Stylistically distinct from
other Japanese designers, his simple, emblematic
imagery combines the Japanese taste for economy with a witty, ironic sensibility.

580. Yusaku Kamekura. *Hiroshima Appeals*
Poster, 1983. Courtesy the designer

581. Shigeo Fukuda. Poster for an exhibition
of the designer's work, 1984. Courtesy the
designer

582. Shigeo Fukuda. Poster for a private exhibition, 1986. Courtesy the designer

583. Shigeo Fukuda. Poster for a one-man
exhibition, 1986. Courtesy the designer

583

JAPANESE

Though not easily codified or defined, Japanese graphic style is recognizable—and not merely by its typography or the occasional Japanese visual reference. Called upon to advertise products and disseminate ideas, both to their compatriots and to the world, Japanese designers speak in a curiously national yet international voice. By employing the full range of photographic and computer communication-arts tools available today, they are able to transform the poster's two-dimensional surface. Their newly created three-dimensional playgrounds may bear either typically elegant harmonies or discordant colors, random shapes, and explosive images. Kazumasa Nagai and Ikko Tanaka are two pioneers of contemporary design, each having made a distinct contribution to Japanese graphic style.

584. Kazumasa Nagai. Poster for Japanese graphic art exhibition in Paris, 1984. Courtesy the designer

585. Kazumasa Nagai. *Zero Nuclear Weapons.* Poster for the Hiroshima-Nagasaki Publishing Committee, 1982. Courtesy the designer

586. Ikko Tanaka. *Asian Performing Arts Institute, UCLA.* Theater poster, 1981. Courtesy the designer

587. Ikko Tanaka. *Noh.* Performance poster, 1981. Courtesy the designer

584

585

Nihon Buyo
UCLA
Asian Performing Arts
Institute 1981
Los Angeles
Washington, D.C.
New York

586

587

BLACK SABBATH

TECHNICAL ECSTASY

588. George Hardie and Richard Manning (Hipgnossis). *Black Sabbath: Technical Ecstasy.* Record album cover, 1976. Courtesy the designers

Within the basically eclectic design environment of the eighties, the term *Post-Modern* has come to apply to a distinctive international style based not on dogma but on the somewhat haphazard confluence of various theories and practices of individual designers worldwide. In current architectural criticism, the term formally and effectively describes the rejection of orthodox Modernist purity in favor of an updated Neo-classical ornamentation; in contemporary design, it is less precise, perhaps only a temporary rubric. The most general interpretation of the term for design purposes would include all contemporary practitioners who are not strict Bauhausians and would embrace such eighties' substyles as Neo-Dada, Neo-Expressionism, Punk, and Pacific Modern.

Like Art Deco, the last major international style, Post-Modern blends art history and new technology with a decorative tendency to achieve a broad-based, commercially acceptable look. Linking its various substyles are certain distinctive visual, if not philosophical, characteristics: a playful kinetic geometry featuring floating forms, sawtooth rules, and randomly placed blips and lines; multiple layered and fragmented images; pleasant pastel harmonies; discordant, letter-spaced typography; and frequent references to art and design history.

The Post-Modern design aesthetic was in the wind long before the name was coined. In the late fifties and the sixties, certain premature Post-Modernisms appeared in the Art Nouveau and Art Deco mannerisms reprised in the work of Push Pin Studios. Even earlier, in 1947, Ettore Sottsass, Jr., had executed a series of graphics combining Constructivist forms and gaily colored geometric debris in a prefiguration of his influential yet short-lived Memphis Style. When he realized, in the early 1980s, that he had little chance of significantly improving the broader urban environment, Sottsass decided to focus on redesign of the home, the last domain of individual freedom. His cartoon-like, pastel-colored Memphis furniture, textiles, and accessories were at once playful, irreverent, and critical of rigid functionalism. Their nature as three-dimensional collage/assemblages strongly affected the look of graphic design in Milan, Barcelona, Los Angeles, San Francisco, and Tokyo. And it continues today to define how graphic design is applied to consumer durable products.

The earliest Swiss contributions to Post-Modernism can be traced to Basel, where Wolfgang Weingart joined the faculty of the Basel Allegemeine Gewerbeschule in 1968. Rejecting the order and cleanliness of the Swiss grid-locked design and typography, Weingart mixed type weights within the same word, created grids and then violated them, and arranged type into images. Though drawing from Swiss formalism, Weingart's Basel Style provided a kind of computer-age liberation from two-dimensional space. Numerous European and American students who studied with Weingart expanded his creative approach to create a distinct look for the eighties.

The New York designer Dan Friedman, a Basel graduate and later a teacher at Yale and SUNY Purchase, was one of the most effective teachers of the new style. Friedman devised various stimulating student projects that tested the relationship between avant-garde and practical design applications. In 1973, he wrote: "Legibility (a quality of efficient, clear, and simple reading) is often in conflict with readability (a quality which promotes interest, pleasure, and challenge in reading). To what degree can a typographic statement be both functional and at the same time aesthetically unconventional?" Friedman's approach was to ricochet through American design education. In Los Angeles, designer April Greiman and photographer Jayme Odgers took the new language further by using kinetic photography. They combined Basel precepts with California Pop/Funk in what might be termed an image overload, similar in texture to the work of Hipgnosis, the British album-cover design studio, and the Japanese poster artist Tadanori Yoko. Greiman later expanded the boundaries of legibility even more through the use of abstract computer imagery. Concurrently, a group of San Francisco designers, influenced by the architects Robert Venturi and Michael Graves, developed Post-Modern decorative motifs characterized by a streamlined Neo-classicism. Teachers at the Cranbrook Academy in Bloomfield Hills, Michigan, formulated an analytical design approach based on the theory of deconstruction: the limits of abstract visual communication are tested by finding how many levels of meaning can be expressed through complex typographic configurations. While essentially decorative, this theory is best applied in the functional design work of the contemporary Dutch firms Studio Dumbar and Total Design.

Along with such analytical explorations of graphic design, there were the more expressive, serendipitous approaches. Like Psychedelia almost a decade before, Punk (also known as Neo-Expressionism and Neo-Dada) was the spiritual offspring of the sixties' underground press and its anti-design aesthetic. Originating in England as an offshoot of the rock music scene, Punk developed in the context of various local cultures, particularly in London, New York, Los Angeles, and Seattle. Its design was governed by speed and economy, and its posters and tabloid newspapers were characterized by the use of raw-edged torn paper and ruling tape and by a "ransom-note" approach to type and image. As with the underground press, comics played an important role in Punk's overall visual image. Swiss Punk represented a more refined use of type and image—a more violent high-tech attack on the grid—and eventually deteriorated into the more commercially oriented New Wave. As cartoonist Gary Panter laments, "Punk was an honest expression, while New Wave is a packaging term."

Despite the Post-Modern label, design style in the eighties must be defined as the sum of its various parts. Evidence definitely exists of a common period vocabulary, or at least a kindred aesthetic sensibility and artistic cross-pollination, visible in all media and applied to diverse products. Yet the aesthetic continues to evolve primarily from the styles of specific designers and to be propagated through the media as popular fashion. Only time will reveal its true nature and significance. 221

MEMPHIS / BASEL / ZURICH

Founded in Milan in 1980, Memphis developed
from the freewheeling creativity and conscious
rejection of functional design in Italy during
the seventies. The term became synonymous
with cartoon-like furniture and textiles that, as
Emilo Ambasz says, "have made peace with the
ephemeral." In Basel, during the late sixties,
Wolfgang Weingart violated the traditional Swiss
rules of order and cleanliness with his free-form
typography characterized by step rules, wide let-
terspacing, and the mixing of type weights. In
Zurich, Odermatt and Tissi developed a method
of typographic collage that intersperses surface
forms with strips of lettering and creates a sense
of spontaneity that gives the viewer the illusion
of involvement in the design process.

589. Ettore Sottsass. *Casablanca.* Furniture
piece, 1981. Courtesy Artemide Inc., New York

590. Nathalie Du Pasquier. *Cerchio.* Memphis
pattern, 1983. From *Memphis: Una Questione di
Stile,* published by Istituto Mides

591. Nathalie Du Pasquier. *Arizona.* Memphis
pattern, 1983. From *Memphis: Una Questione di
Stile,* published by Istituto Mides

592. Memphis logos

593. Wolfgang Weingart. *18 Didacta Eurodidac.*
Poster, 1979. Courtesy Reinhold Brown Gallery,
New York

594. Wolfgang Weingart. *Das Schweizer Plakat
1900–1983.* Poster to promote the book by
Bruno Margadant, 1983. Courtesy the designer

595. Siegfried Odermatt. *Design aus den
Niederlanden.* Exhibition poster, 1982. Courtesy
the designer

596. Rosmarie Tissi. *Englersatz.* Poster for
a typesetting company, 1983. Courtesy the
designer

589

590

591

592

593

594

595

596

597

598

599

600

601

602

603

604

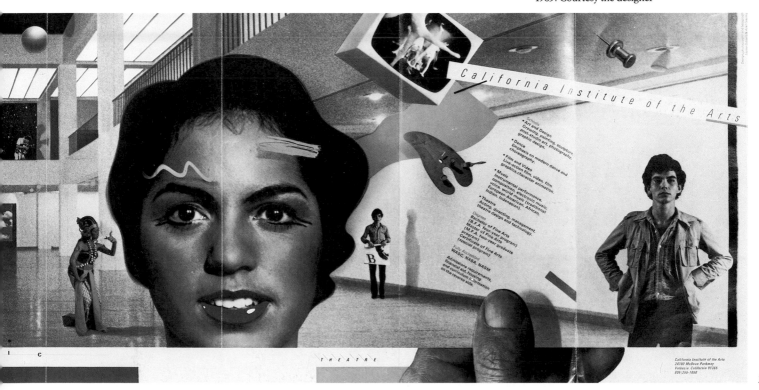

AMERICAN NEW WAVE

Many designers who studied in Switzerland during the late sixties and the seventies returned to the United States to practice what they had learned. Their activities, however, did not reflect the rational design influence of an earlier generation but instead constituted a zealous assault on the fundamental principle of legibility and, thereby, an attempt to define a current graphic vocabulary. Experiments with new optics and computers resulted in the kinetic quality of their designs. The work here answers Dan Friedman's question: "To what degree can a typographic statement be both functional and at the same time aesthetically unconventional?"

597. Hans-U. Allemann. *Package Design.* Poster, 1979. Courtesy the designer

598. Michael Zender. *Cincinnati Symphony Orchestra.* Program cover, 1979. Courtesy the designer

599. April Greiman. *Luxe Magazine.* Magazine headers, 1979. Courtesy the designer

600. Dan Friedman. *Idea.* Cover of *Typography Today,* 1981. Courtesy the designer

601. Inge Druckrey. *Yale Symphony Orchestra.* Poster, 1979. Courtesy the designer

602. April Greiman/Jayme Odgers. *CalArts.* Poster, 1978. Courtesy the designers

603. William Longhauser. *The Language of Michael Graves.* Exhibition poster, 1983. Courtesy the designer

604. Nancy Skolos. *AIGA of Boston.* Poster, 1985. Courtesy the designer

AMERICAN NEW WAVE

A playful eclecticism underlies eighties design of all kinds. Graphic imagery reflects the contemporary fetish for products of the material, commercial, and high-tech culture. Some designers have cleverly updated the typographic and illustration styles of the twenties and reapplied them to various commercial durables, from watchfaces to shopping bags. Others have drawn on computer technology to change the look, if not the substance, of books and magazines.

605. Swatch watches, c. 1987

606. John Jay. *New Year 1983.* Shopping bag for Bloomingdale's, 1982. Richard Hsu (art director) and Melanie Marder Parks (artist). Courtesy Bloomingdale's, New York

607. John Jay. *New Year 1984.* Shopping bag for Bloomingdale's, 1983. Richard Hsu (art director) and Gene Greif (artist). Courtesy Bloomingdale's, New York

608. Carol Bokuniewicz, Maira Kalman, and Tibor Kalman. *David Byrne: Three Big Songs.* Record album cover, 1983. Courtesy M & Co., New York

609. Charles Spencer Anderson and Joe Duffy. *Partners in Performance.* Cover of an invitation to a conference, 1986. Courtesy Duffy Design Group

610. Jane Kosstrin and David Sterling. *Fetish.* Magazine cover, Fall 1980. Courtesy Doublespace, New York

611. Jane Kosstrin and David Sterling. *Fetish.* Magazine pages, Fall 1980. Courtesy Doublespace, New York

612. Rudy Vanderlans. *Emigre, The Magazine That Ignores Boundaries.* Magazine cover, 1986. Courtesy Emigre Graphics, Berkeley

613. Warren Leherer. *French Fries.* Pages from a book published by Ear/Say, 1984. Courtesy the designer

614. Rudy Vanderlans. *Magritte's Hat.* Trademark designed on the Macintosh computer, 1987. Courtesy Emigre Graphics, Berkeley

606

607

605

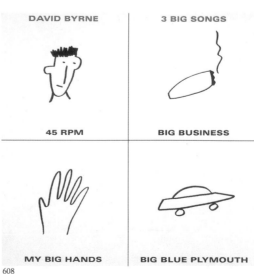

DAVID BYRNE   3 BIG SONGS

45 RPM   BIG BUSINESS

MY BIG HANDS   BIG BLUE PLYMOUTH

608

609

610

611

612

613

Magritte's Hat

614

615

616

617

618

619

620

AMERICAN PUNK

Like other twentieth-century youth movements, current youth culture has invented its own dominant design language. As signals of rebellion, comics are mainstays of the new style, and the basic primitivism of the collage technique helped to express an essential rawness. Collage was therefore the preferred artistic method during the early stages of Punk, and it was ultimately refined as a mainstream design technique.

615. Art Chantry. *Give Peace a Dance.* Poster, 1987. Courtesy the designer

616. Designer unknown. *Fiorucci.* Poster, date unknown. Courtesy Fiorucci, New York

617. Christopher Garland. *Boraxx.* Newspaper cover, 1981. Courtesy the designer

618. Louis Fishauf. Unpublished collage, 1981. Courtesy the designer

619. Gary Panter (artist), Art Spiegelman and Françoise Mouly (designers/editors). *Raw #3.* Magazine cover, 1981. Courtesy Raw Books, New York

620. Sue Huntley and Donna Muir (artists); Susan Hochbaum and Peter Harrison (designers). *Annual Report for Warner Communications.* Spread, 1986. Courtesy Pentagram, New York

621. Mark Marek. *New Wave Comics.* Book cover, 1984. Courtesy the designer

621

AMERICAN POST-MODERN

Prevailing trends in architecture have tradi-
tionally influenced typographic and pictorial
styles. In light of the increased creative interplay
today between architects and interior and
graphic designers, it is not surprising that an
architectonic style of graphics has come to typify
the American Post-Modern style.

622. Michael Manwaring. Hanna wine label,
1986. Courtesy the designer

623. Seth Jaben. *E. G. Smith Color Institute.*
Advertisement, 1987. Courtesy the designer

624. Sussman/Prejza & Company, Inc.
Designs for the 1984 Olympics. *Above:* Environ-
mental graphics for the Arts Festival at Exposition Park; *below:* Entry to track and field events
at the Los Angeles Memorial Coliseum. Courtesy Sussman/Prejza & Company, Inc., Los
Angeles

625. Woody Pirtle and Alan Colvin. *Houston
—A Celebration of Architecture.* Poster, 1983.
Courtesy the designers

626. Michael R. Orr, Donna Bagley, and
Rachel Schreiber Levitan. *16th Annual Exhibition of the Rochester Society of Communicating
Arts.* Catalogue cover, 1985. Courtesy the
designers

627. Michael Vanderbyl. *Sources.* Lecture
series announcement, 1984. Courtesy the
designer

628. Steve Snider. *Zipper Hospital.* Trademark,
1985. Courtesy the designer

629. Woody Pirtle. *Aubrey Hair.* Trademark,
1973. Courtesy the designer

630. John Casado. *Sir Cecil Beaton.* Exhibition
invitation, 1974. Courtesy the designer

631. Susan Johnson. *The Current Thing.* Trademark, 1979. Courtesy the designer

622

623

624

625

626

S O U R C E S

628

629

630

631

627

632

633

634

635

636

637

638

639

EUROPEAN NEW WAVE

Responding to the need to communicate forcefully with participants in the 1968 general strike, French graphic designers developed an effective visual language of solid graphic forms and unadorned hand lettering. The vocabulary of the design collective Grapus has become more sophisticated over the years—with layered photography, intricate typographical and pictorial designs, and unique color and black and white experiments. The posterist Alain Le Quernec has fine-tuned the permutations of the type and image combination. Studio Dumbar, one of Holland's perpetually innovative design firms, has extended the boundaries of acceptable corporate, government, and service-oriented communications. The Dutch designer Joost Swarte draws upon past cartoon masters and vintage decorative typefaces for a contemporary style that works as well in a comic book as on Dutch postage stamps. Paul Wearing's fabric print typifies the return to humorous decorative motifs in graphics and fabric design.

632. Grapus (Alexander Jordan, Garald Paris-Clavel, and Pierre Bernard). *Atelier Théâtral.* Theater poster, 1981. Courtesy Grapus, Paris

633. Grapus (Alexander Jordan, Garald Paris-Clavel, and Pierre Bernard). *Créanciers.* Theater poster, 1980. Courtesy Grapus, Paris

634. Grapus (Alexander Jordan, Garald Paris-Clavel, and Pierre Bernard). *Grapus.* Exhibition poster, 1982. Courtesy Grapus, Paris

635. Alain Le Quernec. *Thursdays of the Marionette.* Poster, 1983. Courtesy the designer

636. Gert Dumbar. *Mondrian.* Poster, 1972. Courtesy Studio Dumbar, The Hague

637. Joost Swarte. Postage stamps, 1986. Courtesy the designer

638–39. Studio Dumbar. Floor-identification system in a hospital, using bouncing balls, 1979–80. Courtesy Studio Dumbar, The Hague

640. Paul Wearing. Crocodile fabric print, 1985. Courtesy the designer

640

233

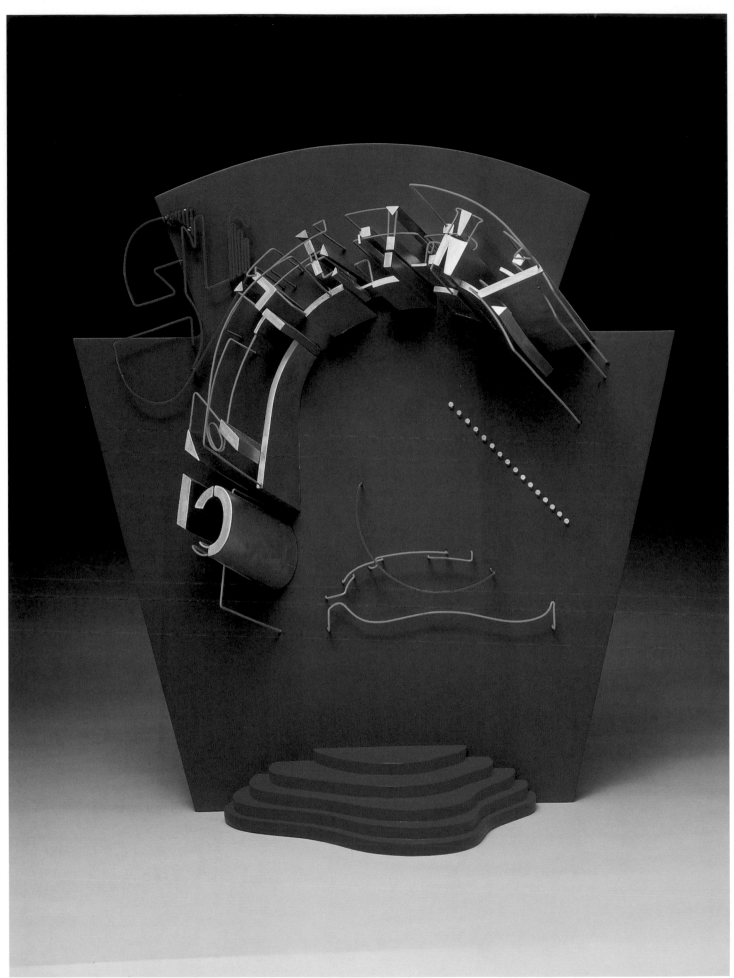

641. Robert Nakata. *Heinz Ketchup model degree project,* Cranbrook Graduate Design, Cranbrook Academy of Art, 1985. Courtesy Katherine McCoy

During the eighties, Post-Modern was the rubric under which emerging design sensibilities were loosely lumped together. Contrary to European Modernism during the mid-teens and twenties, Post-Modernism was not a unified movement based on utopian ideology. Rather, it was alternately radical, pseudoradical, or mannerist. In fact, what began in the early eighties as a young generation's genuine rebellion against the rigidity of cold, corporate Modernism, ultimately evolved into a lure that marketers used to hook youthful consumers. Commercial entrepreneurs appropriated even the most scourge-of-Western-civilization-like approaches.

Nonetheless, a few graphic designers with convention-busting methodologies altered the nature of design by challenging accepted tenets of beauty and function. While this provoked some jousting with older critics over "the rightness of form," Late-Modernist ideals of clarity and logic were eventually supplanted, if only temporarily, by multilayered type design, kinetic images, jarring spatial juxtapositions, and illegible texts.

Cranbrook Academy of Art was a hothouse of insurgent visual linguistics known as Deconstruction, which was defined as an antilinear exploration of graphic form and visual communication based on the subversion of fixed meanings and manipulative codes. Before the personal computer made it easy, Cranbrook students scrupulously deconstructed the components of graphic design just as Marxist or Post-Structuralist literary theoreticians in the sixties parsed texts for hidden meanings. The equivalent visual manifestation was chaotic typography and jumbled page layout that rejected conventional placement of headlines, body copy, and images. "Hierarchy [was] seen as an authoritarian technique used to manipulate the reader and stabilize meaning," stated the Cranbrook design department co-chairperson Katherine McCoy.

In this environment graphic design no longer functioned simply as a neutral frame but as a theoretical armature on which structure and meaning were continually challenged. However, not all contemporary practitioners addressed design problems with academic rigor. Rudy VanderLans, who in 1985, together with type designer Zuzana Licko, founded *Emigre* magazine – the clarion of the new digital typography – developed a methodology that wed technology and intuition. The tabloid-sized quarterly defied the tenets of Modern layout much in the same way that sixties Psychedelic poster artists upended the rules of legibility—laying down rules of their own. Under Modernism, type had become a neutral frame within which crisp and clean photographs or abstract illustrations were composed. *Emigre* was typocentric. Its typography was its content. By eradicating any semblance of the Modernist grid, VanderLans opened up the printed page to unfettered, raucously artful typographic configurations.

Emigre was the main stage for experimental typographic design. It was also a laboratory for the Macintosh computer, the box that launched the digital revolution. The Mac helped thrust type (and the word "font") into the popular culture as a form of personal expression. Although the Mac was a production tool, its miraculous capabilities encouraged designer/artists to play with its numerous defaults and thus challenge its limitations. Initially designers toyed with bitmapped letters and tested the extent to which alphabets could be pushed and remain functional. This resulted in typefaces that were more akin to miniature Expressionist artworks than mere letters. In the computer era various "distressed" typefaces were devised – often by designers who had never created alphabets before.

Fuse was a mother-lode of experimentation that spawned a new aesthetic. Sponsored by the FontShop International, and founded by Neville Brody—one of the pioneers in the first wave of Post-Modern expressionism—and John Wozencroft—a political polemicist—*Fuse* was the petri dish of type culture, a "digital magazine" that showcased conceptual type-play. Type was designed around such themes as politics, sexism, and pornography. Each of *Fuse*'s conceptual alphabets aimed to express and symbolize issues rather than serve the functional demands of type.

After enduring decades of Helvetica, distressed and degraded type designs signaled freedom.

Ray Gun – art directed and designed by David Carson—which was devoted to nineties alternative music, was defiantly anarchic and yet codified a period style. Although inspired by *Emigre*, Carson went further in exploiting the Mac's programmatic tics, including negative leading, overlapping, layering, and creating absurd compositional conceits, such as backwards text settings and columns of text that bled off the page. Carson's layouts were reminiscent of early twentieth-century Cubist and Futurist painting, yet were resolutely contemporary. Like raw-edged music, his design exalted in harmonic dissonance. *Ray Gun*'s visibility gave the style credibility, and Carson's design tropes became the youth culture's aesthetic.

Not all designers were comfortable following the pack; not all clients wanted "edgy" design. A bridge connecting classicism and pure simplicity enabled designers to return to formal purity without being labeled retrograde or nostalgic. The new minimalism was not a dogmatic elimination of all ornament, it was more of a clearinghouse—a separating of the ambiguous from the necessary.

Cranbrook, *Emigre*, *Fuse*, and *Ray Gun*, as well as a score of individual designers, contributed to the overall nineties style. But the Mac's catalytic influence cannot be underestimated in this equation. Its desktop/laptop power and convenience enabled designers to experiment more directly and freely than at any other time throughout graphic design history. Digital media further encouraged designers to leap into comparatively uncharted territory, including motion and sound: film and TV title sequences, music videos, animation, and websites. Each demands eternal newness—making novelty laborious and timelessness dubious. Fashion's fickleness has led to fumbled forecasting. Deconstruction and minimalism vied for stylistic ascendancy as anti-Modernism slid into Neo-Modernism. All in all, the late nineties were characterized by both individual vision and mass mimicry.

235

DECONSTRUCTION

The last decade of the twentieth century saw a clash of new technologies and old styles, "hybrids" and "mutants." Among the early founts of the graphic revolution, Cranbrook Academy helped to spawn various theoretical alternatives. Deconstruction theorists proposed that a participatory audience "constructed meaning" through individual interpretations and common messages. Deconstruction questioned the authority of traditional communications. The merging of dissonant type styles expressing two or more ideas on a single page offered the "receiver" optional pathways. This approach symbolized the new politics of diversity found in academia during the late eighties. In addition, Deconstruction revealed levels of transparency and showed the inner structure of a designed page: "These pieces talk about themselves, expose their own mechanics, and hold a dialogue about their own constructs," wrote Katherine McCoy. In this way *Ray Gun*'s layouts celebrated the defaults of computer programming. *Fuse* addressed the nexus where political and aesthetic issues met. Some of the *Fuse* typefaces were speculative without pretense of functionality, aimed only at challenging the status quo. Others appealed to designers who sought novelty. A style characterized by chaotic type and image quickly emerged. The "End of Print" aesthetic, as David Carson dubbed his own style (and his first monograph), was quickly implanted in the body of commerce. Ideas that were once truly radical evolved into commercial radicalism.

642. Katherine McCoy. *Cranbrook Graduate Design.* Poster for Cranbrook Academy, 1989. Courtesy the designer

643-4. David Carson. *Ray Gun.* Premiere cover and interior spread set entirely in Dingbats, 1992

645. Neville Brody. *Fuse 10.* Poster promoting the fashion issue, 1996. Courtesy FontShop International

646. P. Scott Makela. *Live To Death.* Poster, 1991. Courtesy Laurie Haycock Makela

647. Ed Fella. *Phillip Fike/Bill Rauhauser.* Poster for the Detroit Artists Market, 1987. Courtesy the designer

642

643

644

645

646

647

EMIGRE

In 1983, a year before the introduction of the Macintosh, Rudy VanderLans and Zuzana Licko founded *Emigre*, the vanguard of digital graphic design. What began as a generalist alternative culture magazine developed into the harbinger of the newest "new typography." After sampling the earliest Macintosh with its primitive, bitmapped default faces, *Emigre*'s founders presciently saw the potential of this new tool. Deciding the world did not need another culture tabloid, they focused exclusively on graphic design—but not as passive observers. The quarterly was a hothouse that wed advanced technology to unconventional aesthetics. VanderLans and Licko foresaw that digital typesetting was more than a mere technological advancement, it would forever alter typographic tradition. And Emigre Graphics (later dubbed Emigre Fonts), a type foundry, was a pioneer in alphabet design, introducing the earliest dot-matrix and, as the technology improved, high-resolution digital typefaces. *Emigre*, the magazine, featured many proponents and exponents who combined youthful rebellion, aesthetic diversity, and intellectual curiosity into a style of graphic design that challenged the canonical rules and modern approaches. Ultimately an "*Emigre* style" was incorporated into youth-oriented mass media.

648. Rudy VanderLans. *Emigre #13: Redesigning Stereotypes.* Cover, 1985

649. Rudy VanderLans. *Emigre #23: Culprits.* Cover 1992

650. Rudy VanderLans. *Emigre #15: Do You Read Me?* Cover, 1990

651. Rudy VanderLans *Emigre #20: Expatriots.* Cover, 1991

652. The Designers Republic. *Emigre #29: The Designers Republic.* Cover, 1994

653. Rudy VanderLans. *Emigre #24: Neomania.* Cover, 1992

654. Rudy VanderLans (designer), Gail Swanlund (photographer). *Emigre Fonts.* Catalogue cover, 1998

655. Barry Deck (right page), P. Scott Makela (left page). *Arbitrary.* Editorial and ad page in *Emigre #23*, 1994

656. P. Scott Makela. *Dead History.* Poster for typeface by Makela, 1990. All pieces courtesy *Emigre*

648

649

650

651

652

653

654

655

656

657

658

659

660

661

design in the global digital commune

662

663

664

FONTISM

Of all the terms to emerge from the graphic arts during the personal computer era, "font" (originally signifying a unified set of hot metal letters, which precedes the digital epoch by centuries) has been most integrated into the mass culture. Your average computer user talks of fonts as though the word was never arcane professional jargon. The reason is that software for the Macintosh and PC democratized both the use and manufacture of type. Until the advent of the computer, type creation was the sole province of skilled draftsmen, punch-cutters, and letterform designers who toiled at perfecting every nuance of a particular alphabet. The process could take months, even years. Yet during the nineties, programs like Fontographer enabled craftsmen and neophytes to create type. Both contributed to new methods and aesthetics practiced today. Graphic designers and artists saw type as another expressively interpretative medium. Without the strictures imposed by tradition, designers did not follow the same rules that had always governed production. Type no longer had to be pristine or legible, as long as it evoked a mood, established an aura, or signaled a code. Weird, quirky, and discordant typo-imagery, similar to early-twentieth-century Cubist painting, developed into a raucous, layered graphic style. The mutability of digital letters and the accessibility of custom faces contributed to typocentrism in graphic design.

657-8. Elliott Peter Earls. *The Pitch,* Vol. 1. Type specimen catalogue, 1998

659. Stephen Coates. *EYE;[Type].* Magazine cover, 1994. Courtesy Rick Poynor

660. Betsy Kopshina. *Garage Fonts.* Catalogue cover for type foundry, 1997

661-4. Rick Valicenti and Petra Klusmeyer/Thirst. *First Impressions.* Promotional campaign for Gilbert Paper Co., 2000. Courtesy the designer

FONTISM

When digitalization was introduced to the recording industry in the late 1980s, thousands of existing LPs were eventually re-released in CD format. Similarly, numerous classic typefaces were "redrawn" and re-released in digital formats for use on computers. New typefaces were generally greeted with the same enthusiasm as new music or fashions. In addition to the old stand-bys, the speed and economy of the new technology enabled type designers and graphic designers to create custom alphabets. While some of these fonts were rooted in the history of type's form and function, countless others were idiosyncratic interpretations of what an artist believed type should be; the creators viewed letterforms as just another artistic means to challenge the status quo. The witty titles of faces, such as "Erosive," "Entropy," and "Viscosity," illustrate that these forms had metaphorical weight, even more than practical application. With widespread accessibility to type design software, desktop digital type foundries issued distressed, degraded, and grunge fonts. Before digital media these works were cut and pasted as one-of-a-kind ransom-letter-style specimens, but the computer opened the floodgates of production and is a platform for distribution. Hundreds of fonts have been created, and most conceivable approaches have been tried, from ones that are programmed to erode during typing, to others that look like eighteenth-century handwriting. These typefaces changed the look of print. Layouts using "Pulsitalia" or "NeoDeko" will always be somewhat anarchic in a self-conscious manner.

665. Pete McCraken. *Erosive.* Typeface, 1993
666. Dave Henderlieter, *Pulsitalia.* Typeface, 1994
667. Pete McCraken. *NeoDeko.* Typeface, 1993
668. Scott Yoshinaga. *Grunge.* Typeface, 1993. All courtesy Plazm Fonts
669. Stephen Farrell. *Entropy.* Typeface, 1993. Courtesy Slipstudios
670. Stephen Farrell. *Volgare Proclamation.* Type prospectus (Daniel X. O'Neil, poet), 1996. Courtesy Slipstudios
671. Kathy Warinner and Bob Aufuldish. *Viscosity.* Typeface, 1996. Courtesy the designers

665

666

667

668

669

Volgare Proclamation

Here lie Volgare,
wrought from the hand of X,
birthed inside a type designer's studio,
and being only the latest product
in a long line of American things
fashioned from the raw material of Europe.

Thinkers and writers:
Take and patch these marks onto your own speech.
Receive and place this set of characters,
forever re-written,
living as endless words-in-waiting,
an infinite event yanked from a
hundred unconscious moments in the life of a skeletal clerk.
May the automatic feeling of Diction be with you always.

Imagine a fisherman standing on the shore and casting a line into the ocean. Imagine the immensity of the Pacific and the inconsequential frame of a human being.

CONTROLLED CHAOS

Modernism stressed order and cleanliness. Post-Modernism exhibited chaos and clutter. During the nineties this raucous sensibility evolved into a mannerism that reveled in the complex integration of type and image, but was nonetheless controlled and disciplined—improvisational yet premeditated. The computer allowed designers to create irrational-looking design. Ironically, it was a counterpoint to the mathematical constructs on which computer science is built. But the computer also allowed for easier access to once costly special effects, making the experimental more commonplace. The resulting designs are summed up by the word "hybrid." Although inspired by Deconstruction, *Emigre*, *Fuse*, and grunge, controlled chaos was assimilation ranging from the most advanced technology to the least sophisticated vernacular. A period style emerged, but it was the sum of disparate parts. From the raw, distressed look of MTV's *Unplugged* to the computer generated sheen of *Architecture Must Burn*, chaos was symptomatic and symbolic of culture's relentless media bombardment.

672-3. Jeffrey Keaton (creative director), Christopher Davis (art director/designer). *MTV Unplugged*. Book cover and interior design, 1995. Courtesy Jeffery Keaton

674. Why Not Associates (designers), Rocco Redondo (photographer). *Smirnoff*. Poster campaign for Smirnoff Vodka, 1990. Courtesy the designers

675. Erik Adigard and Patricia McShane (designers), Erik Adigard (illustrator). *Architecture Must Burn*. Book interior, 2000. Courtesy Erik Adigard

676. Why Not Associates (designers), Rocco Redondo (photographer). *U&lc*. Magazine cover, 1997. Courtesy the designers

672

673

674

A_WORLD_OF__CONTINUAL_MOTION

675

tom ford futurism

675

Volume 23, Number 1, Summer 1996

For a free issue of U&lc please write to U&lc,
866 2nd Ave, New York, NY 10017, USA
or fax to U&lc at 212 752 4752.

UPPER and lower case
The International Journal of Graphic Design and Digital Media
Published by International Typeface Corporation

Type the medium and the message

676

CONTROLLED CHAOS

The graphic design of the nineties was also a rebellion against the slick professionalism and corporate design ethos that replaced idiosyncratic methods with bright varnishes and coated papers. Reacting to the conformist sensibility of the times, designers introduced personality into various kinds of work for cultural, arts, and nonprofit institutions. While strictly conveying messages, these were art-based compositions that consciously skewed the rules of balance, harmony, and proportion to enhance visual interest, and shock the viewer into attention. The anarchic letterforms were used as keys to unlock emotions. The needle exchange posters use distressed typography—headlines such as "Death Is Not an Option"—as a visual metaphor for the unbearable chaos of a drug-user's life. The disorder of the "San Francisco Performances" silk screen echoes the unconventional dancing of its subject. The razor-cut body lettering (formed by scabs) on the "Sagmeister" lecture announcement is an extreme sacrifice to art. Although linked by similar aesthetics, these works celebrate the presence of the iconoclast in commercial art.

677. Somi Kim (Reverb, LA), Barbara Glauber (Heavy Meta, NY). *Cal Arts.* Catalogue cover, 1994. Courtesy the designers

678. Jennifer Sterling. *San Francisco Performances.* Silk-screen poster, 1997. Courtesy the designer

679-81. Martin Venezky (designer), U-cef Hanjani (art director), Robert Olding (photographer), Bob Rickert (copywriter). *NXCH: (888) 48 YOUTH.* Posters for a needle exchange, 2000. Courtesy the designer

682. Stefan Sagmeister (designer), Martin Woodtli (cut lettering). *Sagmeister.* Poster for designer's lecture, 1999. Courtesy the designer

683. Jennifer Morla (creative director, designer), Petra Geiger (designer). *California College of Arts and Crafts New Building.* Poster, 1998. Courtesy the designer

677

678

679

680

681

682

683

RAVE

The most grateful beneficiaries of computer-aided desktop publishing in the nineties were not the wannabes who churned out bland newsletters, but the artists and designers (the amateurs and neophytes) who create club and rave flyers. Used to promote dance parties and rave events in clubs and after-hours haunts, these postcard invitations were introduced in late 1990 and soon after defined the dance party aesthetic of the age. The design style married neo-psychedelia, Japanimation, video game imagery, and futuristic lettering with a fetish for technology (the word "techno" is used to describe both the digitally mixed music and the graphic style). Rave-like events date back to the seventies, but the electronic music free-for-alls that erupted spontaneously in England, Germany, Spain, and America were unique in defining the ethos (music, drugs, fashion) of the day. The flyers, which became souvenirs of each event, were designed with great precision and originality. Frequent motifs included parodies of well-known product logos, scary gothic imagery, space-age-technology graphics, and digital collage. The outlandish flyer style was subsequently co-opted by the advertising industry as a code and lure for selling products to the youth culture.

684. Kristina Steubner and Katrin Wiens (designer/illustrator). *Tokyo Techno Tourism. Exhibition flyer, 2000.* Courtesy Toursalon, Berlin

685. Swifty (Ian Swift). *Far Out in Dub Space.* Club flyer, 1999. Courtesy the designer

686. Lopez 97: büro destruct Bern Capital. *Sun Electric.* Club flyer, 1997. Courtesy the designers

687. Daryl Obert, Eric Stauder (designers), David Phorilak (packaging consultant). *Zoolu Five.* Invitation flyer, 1999-2000. Courtesy Dots Per Minute

688. Zack Detox, Eric Stauder (designers). *Digital Overdose.* Invitation flyer, 1999. Courtesy Dots Per Minute

689. Eric Stauder. *Friday Night Funktions.* Invitation flyer, 1999. Courtesy Dots Per Minute

684

685

686

687

688

689

KINETICS

Graphically designed film title sequences date back to the fifties. Saul Bass's unprecedentedly expressionistic titles for *The Man with the Golden Arm* launched a whole genre, spawning many exemplars for decades to follow. But with the advent of computer animation programs and desktop film editing software, sophisticated titling is more common than when, in Bass's day, it was a costly extravagance. Contemporary motion typography began, ironically, in the print medium and with deconstruction experiments. Before technology enabled these methods to be uploaded to the computer screen, however, designers simulated motion on paper by using shadows, blurs, and other kinetic effects. This was, in part, a symbolic reference to the digital age. But it was Kyle Cooper's mysterious, multi-layered, scrawled and blurred title sequence for the film *Seven* that brought the "new" new typography full circle to its original inspiration—the notion of motion. It also inspired other designers in film, television, and "new media" to make typo-pictorial narratives. The computer allows for a wide range of kinetic effects, from long to tight shots of type, animated three-dimensional lettering (playing basketball, in the case of *Scout's Honor*), and colorful abstractions that intersect with static and moving pictures.

690. Kyle Cooper (director), Kyle Cooper, Jenny Shainin (designers), *Seven.* Film title sequence, 1995. Courtesy Imaginary Forces

691. Matts Hakkanson, Marlene McCarty (designers) Marlene McCarty, Donald Moffett (art directors). *I Shot Andy Warhol.* Film title sequence, 1994. Courtesy Marlene McCarty

692. Walter Bernard, Mirko Ilic (creative directors), Lauren Denapoli (animator). *Scout's Honor.* Film title sequence, 1999. Courtesy WBMG Inc and Mirko Ilic Corp.

693. Emily Oberman, Bonnie Siegler (director/designers), Edie Baskin (photographer). *Saturday Night Live.* Television title sequence, 1998. Courtesy Number Seventeen

A NEIL·LEIFER FILM

SNL

Martha PLIMPTON.

Martha PLIMPTON.

LS HONOR

CHERI OTERI

Jamie HARROLD. Donovan LEITCH.

SCOUTS HONOR

CHRIS KATTAN

KINETICS

Once the Internet was merely a receptacle for chunks of text. Then software was developed, first to show static type and image, and ultimately to animate them. Although still in its formative stages, the Web's capacity for movement has advanced to the commonplace. While still limited by modem speeds and browser capacities, motion has moved from beyond the bells-and-whistles stage, through the experimental phase, into the realm of the sophisticated. Some of this kinetic content is delivered as "streaming media," clips of sound and picture (including movies and video) that are fed through the ether onto hard drives. For designers, the challenge is to continually make original content for the Web that employs the traditional design tools—type and image—with the developing Internet technologies. There is no codified style, though there are models. But as of now, the medium is in such flux that the paradigm one minute is an artifact the next.

694. Erik Adigard, Patricia McShane. *Power.* Website ad campaigned for MADxs, 1998. Courtesy the designers

695. Erik Adigard (designer), John Plunket (art director) *Wired Digital.* Website, 1998. Courtesy the designer

696. Richard McGuire, Dave Redl (designers), Funny Garbage. *Willing to Try,* website for Japanese tutoring company, 1999. Courtesy Funny Garbage

697. Peter Girardi, Chris Capuouzzo, John Giordani, Agnieszka Gasparska (designers), Funny Garbage. *Making the Web Worth Watching.* Promotional website, 2000. Courtesy Funny Garbage

694

695

696

697

698

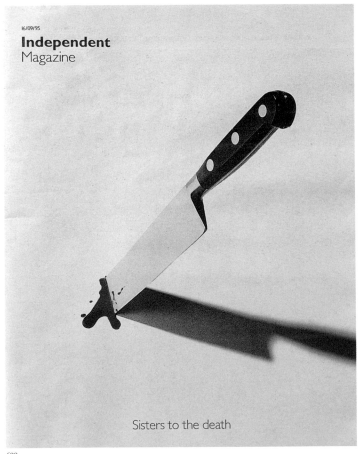

16/09/95

Independent
Magazine

Sisters to the death

699

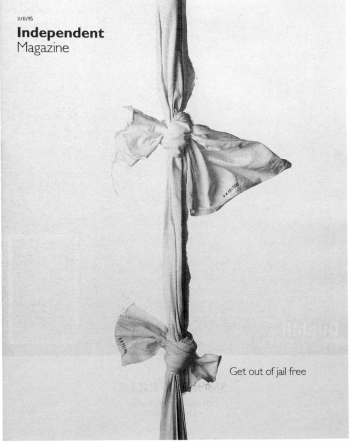

11/11/95

Independent
Magazine

Get out of jail free

700

701

702

703

NEW SIMPLICITY

Every style fosters a counterstyle. The chaotic complexity that underscored the Post-Modern era and continued through into the Digital ultimately met resistance in the mid-nineties. A new simplicity (sometimes referred to as Neo-Modern)—a reduction of layers of type and image to rudimentary forms and messages—was not a reprise of the orthodox Swiss International Style but rather a more playful fundamentalism. The lessons of Post-Modern were clear: graphic design should have personality; it should express diversity. Excess was rejected but allure was not. Plain geometry and unfettered type were reintroduced. Pleasing pastels and Minimalist ornament were invoked. Complexity was never an appropriate solution to all design problems, or a comfortable approach for all designers—excessive amounts of texture often overpowered an idea. Simplicity gathered steam because the unprecedented increase in information, both in print and on the Internet, compelled designers to aid the receiver efficiently navigate a page, package, or screen.

698. Stephen Doyle and Tom Kluepfel. *Martha Stewart's Everyday Colors.* Labels for paint cans, 1997. Courtesy Doyle and Partners

699-700. Vince Frost. *Independent Magazine.* Covers, 1995. Courtesy Frost Design Ltd.

701. Meta Design, San Francisco. *A6.* Booklet for the Aspen Conference, 1995. Courtesy Erik Spiekermann

702. Rob Stone. *Versus #4.* Magazine cover, 1995. Courtesy the designer

703. Haley Johnson Design Company. *What We Do.* Newsletter for Redgroup, 1998. Courtesy Haley Johnson

NEW SIMPLICITY

Simplicity is to Minimalism what complexity is to chaos, a component, not the whole. Minimalism and chaos are the fanatical sides of both coins. Reducing graphic design to its minutest parts while retaining personality and conveying ideas—and at the same time attracting an audience's interest—is a true challenge. Minimalism works best as a counterpoint to more elaborate design; then, its radical simplicity steals the stage. Michael Bierut's *Scale* poster illustrates how maximum impact can be achieved through the minute manipulation of one of the most elementary forms, a circle. Indeed its grand scale is what evokes power. Alexander Gelman's less austere (he injects color), but no less reductive, posters prove that graphic strength is, despite the counter movements and styles of the late twentieth century, rooted in the Mies van der Rohe dictum that "less is more."

704. Alexander Gelman. *Five Fifty Five Gallery.* Poster, 1998. Courtesy the designer

705. Alexander Gelman. *Golden Bee Biennale.* Poster, 1999. Courtesy the designer

706. Howard Brown, Mike Calkins (designers), Howard Brown (art director). *Urban Outfitters.* Poster, 1999. Courtesy Urban Outfitters

707. Michael Bierut. *The Architectural League of New York's Young Architects' Forum: Scale Purpose.* Call for entries, 1999. Courtesy the designer

704

705

706

707

Killer sudoku, whodunnit?, **giant crossword**…plus Christmas TV and radio guide

708: Marian Bantjes, designer. *G2 : Puzzle Special. The Guardian,* 2007. Courtesy Marian Bantjes

Although style has taken a holiday in the early twenty-first century, New Century graphic style is not style-less and amorphous. During the first decade of the new millennium, designers were stylish and stylized in ways that were clearly distinguishable from the previous two decades. What some critics call the "post-digital" age is notable for eclectic paradoxes—polished minimalism and do-it-yourself (DIY) complexity and even a bit of orthodox rationalism thrown in—but there is little if anything that could be labeled a period style—at least not yet.

There is no equivalent to Art Nouveau, Modernism, even Post-Modernism, but all these venerable stylistic manifestations and more are discernable in contemporary methods. New Century is comprised of thematic genres, rather than traditional styles, through which various typographic and pictorial mannerisms are expressed.

Style is no longer solely determined, as in previous eras, by commerce on the one hand or ideology on they other. Nor have the 2000s seen the kind of design-culture wars that flared up during the outset of the digital age in the mid-1980s, when Modern and anti-Modern aesthetics were at odds, and generational animosity seemed to blow the lid off of propriety. In the late 2000s graphic design settled into a period of redefinition and reevaluation. Contemporary designers are less rebellious and less contentious. Grunge is out but handicraft is in. Ugly is passé, but raw and naïf is accepted. Designers experiment with new media—motion and sound, and spectacles—but they don't rock the stylistic boat. In many ways, designers are more individual in their choice of graphic signature yet curiously more conformist in their selection of type and ornament.

New technology is usually the engine. But that does not mean "futuristic" technology routinely triggers futurist design. Drawing inspiration from history is very attractive today, particularly Modernism, which leads to neo-Modernism. The verities of a less-is-more sensibility serve as a symbolic refuge from the chaotic information overload so prevalent on too many websites today. Neo-Modern is not only retro nostalgia but expands upon the "gaily functional" approach that was essential to Modernist forebearers like Paul Rand and Lester Beall.

It is ironic that before the computer some of the more orthodox Modernist designers did their utmost to rid graphic design of all excessive ornamentation. As if anticipating computer templates, the grid was introduced as a means of attaining orderly and conformist design. So when the computer was introduced, it might have been viewed as though the Modernists had died and gone to heaven, where they were greeted by a tool that would quickly and easily clean standardized formats. What a boon to rationalism. What a joy for—well, joyless design. But fortunately, the computer was not the instrument of dogma and rigidity it appeared to be.

Technology aids and abets a kind of counter-neo-Modernism, which is built on intricate ornamental structures. Swirling and twirling tendril motifs made from arabesques and baroque designs hold a special fascination for designers. The computer has made their contemporaneous execution easier than when such things relied exclusively on tedious hand work.

With the computer came the "Information Age," and with the personal computer and Internet came the "Information Overload Age." And this is where graphic style and theme intersect. If one signature New Century stylistic attribute exists, an information style would have to be it. Over the past decade (although it started emerging in the 1980s), information graphics, otherwise known as information architecture (a term coined by Richard Saul Wurman) or information style, has become a major genre in all publishing venues. Information design is not a style in the strictest sense, but as a genre it uses many common visual idioms that could be construed as a style. It is, however, arguably the most frequently practiced of the New Century graphic developments. As more information gluts the media, more information visualization is produced.

Using visual methods to convey both detailed and simple data is a means of capturing a viewer's attention with information, which might easily be overlooked if rendered as pure text.

In the 1970s, graffiti infested (or brightened, in some cases) urban neighborhoods. It was both reviled as vandalism and celebrated as expressive art. Whatever the critical point of view, graffiti evolved into a visible form of guerilla street art, whereby the artists and designers—viral rebels and commercial usurpers—co-opted all manner of public facade to promote personal and institutional messages. The styles are varied but the genre is identified with the New Century.

The street is not the exclusive province for hand lettering, though much of it has been accomplished that way (and through wild postings). But signs and other outdoor manifestations have become inspiration for a New Century genre of handwritten lettering and typography. Although nothing about the practice is new, in the shadow of clean and precise desktop publishing, brush- and pen-scrawling and modern calligraphy are emblematic of an age before design templates took the individuality out of visual expression.

The street is the natural venue for political protest and dissent. While this is also not a new thematic area, in recent years the quantity of political expression has increased on paper and in the virtual world. As always, to thwart the feeling of helplessness in the face of war, racism, and pollution, among other major themes, designers produce missives of support and advocacy. If there is a style here, it is one of immediate communication.

Style has become less definable in the twenty-first century. Part of this trend is attributed to the rise in individuality found in "storytelling." Graphic design has become more about telling stories—narratives—than decorating. With less emphasis on commercial stylizations, there is less demand for new mannerisms to be "invented." The conformity of style is no longer as valuable to marketers and consumers as it was. Style must be redefined for the twenty-first century.

New Century is not a calculus whereby certain graphic tropes equal one manifestation. It is, however, a kind of mosaic of variegated approaches that add up, not to one quantifiable entity, but to an ethos of a time in which graphic design is in flux in terms of media and style.

259

A

NEO-MODERN

The term "Modern" has had various iterations and interpretations—avant-garde twentieth-century Modern, modernistic and moderne, mid-century Modern, Post-Modern and now neo-Modern. Each represents a moment in time and place, a marriage of form and content, a milestone and a millstone. The last and newest term signifies an aesthetic born directly of the Bauhaus and Swiss Modern movements but made modern (read: contemporary) in the non-ideological sense of the term. Neo-Modern is characterized by simplicity, economy, functionality, and subdued elegance. Neo-Modern is not, as Modernism was in the 1920s and 1930s, a mission to rid the world of ugliness; rather, it is an aesthetic preference for the alluringly unadorned. Neo-Modern is typified by no-nonsense sans serif typefaces used in caps and upper- and lowercase. Helvetica has made a comeback, but Gotham, Din, and other sans are popular, too. Neo-Modern has worked its stylistic way into many genres, but perhaps no more so than book covers and jackets. Although the field is as eclectic as can be—in the hope of capturing a dwindling audience in this "post-print" period—the need for clear and clean design mannerisms to package books means designers are increasingly returning to elemental type treatments framed by simple but eye-catching geometries and other low-impact visual tropes.

709. David Pearson, designer. *L'Univers.* Book cover, Éditions Zulma, 2009

710. Gregg Kulick, designer. *The Great Political Theories.* Paperback cover, Harper Perennial, 2008

711. Rodrigo Corral, art director and designer. *The Best Creative Nonfiction: Vol. 1.* Book cover, W. W. Norton, 2007

712. Gregg Kulick, designer. *Seven Days of Peter Crumb.* Paperback cover, Harper Perennial, 2007

713. Bobby C. Martin Jr., creative director and designer; OCD and Ogilvy & Mather, agency. *Museum for African Art.* Logo, 2008

709

710

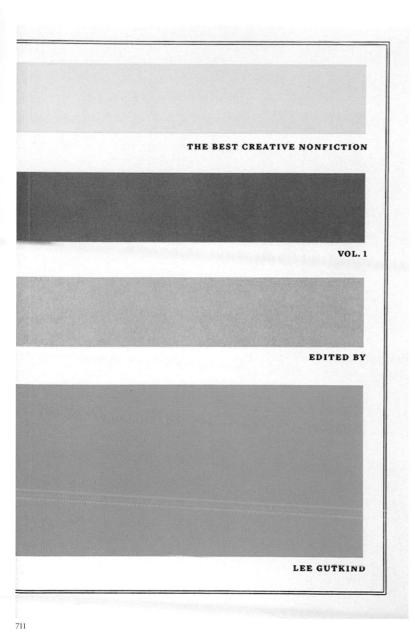

THE BEST CREATIVE NONFICTION

VOL. 1

EDITED BY

LEE GUTKIND

711

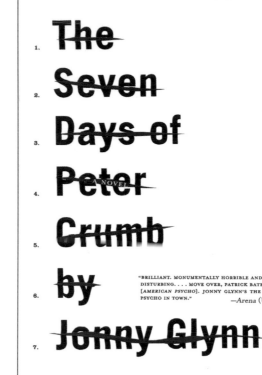

1.
2.
3.
4.
5.
6.
7.

The
Seven
Days of
Peter
Crumb
by
Jonny Glynn

A NOVEL

"BRILLIANT. MONUMENTALLY HORRIBLE AND
DISTURBING. . . . MOVE OVER, PATRICK BATEMAN
[AMERICAN PSYCHO]. JONNY GLYNN'S THE NEW
PSYCHO IN TOWN."
—Arena (UK)

712

MUSEUM
FOR
AFRICAN
ART

713

714

715

716

717

ORNAMENTAL

Despite seismic shifts in popular taste
that effectively alter the design terrain,
ornamentation (considered a "sin" by some
and heavenly by others) always returns in some
form or another. Ornament may indeed mask
poor craftsmanship. It may divert the eyes from
real issues. But it is nonetheless essential to
many designers and consumers who savor the
beauty—and at times, the folly—of decoration,
both exquisite and extreme. The art of intricate
patterns returned to the graphic design fold in
the 2000s coincident with a revival of T-shirts
and other sportswear that rely on intricate and
outlandish graphics to separate one wearer
from another. Moreover, the computer made
the making of repetitive patterns and singular
decorative designs quicker and easier to
accomplish. This does not mean ease is the only
reason for the ornamental revival—but its cut-
and-paste and step-and-repeat techniques should
not be underestimated. In the early twentieth
century, ornament was deemed passé not just
because it was bourgeois, but it was so work
intensive it went counter to the "Machine Age"
and "Streamline" ethics. In the computer age
production is as easy as using a mouse, and the
options for graphic ornamentation are seemingly
infinite. And that embrace of the infinite is what
makes reprising the old and inventing the new
so stylistically pleasurable.

714. David Pearson, designer, and Jim
Stoddart, art director. *Epictetus: Of Human
Freedom.* Paperback cover, Penguin Books, Ltd.,
2010

715. Louise Fili, designer. *Design Italia.* Poster,
School of Visual Arts, 2010

716. Marian Bantjes, designer. *Design Ignites
Change.* Poster (laser cut from white paper),
Academy for Educational Development: AED,
2008

717. Roberto de Vicq de Cumptich, designer,
and Paolo Pepe, art director. *A Game of Thrones.*
Book jacket, Random House, 2008

718–719. Bob Aufuldish, designer. *CCA
Architecture Lecture Series.* Letters, California
College of the Arts Architecture Program, 2007

718   719

```
123456789012
567890123456
901234567890
345678901234
789012345678
123456789012
567890123456
901234567890
```

INFORMATION

It is not clear whether the information graphics revolution has eased the weight of information overload or contributed to it. What is apparent is that the need for more information visualization in the 2000s has grown exponentially with the increased data streams—or rather tidal waves—encouraged and enabled by the Internet. Paradoxically, all of these graphics—and the majority of information displays—are produced for print venues (magazines, books, posters). What began in the late twentieth century as a means of quick, thumbnail explanation (when the *New York Times* introduced information graphics, they were called "sides of beef") has evolved into a graphic design staple with ersatz style all its own. Using universal sign symbols or ISOTYPES (originally developed in the 1920s by Otto Neurath), contemporary designers create information schemes, compositions, and matrices that explain everything from the nature of sexual fetishes to the most favored recreational drugs. The information graphic has become so ubiquitous that it is also the object of sarcasm, ridicule, and satire. The graphics themselves are routinely imbued with wit so as to aid the end user in the navigation process. The most common feature of the serious and comic information graphic is a profusion of type, sometimes the smaller and tighter the better, which often undermines the purpose of a clear information graphic.

720. Michael Bierut and Jennifer Kinon, designers; Katharine Gates, content. *Kink, The Erotic Roadmap*. Information graphic poster, The Museum of Sex, New York, 2007

721. Christoph Niemann, illustrator. "Good Night and Tough Luck." From a visual essay on nytimes.com, 2009

722. Dave Eggers, designer. *McSweeney's No. 3. McSweeney's* magazine cover, 1999

723. Deborah Adler, typographer/designer. Prescription bottle label, Target Inc., 2003

724. Joshua Covarrubias, designer/illustrator; Agnieszka Gasparska, art director. *Our Favorite Drugs*. Information graphic, *GOOD* magazine, 2009

720

721

722

723

Our Favorite Drugs

The war on drugs keeps law enforcement busy—33 percent of all arrests made in 2007 were drug related—but the kinds of battles police are fighting vary widely across the country, from meth labs in California to cocaine dealers in Florida. This is a look at what drugs local law enforcement officials said were posing the greatest dangers to their communities, when asked by the Department of Justice.

724

265

INFORMATION

Homunculi, organizational family trees, directional points and lines, these are some of the visual tropes used in information graphics. Nigel Holmes was one of the first designers to re-introduce this quantitative visualization to American periodicals in a vibrant and alluring way. His curious brand of fundamental information and "follow the bouncing ball" style of graphics helped to launch an editorial practice that is currently an essential means of conveying data. It did not take long for a sub-field of design to grow up around Holmes, who was for two decades the information art director of *Time* magazine. Every news magazine developed a graphics department. And soon, thanks to Richard Saul Wurman, the practice had a name suitable for framing on a plaque: information architecture—ostensibly graphic design working toward the goal of clarifying simple and complex data. The key difference between information design and general graphic design is transparency. Ornament and decoration are unacceptable if they hinder perception. And yet, information has developed its own style, and information graphics have, by virtue of a common visual language, become a sort of style, with each practitioner contributing a personal approach that contributes to the whole genre.

725. Nigel Holmes, designer, art director. *How to Conduct*. Information graphic, Bloomsbury Press/Wordless Diagrams, 2005

726. Nicholas Felton, designer and illustrator. Information graphic, *The 2009 Feltron Annual Report*, 2010

727. Sam Potts, designer. *Geek Love*. Information graphic. *New York Times* op-ed page, 2008

728. Alicia Cheng, Mgmt., designers; Criswell Lappin, art director. *Philip Johnson*. Information graphic, *Metropolis* magazine, 2005

729. Alicia Cheng, Mgmt., designers. *The War in Iraq*. Information graphic, *New York Times* op-ed page, 2005–2010

725

FIGURE 9. REPORTED TRAVEL AND LOCATIONS

726

727

728

729

730

STREET ART

Graffiti reached epidemic proportions in the 1970s and grew like kudzu in most every urban center in the world. The critics called it vandalism and enacted strict ordinances to defeat its spread. The practitioners and fans called it street art, an expressive alternative métier for messaging and self promotion. Today galleries show it, books celebrate it, and advertising agencies exploit the form and graffiti style as "guerilla" art. Coincident with spray-painted graffiti was an upsurge, and later a fashion, for stickers and wild postings of larger fliers and posters. This was not unique to 2000 or 1990 or 1960, but it reached a new crescendo in the past decade. The leader of the pack was Shepard Fairey's 1989 "OBEY the GIANT" ("Andre the Giant Has a Posse") campaign, simply known as OBEY, that launched Fairey on a wild posting mission, which has taken its legal toll. For the 2008 U.S. Presidential election, Fairey created the "Hope" poster for Barack Obama, which was first published on the Web but soon found its way onto streets throughout the United States (it has also caused its share of legal woes). Fairey is but one of many "street artists," both guerilla and mainstream. Starting in the late 1990s, designers took graphics to the streets, from painting advertising and promotion on buildings to building inflatable sculptures to using billboards to convey personal art messages. What's more, the visual idioms of street art, notably the common stencil, have been appropriated for films, plays, and other mainstream entertainment.

730. Shepard Fairey, designer. *OBEY.* Vinyl sticker, c. 1990s

731. Paula Scher, designer. Exterior design, New Jersey Performing Arts Center (NJPAC) 2004

732. Shepard Fairey, designer; The Obama Field Painter, painter. *HOPE.* Poster, painted on a field in Pennsylvania, 2008

733. Drew Hodges, SpotCo., designer. *RENT.* Logo, 1994

734. Ji Lee, designer and illustrator. "Delete Billboard." Part of NY Street Advertising Takeover, 2009. Photo courtesy Ji Lee

735. Stefan Sagmeister, Matthias Ernstberger, designers; Monika Aichele, illustrator. *Everybody.* Inflatable sculpture, Six Cities Design Festival, Scotland

731

732

733

734

735

736

737

738

739

740

HAND LETTERING

Letterforms in all shapes and sizes were drawn, carved, and engraved using the hand—the first digital tool. And the hand created of some of the most beautiful lettering ever devised. In the computer age there has been a renaissance of the hand. Although drawing on the computer is perhaps no less complicated than on paper, the logic inherent in the new tool nevertheless eliminates the serendipitous edge that is endemic to the old one. These days, just the word "expressive" connotes liberation from the confines of technology, even though it may only be an illusion. Designers have practiced ad hoc writing as a respite from the rigor of traditional typography. It was fairly common for designers to use brush- and pen-scrawls as display lettering-cum-personal signature. Ironically, the scanner and digital camera have made it easier to use hand lettering that is painterly and abstract. But digitization inevitably results in mass production and mass production invariably removes the quirkiness from any letterform. Hand lettering enables a designer to make a distinct mark. And yet a level of conformity prevails when so many designers are using similar techniques. Although a good programmer could train the computer to almost anything, as design becomes more computer-generated, as programmed, the human factor must not be underestimated. The hand is graphic design's oldest tool—and for now, it is having a revival.

736. Jonny Hannah, illustrator, and Alex MacFadyen, art director. *Complete Shakespeare*. Editorial illustration, Telegraph Media Group, 2008

737. Bernard Maisner, designer and letterer. *Body Language*. Self promotion, 2009

738. Leanne Shapton, designer and illustrator. *9 Stories* by J.D. Salinger. Book art, 2009

739. Jon Gray, designer and letterer. *Everything Is Illuminated*. Book cover, Houghton Mifflin, 2002

740. Alex Trochut, designer and letterer. *This Is Illustration. Varoom* magazine cover, 2009

POLITICAL

Activist politics and graphic style make strange bedfellows. Yet styles have historically been associated with and so help define certain political movements and ideologies. The Nazi party branded itself with vivid signs, symbols, and colors. The Italian Fascist party, though not as consistent, used a few key images as their brand. Soviet and Communist Chinese symbologies are easily identifiable. Even before "branding" became a buzzword in the 1990s, the practice was perfected for political campaigns and social causes. In the 2000s the world has not shed much of its atavism; wars, prejudice, inequities, hostilities, and more continue to be manifest. And designers continue to protest or advocate certain acts and beliefs. The poster continues to have the most traction as a messaging tool. Even in the so-called printless era, posters remain an efficient means of reaching audiences. With the computer, posters have a life beyond their limited print existence. There are two kinds of political graphics. One is part of a strategic campaign, which is planned and coordinated much like an advertising intervention. Then there are the ad hoc expressions that arise immediately in response to a critical moment or event. The *iRaq* "sampling" of the famous iPod campaign was spontaneously based on an iconic photograph of torture smuggled out of the Abu Ghraib prison. Not all are so "readymade" for protest, but the most effective missives have highly recognizable images that work simultaneously on two levels—wit and truth.

741. Yosse Lemel, designer. *Blood Bath.* Poster, 2002

742. Mirko Ilic and Daniel Young, designers. *Darfur.* Poster, Parodoxy Products, 2006

743. Cooper Green, designers. *iRaq.* Poster, 2004

744. Micha Wright. *Vacancies Available.* Poster, 2004

745. Redback Graphix, designers. *Condoman.* Poster for NACAIDS Canberra, Australia, c. 1994. © Commonwealth Department of Human Services and Health, Aboriginal Health Workers of Australia (Queensland)

741

742

743

744

745

Abdy, Jane. *The French Poster*. New York: Graphiques, 1977.

Ackland-Snow, Nicola; Brett, Nathan; and Williams, Steven. *Fly: The Art of the Club Flyer*. New York: Watson-Guptil Publications, 1996.

Ades, Dawn. *Photomontage*. New York: Pantheon, 1976.

——. *Posters: The 20th Century Poster Design of the Avant-Garde*. New York: Abbeville, 1986.

Anikst, Mikhail, ed. *Soviet Commercial Design of the Twenties*. New York: Abbeville, 1987.

Anscombe, Isabelle, and Gere, Charlotte. *The Arts and Crafts Movement in England and America*. New York: Rizzoli, 1978.

Arnheim, Rudolf. *Art and Visual Perception: A Psychology of the Creative Eye*. Berkeley: University of California Press, 1974.

Art Deco Trends in Design. Chicago: The Bergman Gallery and University of Chicago, 1973.

Arwas, Victor. *Art Deco*. New York: Harry N. Abrams, 1980.

Ashwin, Clive. *A History of Graphic Design and Communication. A Source Book*. London: Penbridge, 1983.

Aslin, Elizabeth. *The Aesthetic Movement. Prelude to Art Nouveau*. New York: Praeger, 1969.

Baljev, Joost. *Theo van Doesburg*. New York: Macmillan, 1975.

Banham, Reyner. *Theory and Design in the First Machine Age*. New York: Praeger, 1967.

Barnicoat, John. *A Concise History of Posters: 1870–1970*. New York: Oxford University Press, 1980.

Battersby, Martin. *The Decorative Thirties*. New York: Walker, 1971.

——. *The Decorative Twenties*. New York: Walker, 1969.

Bayer, Herbert. *Bauhaus 1919–1928*. New York: The Museum of Modern Art, 1972.

——. *Herbert Bayer. Painter, Designer, Architect*. New York: Van Nostrand Reinhold, 1967.

Billcliffe, Roger. *Mackintosh Textile Designs*. New York: Taplinger, 1982.

Bing, Samuel. *Artistic America, Tiffany Glass, and Art Nouveau*. Reprint. Cambridge, Mass.: M.I.T Press, 1970.

Black, Mary. *American Advertising Posters of the Nineteenth Century*. New York: Dover, 1976.

Boe, Alf. *From Gothic Revival to Functional Form: A Study in Victorian Theories of Design*. Oslo: Oslo University Press; Oxford: Blackwell's, 1957.

Bojko, Szymon. *New Graphic Design in Revolutionary Russia*. New York: Praeger, 1972.

Bolin, Brent C. *Flight of Fancy*. New York: St. Martin's Press, 1985.

Branzi, Andrea. *The Hot House: Italian New Wave Design*. Cambridge, Mass.: M.I.T Press, 1986.

Briggs, Asa, ed. *William Morris: Selected Writings and Designs*. Harmondsworth, England: Penguin, 1962.

Broos, Kees. *Pet Zwart 1885–1977*. The Hague: Gemeentemuseum, 1973.

Brown, Robert K., and Reinhold, Susan. *The Poster Art of A. M. Cassandre*. New York: E. P. Dutton, 1979.

Brunhammer, Yvonne. *The Nineteen Twenties Style*. London: Paul Hamlyn, 1969.

Burckhardt, Lucius. *The Werkbund History and Ideology, 1907–1933*. New York: Barron's, 1977.

Busch, Donald. *The Streamlined Decade*. New York: George Braziller, 1968.

Cabarga, Leslie. *A Treasury of German Trademarks*. New York: Art Direction Book Co., 1985.

Callen, Anthea. *Women Artists of the Arts and Crafts Movement, 1870–1914*. New York: Pantheon, 1980.

Campbell, Joan. *The German Werkbund: The Politics of Reform in the Applied Arts*. Princeton: Princeton University Press, 1978.

Carter, Rob; Day, Ben; and Meggs, Philip. *Typographic Design: Form and Communication*. New York: Van Nostrand Reinhold, 1985.

Carter, Sebastian. *Twentieth Century Type Designer*. New York: Taplinger, 1987.

Clark, Robert J. *Arts and Crafts Movement in America*. Princeton: Princeton University Press, 1972.

Constantine, Mildred, and Fern, Alan. *Revolutionary Soviet Film Posters*. Baltimore: Johns Hopkins University Press, 1974.

——. *Word and Image*. New York: The Museum of Modern Art, 1968.

Cooper, Austin. *Making a Poster*. London: The Studio, 1949.

Cooper, Douglas. *The Cubist Epoch*. London: Phaidon, 1970.

Crane, Walter. *Of the Decorative Illustration of Books Old and New*. London: George Bell, 1896.

——. *William Morris to Whistler*. London: George Bell, 1911.

Delhaye, Jean. *Art Deco Posters and Graphics*. New York: Rizzoli, 1978.

Delpire, Robert. *Paris 1925*. Paris: Gallimard, 1957.

Design in America: The Cranbrook Vision 1925–1950. New York: Harry N. Abrams, 1983.

Deslandres, Yvonne, with Lalanne, Dorothea. *Poiret*. New York: Rizzoli, 1987.

Dewey, John. *Art as Experience*. Reprint. New York: Wideview/Perigee 1980.

Dorfles, Gillo. *Kitsch: The World of Bad Taste*. New York: Universe, 1969.

Downey, Fairfax. *Portrait of an Era as Drawn by Charles Dana Gibson: A Biography*. New York: Charles Scribner & Sons, 1936.

Elliott, David, ed. *Alexander Rodchenko and the Arts of Revolutionary Russia*. New York: Pantheon, 1979.

Ferebee, Ann. *A History of Design from the Victorian Era to the Present*. New York: Van Nostrand Reinhold, 1970.

Fortz, Adrian. *Obects of Desire. Design and Society from Wedgwood to IBM*. New York: Pantheon, 1986.

Fraser, James, and Heller, Steven. *The Malik Verlag 1916–1947, Berlin, Prague, New York*. New York: Goethe House; Madison, N.J.; Fairleigh Dickinson University, 1985.

Friedman, Mildred, ed. *De Stijl 1917–1931, Visions of Utopia*. New York: Abbeville, 1982.

Frutiger, Adrian. *Type, Sign, Symbol*. Zurich: ABC Verlag, 1980.

Fuld, James J. *A Pictorial Bibliography of the First Editions of Stephen C. Foster*. Philadelphia: Musical Americana, 1957.

Gallo, Max. *The Poster in History*. New York: American Heritage, 1974.

Garner, Philip. *Contemporary Decorative Arts from 1940 to the Present*. New York: Facts on File, 1980.

Gerstner, Karl, and Kutler, Marcus. *Die Neue Graphik/The New Graphic Art*. New York: Hastings House, 1959.

Glaser, Milton. *Milton Glaser Graphic Design*. Woodstock, N.Y.: Overlook Press, 1974.

Gluck, Felix, ed. *World Graphic Design: Fifty Years of Advertising Art*. New York: Watson-Guptil, 1969.

Gombrich, E. H. *Art and Illusion*. 2nd edition. Princeton: Princeton University Press, Bollingen Series, 1961.

Grannis, Chandler B., ed. *Heritage of the Graphic Arts: A Selection of Lectures Delivered at Gallery 303, New York City*. New York and London: R. R. Bowker, 1972.

Gray, Camilla. *The Russian Experiment in Art 1863–1922*. New York: Charles Scribner & Sons, 1973.

Gray, Nicolette. *A History of Lettering: Creative Experiment and Letter Identity*. Oxford, 1986.

——. *Nineteenth Century Ornamented Typefaces*. Berkeley: University of California Press, 1977.

Greif, Martin. *Depression Modern: The Thirties Style in America*. New York: Universe, 1977.

Hageney, Wolfgang. *Paris, 1928–1929*. Rome and Milan: Editions Belvedere, 1985.

Hammond, Wayne G., and Volz, Robert L. *Book Decoration in America, 1890–1910*. Revision. Williamstown, Mass.: Chapin Library, Williams College, 1979.

Havinden, Ashley. *Advertising and the Artist*. London: The Studio, 1956.

Heartfield, John. *Photomontages of the Nazi Period*. New York: Universe, 1977.

Heller, Steven, and Pomeroy, Karen. *Design Literacy: Understanding Graphic*

Design. New York: Allworth Press, 1997.

Heller, Steven. *Design Literacy (Continued): Understanding Graphic Design*. New York: Allworth Press, 1999.

Heller, Steven, and Fink, Anne. *Faces on the Edge: Type in the Digital Age*. New York: Van Rostrand Reinhold, 1997.

Henderson, Sally, and Landau, Robert. *Billboard Art*. San Francisco: Chronicle, 1979.

Hillier, Bevis. *Art Deco of the Twenties and Thirties*. London: Studio Vista; New York: E.P. Dutton, 1968.

——. *The Decorative Arts of the Forties and Fifties: Austerity Binge*. London: Studio Vista, 1970.

——. *The Style of the Century 1900–1980*. New York: E. P. Dutton, 1983.

——. *The World of Art Deco*. New York: E. P. Dutton, 1971.

Hine, Thomas. *Populuxe*. New York: Alfred A. Knopf, 1986.

Hipgnossis and Hardie, George. *The Work of Hipgnossis*. New York: A & W Visual Library, 1978.

Hlavsa, Oldruich. *A Book of Type and Design*. New York: Tudor, 1960.

Hofmann, Armin. *Graphic Design Manual: Principles and Practice*. New York: Van Nostrand Reinhold, 1965.

Horn, Richard. *Memphis: Obects, Furniture, and Patterns*. Philadelphia: Running Press, 1986.

Hornung, Clarence P., and Johnson, Fridolf. *200 Years of American Graphic Art: A Retrospective Survey of the Printing Arts and Advertising Since the Colonial Period*. New York: George Braziller, 1976.

Howarth, Thomas. *Charles Rennie Mackintosh and the Modern Movement*. London: Routledge and Kegan Paul, 1952.

Hulten, Pontus, organizer. *Futurismo, Futurism and Futurisms*. New York: Abbeville, 1986.

Hurlburt, Allen. *The Design Concept*. New York: Watson-Guptil, 1981.

——. *The Grid*. New York: Van Nostrand Reinhold, 1978.

Huszar, Vilmos. *Schilder en Ontwerper 1884–1960, De Grote Onbekende Van de Stil*. Utrecht: Sjarel Ex, Els Hoek, 1985.

Igarashi, Takenobu, ed. *World Trademarks and Logotypes II*. Tokyo: Graphic-sha, 1987.

Jan Tschichold: Leben und Werk des Typographen. With an introduction by Werner Klemke. Dresden: VEB Verlag der Kunst, 1977.

Japan Package Design Association, ed. *Package Design in Japan. Its History, Its Faces*. Tokyo: Rikuyo-sha, 1976.

Johnson, Diana Chalmers. *American Art Nouveau*. New York: Harry N. Abrams, 1980.

Johnson, Douglas and Madeleine. *The Age of Illusion: Art and Politics in France, 1918–1940*. New York: Rizzoli, 1987.

Jones, Owen. *The Grammar of Ornament*. Reprint. New York: Portland House, 1986.

Jordan, Joel T.; Hoeckle, Summer Forest; Jordan, Jason A. *Searching for the Perfect Beat: Flyer Designs of the American Rave Scene*. New York: Watson-Guptil Publication, 2000.

Jubb, Michael. *Cocoa and Corsets*. London: Public Record Office, Her Majesty's Stationery Office, 1984.

Kahn, Douglas. *John Heartfield: Art and Mass Media*. New York: Tanam, 1985 .

Kallir, Jane. *Viennese Design and the Wiener Werkstätte*. New York: Galerie St. Etienne/George Braziller, 1986.

Karginov, German. *Rodchenko*. New York: Pantheon, 1980.

Kelly, Rob Roy. *American Wood Type, 1828–1900. Notes on the Evolution of Decorated and Large Types*. New York: Da Capo, 1969.

Kepes, Gyorgy. *Language of Vision*. Chicago: Paul Theobald, 1945.

——. *The New Landscape*. Chicago: Paul Theobald, 1956.

Khan-Magomedov, Selim O. *Alexander Rodchenko: The Complete Work*. Cambridge, Mass.: M.I.T. Press, 1987.

——. *Alexander Vesnin and Russian Constructivism*. New York: Rizzoli, 1987 .

Kimura, Katsu. *Art Deco Package Collection*. Tokyo: Rikuyo-sha, 1985.

Koretski, Victor Borisovich. *Comrade Poster*. Moscow, 1978.

Kostelanetz, Richard, ed. *Moholy-Nagy*. New York and Washington: Praeger, 1970.

Koumenhoven, John A. *Made in America: The Arts in Modern Civilization*. New York: Doubleday, 1948.

Kunzle, David. *The Early Comic Strip*. Berkeley: University of California Press, 1973.

Lang, Lothar. *Expressionist Book Illustration in Germany, 1907–1927*. Boston: New York Graphic Society, 1976.

Larner, Gerald and Celia. *The Glasgow Style*. London: Astragal, 1980.

Lewis, John. *Anatomy of Printing: The Influences of Art and History on Design*. New York: Watson-Guptil, 1970.

——. *The Twentieth Century Book*. New York: Van Nostrand Reinhold, 1967.

Lewis, John, and Brinkley, John. *Graphic Design*. London: Routledge and Kegan Paul, 1954.

Lindsay, Jack. *William Morris: His Life and Work*. New York: Taplinger, 1980.

Lippard, Lucy R. *Dadas on Art*. Englewood Cliffs, N.J.: Prentice-Hall, 1971.

Lissitzky-Kuppers, Sophie. *El Lissitzky: Life, Letters, Text*. London and New York: Thames & Hudson, 1980.

Lista, Giovanni. *Le Livre Futuriste*. Modena, Italy: Editions Panini, 1986.

Lodder, Christina. *Russian Constructivism*. New Haven: Yale University Press, 1987.

Lois, George, and Pitts, Bill. *The Art of Advertising: George Lois on Mass Communication*. New York: Harry N. Abrams, Inc., 1977.

Lucie-Smith, Edward. *Cultural Calendar of the Twentieth Century*. London: Phaidon, 1981.

Lupton, Ellen and Miller, Abbot. *Design, Writing Research: Writing on Graphic Design*. London: Phaidon, 1999.

McCarthy, Fiona. *A History of British Design, 1830–1970*. London and Boston: George Allen & Unwin, 1979.

McClelland, Gordon. *Rick Grin*. New York: Putnam and Perigee Paper Tiger, 1980.

McDermott, Catherine. *Street Style: British Design in the Eighties*. New York: Rizzoli, 1987.

Macfall, Haldane. *Aubrey Beardsley: The Man and His Work*. London: John Lane, 1928.

McLean, Ruari. *Jan Tschichold: Typographer*. Boston: David R. Godine, 1975.

——. *Modern Book Design*. New York: Faber & Faber, 1958.

——. *Victorian Book Design*. New York: Faber & Faber, 1963.

McLuhan, Marshall, and Fiore, Quentin. *War and Peace in the Global Village*. New York: Bantam, 1968.

Madsen, Stephen Tschudi. *Sources of Art Nouveau*. New York: Da Capo, 1976.

Marchand, Roland. *Advertising the American Dream: Making Way for Modernity, 1920–40*. Berkeley: University of California Press, 1985.

Margolin, Victor. *American Poster Renaissance: The Great Age of Poster Design, 1890–1900*. New York: Watson-Guptil, 1975.

Marzio, Peter. *The Democratic Art: Pictures for a Nineteenth-Century America*. Boston: David Godine, 1979.

Mayor, A. Hyatt. *Popular Prints of the Americas*. New York: Crown, 1973 .

Meggs, Philip B. *A History of Graphic Design*. New York: Van Nostrand Reinhold, 1983.

Meikle, Jeffrey L. *Twentieth Century Limited Industrial Design in America, 1925–1939*. Philadelphia: Temple University Press, 1979.

Metzl, Ervine. *The Poster: Its History and Its Art*. New York: Watson-Guptill, 1963.

Miller, J. Abbot. *Dimensional Typography: Case Studies on the Shape of Letters, A Kiosk Report*. Princeton: Princeton Architectural Press, 1996.

Moholy-Nagy, Laszlo. *Vision in Motion*. Chicago: Paul Theobald, 1947.

Morison, Stanley. *First Principles of Typography*. Cambridge, England: Cambridge University Press, 1957.

Mouron, Henri. *A. M. Cassandre*. New York: Rizzoli, 1985.

Muller-Brockmann, Josef. *The Graphic Artist and His Design Problems*. New York: Hastings House, 1961.

——. *A History of Visual Communication*. New York: Hastings House, 1967.

Muller-Brockmann, Josef and Shizuka. *A History of the Poster.* New York: Hastings House, 1961.

Murgatroyd, Keith. *Modern Graphics.* London: Studio Vista, 1969.

Naylor, Gillian. *The Arts and Crafts Movement: A Study of Its Sources, Ideals, and Influence on Design.* Cambridge, Mass.: M.I.T Press, 1975.

Neuwmann, Eckhard. *Bauhaus and Bauhaus People.* New York: Van Nostrand Reinhold, 1970.

———. *Functional Graphic Design in the Twenties.* New York: Van Nostrand Reinhold, 1967.

Ozenfant, Amedee. *Foundations of Modern Art.* New York: Dover, 1953.

Packer, William. *The Art of Vogue Covers, 1919–1940.* New York: Bonanza, 1980.

Passuth, Kristina. *Moholy-Nagy.* London and New York: Thames & Hudson, 1984.

Pentagram. *Ideas on Design.* New York: Faber & Faber, 1986.

———. *Living by Design.* New York: Whitney Library of Design, 1978.

Peterson, Theodore. *Magazines in the Twentieth Cenury.* Champaign-Urbana, Ill.: University of Illinois Press, 1964.

Pevsner, Nikolaus. *Pioneers of Modern Design: From William Morris to Walter Gropius.* Harmondsworth, England: Penguin, 1960.

Pitz, Henry C. *The Practice of Illustration.* New York: Watson-Guptill, 1947.

Prokopoff, Stephen. *The Modern Dutch Poster.* Champaign-Urbana, Ill.: University of Illinois, Krannert Art Museum, 1987.

Pulous, Arthur J. *The American Design Ethic: A Hisory of Industrial Design to 1940.* Cambridge, Mass.: M.I.T Press, 1986.

Quilici, Vieri, ed. *Rodchenko, the Complete Work.* Cambridge, Mass.: M.I.T Press,1987.

Radice, Barbara. *Memphis: Research, Experiences, Results, Failures, and Successes of New Design.* New York: Rizzoli, 1984.

Rand, Paul. *A Designer's Art.* New Haven: Yale University Press, 1985 .

———. *Thoughts on Design.* New York: Van Nostrand Reinhold, 1971.

Read, Herbert. *Art and Industry.* New York: Horizon, 1961.

Reed, Orrel P., Jr. *German Expressionist Art: The Robert Gore Rifkind Collection.* Los Angeles: University of California, Frederick S. Wright Art Gallery, 1977.

Rennert, Jack. *Timeless Images.* Tokyo: Isetan Museum of Art, 1984.

Rhodes, Anthony. *Propaganda: The Art of Persuasion, World War II.* Victor Margolin, ed. New York: Chelsea House, 1976.

Rowland, Kurt. *History of the Modern Movement.* New York: Van Nostrand Reinhold, 1974.

Rubin, William S. *Dada, Surrealism, and Their Heritage.* New York: The Museum of Modern Art, 1968.

Rublowsky, John, and Heyman, Ken. *Pop Art.* New York: Basic Books, 1965.

Sanders, Barry. *The Craftsman: An Anthology.* Santa Barbara: Peregrine Smith, 1978.

Sartogo, Piero. *Italian Re-Evolution: Design in Italian Society in the Eighties.* La Jolla, Calif: La Jolla Museum of Contemporary Art, 1986.

Schau, Michael. *All American Girl: The Art of Coles Phillips.* New York: Watson-Guptil, 1975.

Schmidt, Joost. *Lehre und Arbeit am Bauhaus 1919–32.* Dusseldorf: Editions Marzona, 1984.

Schweiger, Werner J. *Wiener Werkstätte: Design in Vienna, 1903–1932.* New York: Abbeville, 1984.

Selz, Peter, and Constantine, Mildred. *Art Nouveau.* New York: The Museum of Modern Art, 1976.

———. *Art Nouveau: Art and Design at the Turn of the Century.* New York: The Museum of Modern Art, 1959.

Sembach, Klaus-Jurgen. *Exactitude: Style 1930.* New York: Univerg, 1986.

Shahn, Ben. *The Shape of Content.* Cambridge, Mass.: Harvard University Press, 1957.

Snyder, Gertrude, and Peckolick, Alan. *Herb Lubalin: Art Director, Graphic Designer, and Typographer.* New York: American Showcase, 1985.

Sparke, Penny. *An Introduction to Design and Culture in the Twentieth Century.* London: Allen & Unwin, 1986.

Sparke, Penny; Hodges, Felice; Coad, Emma Dent; and Stone, Anne. *Design Source Book.* Secaucus, N.J.: Chartwell, 1986.

Sparling, H. Halliday. *The Kelmscott Press and William Morris, Master-Craftsman.* New York: Macmillan, 1924.

Spencer, Herbert. *Pioneers of Modern Typography.* New York: Hastings House, 1970.

———. *The Liberated Page: A Typographical Anthology.* San Francisco: Bedford, 1987.

Spencer, Isobel. *Walter Crane.* New York: Macmillan, 1975.

Spiegelman, Art, and Mauly, Françoise, eds. *Read Yourself Raw.* New York: Pantheon, 1987.

Sutnar, Ladislav. *Package Design: The Force of Visual Selling.* New York: Arts, 1953.

Taylor, Joshua C. *Futurism.* New York: The Museum of Modern Art, 1961.

Thorgerson, Storm, and Dean, Roger, eds. *Album Cover Album: A Book of Record Jackets.* New York: Dragon's World Book, 1977.

Thorgerson, Storm, and Powell, Aubrey. *100 Best Album Covers.* London, New York, Sydney: DK Publishing, Inc., 1999.

Tichi, Cecelia. *Shifting Gears: Technology, Literature, Culture in Modernist America.* Chapel Hill, N.C.: University of North Carolina Press, 1987.

Tolmer, A. *Mise en Page: The Theory and Practice of Layout.* London: The Studio, 1930.

Tracy, Walter. *Letters of Credit: A View of Type Design.* Boston: David Godine, 1987.

Twyman, Michael. *Printing, 1770–1970: An Illustrated History of Its Development and Uses in England.* London: Eyer & Spottiswoode, 1970.

Updike, Daniel Berkeley. *Printing Types, Their History, Forms, and Use: A Study in Survivals.* New York: Dover, 1980.

Vallance, Aymer. *William Morris: His Art, His Writings, and His Public Life.* London: Studio Editions, 1986.

Van Doesburg, Theodore. *Principles of Neo-Plastic Art.* London: Lund Humphries, 1969.

Varnedoe, Kirk. *Vienna 1900: Art, Architecture and Design.* New York: The Museum of Modern Art, 1986.

Veronesi, Guilia. *Style and Design 1909-1929.* New York: George Braziller, 1968.

Watkinson, Raymond. *Pre-Raphaelite Art and Design.* New York, 1970.

Weber, Eva. *Art Deco in America.* New York: Bison, 1985.

Weill, Alain. *The Poster: A Worldwide Survey and History.* Boston: G. K. Hall, 1985.

Weisberg, Gabriel P. *Art Nouveau Bing, Paris Style 1900.* New York: Harry N. Abrams, in association with the Smithsonian Institution Traveling Service, 1986.

Welo, Samuel. *Trademark and Monogram Suggestions.* New York: Pitman, 1937.

Wember, Paul. *Johan Thorn Prikker.* Krefeld, Germany: Scherpe Verlag, 1966.

Wingler, Hans M. *The Bauhaus: Weimar, Dessau, Berlin, Chicago.* Cambridge, Mass.: M.I.T Press, 1969.

Wornum, Ralph N. *Analysis of Ornament.* London: Chapman & Hall, 1879.

Yasinskaya, I. *Revolutionary Textile Design. Russia in the 1920s and 1930s.* New York: Viking, 1983.

Young, Frank H. *Advertising Layout.* New York: Pascal Covici, 1928.

ANNUALS

American Institute of Graphic Arts. *AIGA Graphic Design, USA.* New York: Watson-Guptill, 1980.

Art Directors Club. *Annual of Advertising and Editorial Art.* New York: 1921–present.

Coyne, Richard. *CA Annual of Design and Advertisng.* Palo Alto: Communications Arts Books, 1958.

Herdeg, Walter. *Graphis Annual Zurich: Graphis Press.* New York: Hastings House, 1952.

Print Casebooks. Three six-volume editions of the best in graphic design from 1975 to 1980. Bethesda, Md.: R. C. Publications.

"The Society of Illustrators." *The Illustrators' Annual.* New York: Hastings House, 1959.

Typography: The Annual of the Type Directors' Club. New York: Watson-Guptill, 1985.

The name of every designer of an illustration work is listed below, by the page number on which the work appears.

Adigard, Erik, 245,252
Adler, Deborah, 265
Agah, M.F., 159
Aichele, Monika, 269
Allemann, Hans-U., 224
Amato, Fortunato, 156
Anderson, Charles Spencer, 226
Andri, Ferdinand, 60, 63
Armitage, Merle, 156
Ashbee, C. R., 35
Aufuldish, Bob, 243, 263

Baargeld, Johannes, 171
Bagley, Donna, 231
Bantjes, Marian, 258, 262
Barbier, Georges, 135
Bass, Saul, 201
Batty, Dora, 153
Baumberger, Otto, 142
Bayer, Herbert, 88, 112, 114, 115, 116
Beall, Lester, 162, 191
Beardsley, Aubrey, 32, 33, 34, 35
Beggarstaff Brothers, 72
Behrens, Peter, 75
Bell, Robert Anning, 39
Benirschke, Max, 80
Benito, Eduardo, 129
Bereny, Robert, 144
Berlewi, Henryk, 109
Bernard, Pierre, 232
Bernard, Walter, 251
Bernhard, Lucian, 79
Bernhard, Ruth, 163
Bershadeskii, G., 104
Bierut, Michael, 257, 264
Bill, Max, 196
Binder, Joseph, 192
Blue, E. N., 21
Bokuniewicz, Carol, 226
Bolin, 129
Bonnard, Pierre, 43, 49
Borisov, Grigory, 106
Bradley, Will, 8, 64
Breuer, Marcel, 112
Brodovitch, Alexey, 161, 201
Brody, Neville, 237
Brown, Howard, 257
Brownjohn, Chermayeff, and Geismar Associates, 200
Bruckmuller, Josef, 80
Burchartz, Max, 119
Burne-Jones, Edward, 34
büro destruct, 248

Calkins, Mike, 257
Camara, Thomaz Leal, 48

Cappiello, Leonetto, 71, 133
Capuouzzo, Chris, 253
Carlu, Jean, 126, 134, 163
Carqueville, William L., 64
Carson, David, 237
Casado, John, 231
Cassandre, A. M., 132, 134, 135, 158
Chantry, Art, 228
Chappel, Charles, 155
Cheng, Alicia, 267
Cheret, Jules, 29, 43, 51
Christiansen, Hans, 55
Chwast, Seymour, 202
Cieslewicz, Roman, 207
Clavel, Garald-Paris, 232
Clay, John Cecil, 66
Coates, Stephen, 240
Collins, Ray, 212
Colvin, Alan, 231
Cooper, F. G., 76
Cooper, Kyle, 250
Corral, Rodrigo, 261
Cosl-Frey, 144
Covarrubias, Joshua, 264
Crane, Walter, 37, 39
Crumb, R., 204
Culin, Nembhard N., 165
Czeczot, Andrzej, 207
Czerniawski, Jerzy, 209

D'Albisola, Tullio, 91
Davis, Christopher, 244
Davis, Paul, 202
Deck, Barry, 238
De Cumptich, Roberto de Vicq, 263
De Harak, Rudolph, 200
Depero, Fortunato, 94, 95
Detox, Zach, 249
Dix, Otto, 82
Doesburg, Theo van, 110, 111, 168, 170, 173
Dorfsman, Lou, 201
Dow, Arthur, 65
Doyle, Richard, 16
Doyle, Stephen, 254
Druckrey, Inge, 224
Drzewinski, Leszek, 208
Dudovich, Marcello, 71
Duffy, Joe, 226
Dumbar, Gert, 233
Du Pasquier, Nathalie, 222
Dwurnick, Edward, 208

Earls, Elliot Peter, 240
Eckersley, Tom, 187, 188
Eckerstrom, Ralph, 192
Eggers, Dave, 265
Egri, Charles, 164
Ehrenberger, Ludwig Lutz, 55
Elingater, Solomon, 100, 105
Erdt, Hans Rudi, 79
Erkens, P., 172

Ernst, Max, 171
Ernstberger, Matthias, 269
Erry-Adler, Margit, 113
Fairey, Shepard, 268
Falls, C. B., 76
Farrell, Stephen, 243
Federico, Gene, 200
Fella, Ed, 237
Felton, Nicholas, 266
Ferriss, Hugh, 164
Fili, Louise, 262
Fishauf, Louis, 228
Fleckhaus, Willi, 205
Follis, John, 195
Fontanet, Noel, 143
Freundlich, Otto, 86
Friedman, Dan, 224
Frost, Vince, 254
Fuchs, Heinz, 86
Fukuda, Shieo, 217
Funny Garbage, 253

Galanis, Dimitrios, 48
Galantara, 49
Games, Abram, 188, 189
Garland, Christopher, 228
Garretto, Paolo, 132, 159
Gasparska, Agnieszka, 253, 265
Gastyne, Marco de, 49
Gates, Katherine, 264
Geiger, Petra, 247
Gelman, Alexander, 256, 257
Gerstner, Karl, 196
Gibson, C. D., 66
Giordani, John, 253
Girardi, Peter, 253
Glaser, Milton, 202, 203
Glauber, Barbara, 246
Goines, David Lance, 202
Golden, William, 200
Gorowski, Mieczyslaw, 208
Graf, Kaspar, Ernst, 143
Grapus, 232
Grasset, Eugene, 44
Gray, Jon, 270
Green, Cooper, 273
Greif, Gene, 226
Greiman, April, 224
Griffin, Rick, 213
Gropius, Walter, 113
Grosz, George, 173, 174
Guimard, Henri, 42

Hakkanson, Matts, 251
Halliwell, 150
Hamilton, Grant, 20
Hannah, Jonny, 270
Hardie, George, 220
Hardmeier, Robert, 77
Harrison, Peter, 229
Hausmann, Raoul, 170

Havinden, Ashley Eldrid, 152
Hazenplug, Frank, 64
Heartfield, John, 172, 174, 175
Held, John Jr., 159
Henderlieter, Dave, 242
Henrion, F. H. K., 187
Herdeg, Walter, 185
Herrn, 180
Herzig, 137
Hipgnossis, 220
Hirschfeld-Mack, Ludwig, 114
Hoch, Hannah, 172
Hochbaum, Susan, 229
Hodges, Drew, 269
Hodler, Ferdinand, 61
Hoerl, Hans, 85
Hofbauer, Arnost, 54
Hoffmann, Josef, 80
Hofman, P. A. H., 167
Hofmann, Armin, 198, 199
Hofmann, Krystyna, 207
Hohlwein, Ludwig, 74, 178, 179
Holmes, Nigel, 266
Holtom, Gerald, 210
Hope, Will, 68
Hornung, Clarence, 157
Huntley, Sue, 229
Huszar, Vilmos, 110, 111

Ilic, Mirko, 251, 272
Image, Selwyn, 32, 34
Iribe, Paul, 49
Itoh, Kenji, 214
Itten, Johannes, 112

Jaben, Seth, 230
Janco, Marcel, 170
Janselow, M., 54
Jay, John, 226
Johnson, Haley, 255
Johnson, Susan, 231
Johnston, Edward, 186
Jordan, Alexander, 232
Jung, Moritz, 80, 81

Kalman, Maira, 226
Kalman, Tibor, 226
Kamekura, Yusaku, 216
Kampmann, Walter, 75
Kauffer, E. McKnight, 97, 150, 151, 187, 188, 194
Kepes, Gyorgy, 190
Keyton, Jeffery, 244
Kim, Soni, 246
King, David, 210
King, Jessie M., 59
Kinon, Jennifer, 264
Kirchner, Ernst Ludwig, 84
Klimaschin, 176
Klimt, Gustav, 63
Klinger, Julius, 144, 145
Kluepfel, Tom, 254

Klutsis, Gustav, 100
Kokoschka, Oskar, 81, 86
Komardenkov, Vassily, 9
Kopshina, Betsy, 240
Koretski, Victor Borisovich, 179
Kosstrin, Jane, 226
Kuhn, Charles, 184
Kulik, Gregg, 260, 261
Kurlansky, Mervyn, 205

Lapape, Georges, 129
Law, Roger, 210
Lee, Ji, 269
Leherer, Warren, 227
Leibowitz, Mathew, 194
Lemel, Yosse, 272
Leni, Paul, 87
Lenica, Jan, 206
Leonard, 139
Le Petit, Alfred, 28
Le Quernec, Alain, 232
Leupin, Herbert, 185
Levitan, Rachel Schreiber, 231
Lewis, Wyndham, 96
Leyendecker, J. C., 160
Lightfoot, M. G., 58
Lionni, Leo, 192
Lissitzky, El, 10, 98, 99, 100, 101,
    104, 105
Livemont, Privat, 42
Lohse, Richard P., 196
Longhauser, William, 225
Loupot, Charles, 128
Lubalin, Herb, 204
Lustig, Alvin, 195

Macdonald, Margaret and
    Frances, 59
MacFadyen, Alex, 270
Mackintosh, Charles Rennie, 58, 59
Mackmurdo, Arthur H., 35, 37, 42
MacNair, J. H., 58, 59
Maisner, Bernard, 270
Makela, P. Scott, 237, 238
Mangold, Burkhard, 76
Manning, Richard, 220
Man Ray, 186
Manwaring, Michael, 230
Marc, Franz, 85
Marek, Mark, 229
Marinetti, Filippo T., 90, 91
Martin, Bobby C. Jr., 261
Mattaloni, Giovanni, 70
Matter, Herbert, 141, 182, 192, 195
Mayakovsky, Vladimir, 101, 105
Mayer, Hy, 69
McCarty, Marlene, 251
McCoy, Katherine, 236, 237
McCraken, Pete, 242
McGuire, Richard, 253
McMullan, James, 204
McShane, Patricia, 245, 252

Meta Design, 255
Meunier, Henri, 42
Micic, Ljubomir, 121
Moenring, John R., 212
Moholy-Nagy, László, 111, 112, 116,
    117
Morla, Jennifer, 247
Morris, William, 30, 33, 34
Moscoso, Victor, 211
Moser, Koloman, 61, 62, 63
Mouly, Françoise, 229
Mucha, Alphonse, 46, 50
Muchley, Robert, 163
Muir, Donna, 229
Muller, Fridolin, 196
Muller-Brockmann, Josef, 196, 199

Nagai, Kazumasa, 218
Nagatomo, Keisuke, 214
Nakata, Robert, 234, 236
Nash, Jim, 164
Neuberg, Hans, 196
Nicholson, William, 72
Niemann, Christoph, 264
Noguchi, Isamu, 190
Nolde, Emil, 85
Number 17, 251

Oberman, Emily, 251
Obert, Daryl, 249
Odermatt, Siegfried, 223
Odgers, Jayme, 224
Okamoto, Shigeo, 214
Olbrich, Joseph Maria, 62
Orazi, Emmanuel, 51
Orr, Michael R., 231

Pagowski, Andrzej, 207
Paladini, V., 93
Paleologue, Jean de, 44
Pannaggi, Ivo, 92
Panter, Gary, 229
Parks, Melanie Marder, 226
Parrish, Maxfield, 64
Paul, Bruno, 53, 57
Pearson, David, 260, 262
Pechstein, Max, 86, 87
Penfield, Edward, 65
Peske, Jean Miscelas, 44
Pfund, Paul, 138
Phillips, Coles, 66, 67
Pick, Frank, 186
Pirchan, 75
Pirtle, Woody, 231
Poelzig, Hans, 87
Potts, Sam, 267
Prampolini, Enrico, 93
Preetorius, Emil, 145
Prikker, JohanThorn, 57
Prusakov, Nikolai, 106
Pryde, James, 72
Purvis, Tom, 150

Rackow, Leo, 164
Rand, Paul, 11, 191, 193, 200
Redback Graphix, 273
Redl, Dave, 253
Reno, 140
Rhead, Louis, 65
Riccobaldi, Giovanni, 146
Rich, A. L., 69
Ricketts, Charles, 34, 35
Robbins, Tom, 212
Roberts, William, 96
Rodchenko, Alexander, 101, 102,
    103, 105
Rogers, A., 152
Roller, Alfred, 62
Roshkov, Juryi, 108
Rossmann, Zdenek, 121
Rouchon, 29
Rummler, 20

Sagmeister, Stefan, 247
Salisbury, Michael, 205
Schawinsky, Xanti, 116
Scher, Paula, 268
Schlemmer, Oskar, 112
Schmidt, Joost, 113, 115, 116, 119
Schnackenberg, Walter, 75
Schreiber, Georges, 159
Schuitema, Paul, 124
Schulpig, Karl, 136
Schulz Neudamm, 137
Schwartz, Samuel L., 166
Schwitters, Kurt, 168, 170, 171, 173
Seguini, Antonio, 148
Seigler, Bonnie, 251
Semionov, Semion, 107
Seneca, Federico, 148
Severini, Gino, 90
Shainin, Jenny, 250
Shapton, Leanne, 270
Shepard, Otis, 160, 161
Silverstein, Louis, 201
Skolos, Nancy, 225
Smith, J.D., 74
Snider, Steve, 231
Sottsass, Ettore, 222
Spiegelman, Art, 229
Stankowski, Anton, 118
Stauder, Eric, 249
Starowieyski, Franciszek, 206
Steinitz, Kathe, 173
Steinlen, Theophile Alexandre, 43
Steinweiss, Alex, 190
Stenberg, Georgy and Vladimir, 107
Stepanova, Varvara, 103
Sterling, David, 226
Sterling, Jennifer, 246
Stern, Julius J., 157
Steubner, Kristina, 248
Stickley, Gustav, 38
Stoddart, Jim, 262
Stoecklin, Niklaus, 184, 185

Stone, Wilbur Macey, 32
Stone, Rob, 255
Storch, Otto, 203
Strauss, H. M. A., 160
Studio Dumbar, 233
Sussman/Prejza & Company, Inc., 230
Sutnar, Ladislav, 120, 122, 123, 190
Swarte, Joost, 233
Swift, Ian (Swifty), 248

Tanaka, Ikko, 219
Teige, Karel, 109, 120, 121, 122
Thompson, Bradbury, 194
Tiernan, 151
Tissi, Rosmarie, 223
Toulouse-Lautrec, Henri de, 40,
    43, 45
Trochut, Alex, 271
Tschichold, Jan, 118, 119
Turpain, A., 45

Updike, Daniel Berkley, 39

Vadasz, Miklos, 48
Valicenti, Rick, 241
Vanderbyl, Michael, 231
VanderLans, Rudy, 227, 238
Van Hamersveld, John, 212
Velde, Henri van de, 57
Venezky, Martin, 247
Venna, Lucio, 148
Vincent, Rene, 132
Vivarelli, Carlo L., 196
Von Reznicek, Franz, 53

Wallace, 151
Warinner, Kathy, 243
Wearing, Paul, 233
Weiluc, 48
Weingart, Wolfgang, 223
White, Gleeson, 35
Why Not Associates, 245
Wiens, Katrin, 248
Willrab, 77
Wilson, Wes, 210, 211, 213
Wolf, Henry, 205
Wright, Frank Lloyd, 155
Wright, Micha, 273

Yokoo, Tadanori, 214, 215
Yoshinaga, Scott, 242
Young, Daniel, 272

Zaid, Barry, 203
Zender, Michael, 224
Zwart, Piet, 111, 124, 125